THE PAN BOOK OF
CARD GAMES

The Pan Book of

CARD GAMES

Hubert Phillips

Pan Books London, Sydney and Auckland

First published 1953 by H. F. & G. Witherby Ltd
This edition published 1960 by Pan Books Ltd,
Cavaye Place, London SW10 9PG
49 48 47 46 45
© Hubert Phillips 1960
ISBN 0 330 20175 1
Set, printed and bound in Great Britain by
Cox & Wyman Ltd, Reading

FOREWORD

THE present book is to some extent based on *The Complete Book of Card Games* (written in collaboration with my friend B. C. Westall) which first appeared in 1939 and has been many times reprinted. But, as a comparison of the texts will show, the sections dealing with the more significant games have been completely rewritten. For the chapters on Contract Bridge and Canasta I am indebted to Terence Reese, who has been associated with my work on Bridge for nearly twenty years. I have also revised the chapters on Solo Whist, Black Maria and Poker.

In addition, there are here presented a number of important games not included in the earlier work: Kalabriasz; Gin Rummy; Canasta; Booby; Challenge. Booby is a game which I invented during World War II. Challenge is the name I give to a Russian game to which I was recently introduced by Mr J. A. Fotheringham of Trinity College, Cambridge.

My thanks are due to my friend and former secretary Chris Dishington, who was largely responsible for the revision of the typescript.

HUBERT PHILLIPS

CONTENTS

CONTENTS

CONTENTS
GAMES FOR FROM THREE TO SEVEN PLAYERS

PARTY GAMES

PATIENCE GAMES

CONTENTS

INTRODUCTION

A PACK of cards, reduced to its essentials, is a collection of pasteboards with numbers on them. In the normal pack (as used for Contract Bridge) there are fifty-two such pasteboards: four series, each bearing (in effect) the numbers one to thirteen, or (in games where the Ace is high) two to fourteen. The court cards—Knave, Queen, King—are, considered from this point of view, the numbers eleven, twelve, thirteen, adorned with pictures just to give the game liveliness and colour. Some games do not require fifty-two cards. Piquet, for example, is played with a thirty-two card pack (the numbers 2, 3, 4, 5, 6 being eliminated); while the latest game to become popular—Canasta—is played with no fewer than 108 cards: two ordinary packs shuffled together and four Jokers added. Six-pack Bezique is played (as its name implies) with six Bezique (*ie* Piquet) packs shuffled together: 192 cards.

The number of possible card games is literally unlimited. In this book I describe all the standard games played in this country and a great many others that, while not generally known, are worth knowing, including two or three of my own invention. But every one of these games has numerous variants, and a number of them are played under different codes of rules. Indeed, I believe the only game for which there is a universally accepted code of rules is Contract Bridge. For other standard games—such as Solo Whist, Gin Rummy, Canasta and Poker— there are what may be called local variations in the rules; if, therefore, you are playing any of these games, points where there is likely to be disagreement should be resolved beforehand. In all cases I have given the rules which, to the best of my belief, are generally accepted.

I have given much thought to the arrangement of this book, and have to some extent varied my original plan: the classification of card games with reference primarily to the numbers taking part. This aspect of my theme has not been overlooked. But I have thought it worth while to stress also the organic relationship of games of the same family.

As I have said, cards are pasteboards bearing numbers. The interest of card games, must, therefore, be primarily derived from

11

the fascination of numbers. And numbers were invented to facilitate the processes of counting, comparison, and arrangement. But these processes can be considered from several standpoints, and that is why there are so many card games which differ basically from one another.

At one end of the scale are games of pure chance: these turn, in effect, on matching one random number against another. Of such games, 'Chase the Ace' affords a simple example. At the other end of the scale are games like Contract Bridge, where play depends on organizing numbers—each of which has its own ordinal value—in such a way as to get the best results in conformity with the rules.

When you play a hand at Bridge, what you are really doing is deciding (so far as the decision rests with you) in what order your cards can be played to maximum advantage. If you are declarer, twenty-six of the fifty-two cards are under your control; if you are one of the defenders, you have thirteen of the fifty-two cards, and your partner—whose mind, if you are both good players, should be attuned to yours—is collaborating with thirteen cards more.

Contract Bridge may be taken as the type of what is perhaps the senior family of established card games. They are sometimes known as the 'trump and partnership games' and they derive from the seventeenth-century games 'Ombre' and 'Triumph' (whence the word 'trump'), in which is latent the basic idea of Whist and Contract Bridge. In these games the face values of the cards are not in themselves significant.[1] What is significant is that every card has a particular status, from the point of view of taking tricks. And it is the tricks that count. Where there is a trump suit, this suit has priority over the others.

Perhaps the simplest of the games which turn upon trick-organization, and embody the trump idea, is Nap. The principle is well illustrated by the story of the player who, believing he was up against a card-sharper, found himself dealt the four highest Spades and the Ace of Diamonds. As he suspected, the dealer held five Spades. He turned the tables neatly by leading the Ace of Diamonds.

Derivative from the Whist family are games in which there is no trump suit, but organization (in play) is still all-important. The introduction of the no-trump element in Bridge was a marked departure from the principles of Whist (though there

[1] Except in games where bonuses are scored for 'honours'.

is, of course, no reason why Whist should not be played at No Trump).

Solo Whist—a game which tends to be underrated—embodies yet another idea in the Misère call. The play of a Misère hand and, perhaps even more, the play against it, calls for card ability of a high order.

Again, in what is known as the 'Hearts' family of games, everything can depend on playing one's cards in the right order. The best of these games—eg Black Maria—are as difficult as they are fascinating. Their basic tactics are similar to those required when playing a Misère hand: one may, indeed, say that three Misère hands are being played simultaneously.

A quite different principle appears in games of the Rummy family. In the simplest of these games there is no trick-play: the object is merely to 'meld' prescribed selections of cards. In even the simpler Rummy games there is some element of skill, and in the latest member of the family—Canasta—the skill factor is relatively high. Canasta, like Contract Bridge, requires not only concentration and a good card memory, but the capacity to plan one's play.

A third group of games combines the basic idea of Whist with the basic idea of Rummy, ie they involve both the 'melding' of scoring combinations and also the taking of tricks; so that, in their earlier stages, one has a twofold objective. There are three outstanding games in this group: Piquet, Bezique and Kalabriasz. Their variants are innumerable. Piquet has been standardized for over a century: it is one of the games that were played when gaming was gaming, and landed estates changed hands at the turn of a card. But Bezique has many forms—the American game of Pinochle is very nearly the same game—and Kalabriasz has as many variants as it has names, and they are legion. Kalabriasz presents fascinating problems to the student of card history. Its terminology suggests that many different peoples have had a hand in shaping it.

Finally, there are three card games each in its way *sui generis*. One is Cribbage, which resembles the games just mentioned in that it involves both melding and play, but on lines sufficiently distinctive to suggest a quite different origin. A second is Poker, a development of the ancient game of Brag. Poker is the one game which must be played for stakes or there is no point in it at all, and which has very little point unless played for stakes sufficiently large to hurt.

And the third game is the Russian game to which, in this book, I give the name of Challenge. So far as I know, it has not before been presented to the English-speaking public. It is the only important card game known to me which eliminates, just as the game of Chess does, the element of chance.

SYNOPSIS OF THE PRINCIPAL GAMES
INCLUDED IN THIS BOOK

CONTRACT BRIDGE

The best-known and most widely-publicized of all card games. Contract Bridge, a development of the old game of Whist, is a partnership game for four players. To learn to play it even reasonably well demands study and a good deal of practice.

BOOBY

Contract Bridge for three players. This variant (invented by the writer) gives more scope than any other for the exercise of skill and imagination.

SOLO WHIST

Another derivative of Whist, in which four players participate: two players may find themselves playing in partnership against the other two, or one may be called upon to battle single-handed against the other three. This is another game in which the technique of play is in the highest degree important.

PIQUET

One of the best-known—and perhaps the best—of card games for two players. Though played with only a short pack (32 cards), Piquet has a high skill factor: it calls for judgment (*a*) in exchanging the cards originally dealt for others, and (*b*) in the play of the hand.

CRIBBAGE

Another game for two (or more) players, with a long and honourable history. Cribbage differs in its basic ideas from all other card games; though, like Piquet, it combines the two elements of card *selection* and *play*.

BLACK MARIA

A development of the old game of Hearts. Black Maria is, in the opinion of many experts, the most exciting of all card games for three players. Its skill factor is very high. This is one of the games of which the object is not to win tricks, but to avoid winning them. Black Maria can also be played as a partnership game for four players, or as a family game for five or more.

POKER

The greatest of all gambling games—in the sense that it is meaningless unless it is played for stakes. But Poker is very much a game of skill: to win demands a knowledge of the relevant mathematics and also a knowledge of psychology.

QUINTET

An amusing adaptation of Poker for two players.

CANASTA

The latest and most popular development of Rummy, played with a special pack of 108 cards. Canasta is primarily a partnership game for four players. There is a lot of luck in it; but skill will tell in the long run.

GIN RUMMY

The basic idea of Rummy games is the 'melding' of matching cards. Before the introduction of Canasta, Gin Rummy—a variant devised for two players—had a considerable vogue. It is not difficult; can be exciting; and offers reasonable scope for the exercise of skill.

SEVEN CARD RUMMY; KINGS AND QUEENS; SEQUENCE RUMMY; PROGRESSIVE RUMMY

A selection of games of the Rummy family which can be played with enjoyment by from three to seven players.

CHALLENGE

A novelty among card games, of Russian origin, which may one day acquire a literature of its own. Success at this game is a matter of pure calculation; the players start with identical hands, and each knows, at any given moment, exactly what cards his adversary holds.

GERMAN WHIST

An adaptation of Whist for two players.

NULLOS; CONTRACT NULLOS

'Nullo' Bridge for two players. This is an exciting game in which the skill factor will very quickly assert itself.

BEZIQUE

Bezique ranks with Piquet and Cribbage among the standard games for two players. It is the forerunner of the game of Pinochle, which has long been popular in America. Bezique, primarily a 'melding' game, is more popular than Piquet, though its skill factor is not so high.

KALABRIASZ

A game played, under different names, and with numerous variations, in many countries of Europe.

WHIST AND ITS DERIVATIVES

CONTRACT BRIDGE—the game which has dominated the card world for more than twenty years—belongs to what is called the Whist family of card games. No other group of games has attained anything like the same degree of social importance, or has bulked so largely in card literature. Whist dominated the London card clubs throughout Queen Victoria's reign, to be superseded by Bridge just about the turn of the century.

Whist was a development of earlier games, first played (so far as we know) in the seventeenth century. One of such games was Triumph (hence the word 'trump'); another was Ombre—a game not now played—of which there is a fascinating account in Pope's poem *The Rape of the Lock*. But Ombre is a game for two, and Whist is a game for four: its underlying principles are the partnership of two players against two, and the nomination of a trump suit. Hence its derivatives are sometimes known as the 'trump and partnership' family of games.

The mechanics of Whist are comparatively simple. The four players taking part cut for partners and each player then deals in turn, a full pack of fifty-two cards being used. Thirteen cards are dealt face downwards to each player, but the dealer turns up his last card: the suit of this card is the trump suit. Now the players pick up their hands and play begins, the player to the dealer's left leading to the first trick. Every player must follow suit if he can: if he can't follow suit, he may either ruff or discard. The winner of a trick leads to the next one. The object of each deal is to take as many tricks as possible.

Here is a deal at Whist. North and South are partners against East and West. South deals, turning up the ♡ 9, so Hearts become trumps, and West leads to the first trick. The play (as it might have occurred) is given, and it will be seen that North-South take eight tricks. For this (under the old Whist scoring) they would have scored two points (*ie* one point for each trick over six).

18

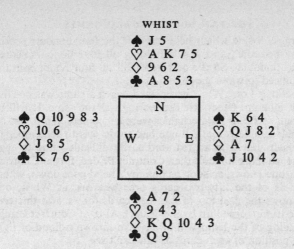

```
                    ♠ J 5
                    ♡ A K 7 5
                    ◇ 9 6 2
                    ♣ A 8 5 3
         ┌─────────────────┐
♠ Q 10 9 8 3 │    N    │  ♠ K 6 4
♡ 10 6       │         │  ♡ Q J 8 2
◇ J 8 5      │ W     E │  ◇ A 7
♣ K 7 6      │         │  ♣ J 10 4 2
         │    S    │
         └─────────────────┘
                    ♠ A 7 2
                    ♡ 9 4 3
                    ◇ K Q 10 4 3
                    ♣ Q 9
```

The card underlined takes the trick.

Trick	W	N	E	S
1	♠ 10	♠ J	♠ K	♠ A
2	◇ 5	◇ 2	◇ A	◇ K
3	♠ 8	♠ 5	♠ 6	♠ 2
4	♠ Q	♡ 5	♠ 4	♠ 7
5	♡ 6	♡ K	♡ 2	♡ 3
6	♡ 10	♡ A	♡ 8	♡ 4
7	◇ 8	◇ 9	◇ 7	◇ Q
8	◇ J	◇ 6	♣ 2	◇ 10
9	♠ 9	♣ 5	♣ 4	♡ 9
10	♣ 6	♣ 3	♡ J	◇ 4
11	♠ 3	♡ 7	♡ Q	◇ 3
12	♣ K	♣ A	♣ J	♣ 9
13	♣ 7	♣ 8	♣ 10	♣ Q

As the game was played in the West End card clubs, play ended when one side or the other had scored a rubber. A rubber (as in Contract Bridge today) went to the side that first won two games. The game was normally five points up, and involved a considerable element of chance, in that honours were scored as well as tricks. The honours were the Ace, King, Queen and Knave of trumps. A side which held three of the four honours scored 'two by honours', and a side holding all four honours scored 'four by honours'. So the odd trick plus all four honours in the deal sufficed to win a game.

Sometimes Long Whist was played, when a game was not five up, but nine up. Otherwise the scoring was the same. It will be seen that, so far as its mechanics were concerned, Whist was an extremely simple game. All one had to do was to remember to follow suit. But it is an extraordinarily difficult game to play well. Much more difficult than Contract Bridge, for, at Contract Bridge, one knows, as soon as dummy's hand goes down, where twenty-six of the fifty-two cards are; whereas, at Whist, one only knows the position of fourteen cards (one's own thirteen, and the trump turned up by the dealer). Also, at Contract Bridge the bidding of the hand will often have thrown a flood of light on the position of such cards as one can't see.

Hence Whist, in the hands of serious players, tended to become more and more elaborate. In the eighteenth century, Edmund Hoyle produced the first textbook on the game: it was then that the phrase 'according to Hoyle' came into common use. By the middle of the nineteenth century, Whist, as played in the West End clubs, had become a very solemn business. Henry Jones ('Cavendish') began to write on the game in the '70s, and his textbook—*Cavendish on Whist*—ran into more than twenty editions. But Cavendish, who became the dictator of the game— arbiter not only of its technique, but of its laws and etiquette— ultimately killed it. He made its rules of play so elaborate that it took months of study (as well as a first-class brain) to master them. When, at the end of the last century, Bridge superseded it, Whist had become more than a game: it was an intellectual ritual. The Edwardians turned with relief to the new game, Bridge, which not only seemed to be much more exciting, but was also nothing like so burdensome from the player's point of view.

So far as I know, Whist, as played under the aegis of Cavendish, has been dead for many years. It is now, I believe, only played at whist drives where most of those who participate know the mechanics of the game and nothing more. At whist drives each hand ranks as a separate event; the trump suit is prescribed beforehand; and honours do not count. We need not concern ourselves with these artless exercises.

Bridge was brought to England from the east—probably from India. But it is believed to have originated in Russia, and the name Bridge is said to be a corruption of Biritch, an anglicized form of the Russian name of the game. During the last half-century the game has changed repeatedly in character, and I daresay it has not yet attained its final form.

In its first form, Straight Bridge, the trump suit was nominated by the dealer, or (at the dealer's option) by his partner. The dealer's partner became the dummy, and his hand went down as soon as a card had been led to the first trick. The scoring was more elaborate than at Whist, and, since calls could be doubled, redoubled, and doubled again, up to 100 points a trick, the game could be very expensive.

Another innovation was the introduction of the No Trump call, which brought with it a whole range of completely new tactical problems.

Auction Bridge came in about 1910. Auction Bridge was a radically different game from Straight Bridge. The selection of the trump suit was no longer determined arbitrarily by the dealer (or the dealer's partner), but was the result of competitive bidding around the table. Thus, any of the four players might become declarer. Moreover, the problem was no longer that of making so many odd tricks, but of making at least as many tricks as had been contracted for. Failure involved penalties 'above the line', so that Auction was not a battle for tricks but, in effect, a battle for points. Latent in it was the idea of the 'optimum contract': the attainment by competitive bidding of the contract beyond which neither side can proceed without standing to lose more points than it can gain. Many years were to pass, however, before the importance of this concept was generally recognized.

Various changes took place in Auction Bridge scoring between 1910 and 1930, when, in most clubs, the game was superseded by Contract. Contract introduced three new features. In the first place, the declaring side could not score 'below the line' more points than had been contracted for. Over-tricks were scored above the line, and did not count towards game. In the second place, there was introduced the element of 'vulnerability': partners who had won a game became vulnerable, and failure to make a contract carried proportionately heavier penalties. Finally, bonuses were awarded where slams were successfully bid. The scoring at Contract has been the subject of a good deal of experiment: the present rules will be found in the section relating to this game.

Three other developments of Bridge—none of which has attained permanence—are perhaps worth recording. First, soon after Auction became popular, there was introduced the idea of the Nullo call. The object was to give players holding bad hands an interest in the bidding. The Nullo call ranked in the auction between Hearts and Spades. One Nullo was an undertaking to lose the odd trick; Two Nullos, an undertaking to lose at least eight tricks; and so on. The Nullo element made bidding a good deal more difficult, and I have not come across it for a good many years now.

A second experiment which was popular for a short time was that of the Goulash. Where the hands had been thrown in, each player arranged his cards in suits: they were then stacked; cut without being shuffled; and dealt out 5, 5, 3 to the four players. A Goulash, of course, produces very unbalanced hands: one may well hold all thirteen cards of a suit. This variant turns Contract into a fantastic gamble, and, like the Nullo call, has not had a lasting appeal.

Finally, an attempt was made in 1938 to introduce five-suit Bridge. The fifth suit, known as Royals, made a sixty-five card pack, so sixteen cards were dealt to each player and the remaining one placed, face upwards, on the table. It could be exchanged by the declarer for any card in his own hand. The symbol for the fifth suit was a crown, and it ranked above Spades and below No Trump. Five-suit Bridge perished almost stillborn: the game is quite difficult enough with fifty-two cards and four suits.

CONTRACT BRIDGE

CONTRACT BRIDGE is, nowadays, by far the most widely played of the various games of the Whist family. The game has developed in this way:

In Whist the trump suit was decided by the turn up of a card.

In Straight Bridge the dealer was allowed to name the trump suit.

In Auction Bridge the players held a competitive auction, in which the sides bid against one another to establish the trump suit. The highest, and last, bid settled the suit. Thus the last bid made might be 'Three Hearts'; this would mean that the declarer contracted to make nine tricks with Hearts as trumps. If he made ten tricks or more, he would score game, and if twelve tricks, a small slam.

The logical development was Contract Bridge, in which players scored the bonus for game and slam only if they bid the required number of tricks. Thus, whereas at Auction an opening bid of One No Trump might well go uncontested, and declarer could score game by making Three No Trump, at Contract he and his partner must contract for Three No Trump if they are to score game.

To secure the best results in bidding, partners must have a good understanding based on one of the popular systems of bidding.

Contract Bridge takes longer to learn than any other card game; in fact, to play an average game in average company takes about six months' study and practice.

This description of the game begins with a brief account of how it is played; there follows a note on the principles of bidding, with a brief introduction to the better-known systems; a summary of the principles of play; and, finally, some hands from match play illustrating the principles of good bidding and play.

How Contract Bridge is Played

1. *Position of Players.* Partners sit at a square table. For simplicity we will call them North, South, East and West.

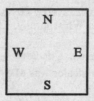

North-South are partners against East-West.

2. *Rank of Cards and Suits.* A full pack of 52 cards is used. The cards of each suit rank in the following order: Ace (the highest), King, Queen, Jack, 10, 9, 8, 7, 6, 5, 4, 3, 2; for the purpose of bidding, though not of play, there is also a ranking order of suits: Spades, Hearts, Diamonds, Clubs. A call in No Trumps ranks above Spades.

3. *Cut for Partners and Deal.* To cut for partners and deal the pack is spread out and each player withdraws one card. The players with the two highest cards are partners against the other two, and the player who has the highest card is the dealer.

4. *Shuffle, Cut and Deal.* The player on the dealer's left shuffles the pack chosen by the dealer (it is usual to play with two packs, using them for alternate hands). The pack is then passed across and cut by the player on dealer's right. Thus, West shuffles and East cuts for South to deal. South deals the cards singly, beginning with the player on his left (West).

5. *Bidding, Tricks and Trumps.* When the deal is complete, the players take up their hands, look at them and arrange them into suits. The dealer then begins the bidding.

In the bidding the two sides attempt to estimate the trick-winning potentialities of their combined hands. In the play that follows, each player plays one card to each of 13 'tricks'. Bidding also establishes whether one suit shall be trumps or whether there shall be no trumps. If there are no trumps, each trick is won by the player who plays the highest card; but if, say, Spades are trumps, then any card in Spades has power to win the trick against any card of another suit. It is, however, obligatory to follow suit when possible.

6. *Meaning of Contract.* Every hand is played at some 'contract'. One side or the other contracts to make a certain number of tricks either at a suit contract or at No Trump. The contract is expressed in terms of odd tricks beyond the number of six. Thus, if North-South made the final bid of Four Spades, perhaps over-calling the opponents' bid of Four Hearts, they are contracting to make 6 + 4, that is, 10 of the 13 tricks, with Spades as trumps.

7. *Double and Redouble.* In addition to making a bid of a specified number of tricks in No Trump or in a suit, a player may pass, saying 'No bid'. It is also possible to 'double' an opponent's contract; the effect of this is to increase the penalties for undertricks if the opponents fail to fulfil their contract. The side which has been doubled may redouble, thereby increasing the score yet again. These calls of double and redouble do not increase the size of the contract; thus, Five Diamonds overcalls Five Clubs redoubled.

8. *Declarer, Lead and Dummy.* The final contract is established when the last, and highest, bid has been followed by three passes. The player who has first mentioned the denomination named in the final contract becomes the declarer. Say that the final bid is Three No Trump, called by North, but that the first mention of No Trump was by South. Then, South is the declarer. The opening lead is made by the player on his left, West. North places all his cards face upwards on the table. North is dummy and can take no part in the play of the hand, except that he has certain limited rights, such as drawing attention to irregularities. Dummy's cards are played by declarer.

9. *Subsequent Play and Leads.* The cards to each trick are played in clockwise order—West, North, East, South for the first trick. The side that wins the trick gathers the four cards and places them face downwards. The player who has won the trick makes the lead to the next trick. Subsequent tricks won by each side are gathered and placed aslant the previous tricks.

10. *An example Hand.* Here is an example hand to illustrate some of the points discussed:

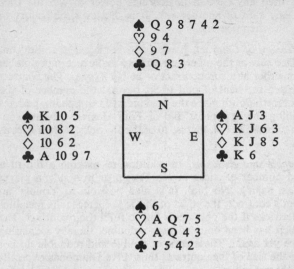

```
                    ♠ Q 9 8 7 4 2
                    ♡ 9 4
                    ♢ 9 7
                    ♣ Q 8 3

  ♠ K 10 5              N           ♠ A J 3
  ♡ 10 8 2                          ♡ K J 6 3
  ♢ 10 6 2         W       E        ♢ K J 8 5
  ♣ A 10 9 7                        ♣ K 6
                      S

                    ♠ 6
                    ♡ A Q 7 5
                    ♢ A Q 4 3
                    ♣ J 5 4 2
```

When this hand was played in the course of the Culbertson-Lenz match of 1932, East was the dealer and the score was love all. This was the bidding:

SOUTH	WEST	NORTH	EAST
			1 ♡
No	1 N.T.	No	2 N.T.
No	3 N.T.	No	No
Double			

The bidding here was non-competitive; that is to say, the two sides were not bidding against one another. The only bid made by North-South was South's double of the contract of Three No Trump. In the match, North led a Spade and West succeeded in making nine tricks at No Trump, thus fulfilling his doubled contract.

The Scoring

1. *Bridge Marker*. The score is entered on a marker printed thus:

Scores are entered above or below the line, as explained below.

2. *Scoring Below the Line*. Scores are entered below the line in respect only of tricks scored by a side which has bid and made its contract. The trick values for the various contracts are as follows:

No Trump, first trick 40 points, subsequent tricks 30.
Spades and Hearts (the major suits), 30 points each trick.
Diamonds and Clubs (the minor suits), 20 points each trick.

Suppose that the contract is Four Diamonds, and that eleven tricks are made. The score is entered below the line as 80 (4 × 20); the overtrick also counts 20 points, but this is entered above the line.

3. *Game and Rubber*. When a side has scored 100 points below the line, it has made a game. A game can be made on one hand (*eg* Three No Trump, 40 + 30 + 30) or in two or more part scores (*eg* Two Diamonds, 40, followed by Two Hearts, 60). When game has been scored by either side, a line is drawn beneath it. A part score does not count towards game if in the meantime game has been scored by the other side. Thus, if on the first hand North-South scores 60, and on the next hand opponents score 120, making game, the 60 scored by North-South does not assist them towards their next game.

The side that first wins two games wins the rubber. For this there is a high bonus, and to bid and make game is therefore one of the primary objects. The bonus for a rubber won in two games is 700; for a rubber won in three games, opponents having won one game, 500. No bonus is scored directly for a side's first game, nor for a part score; but if for any reason a rubber cannot be finished, there is a bonus of 300 for a side that has a game, and of 50 for a side that has a part score.

4. *Vulnerability*. When a side has scored a game, it is said to be vulnerable, and if both sides have scored one game, both sides are vulnerable. The effect of being vulnerable is that the penalties for failing to make a contract are increased.

5. *The penalties for undertricks*. A side that fails to fulfil its contract is penalized as follows:

For a side that is not vulnerable:
    Undoubled—50 for each trick short of contract.
    Doubled—100 for the first trick; 200 for subsequent tricks.
    Redoubled—200 for the first trick; 400 for subsequent tricks.

Three down doubled, not vulnerable, therefore costs, 500 (100 + 200 + 200).

When a side is vulnerable, the penalties are as follows:
    Undoubled—100 for each trick short of contract.
    Doubled—200 for the first trick; 300 for subsequent tricks.
    Redoubled—400 for the first trick; 600 for subsequent tricks.

Three down doubled and vulnerable, therefore, costs 800 (200 + 300 + 300).

6. *Bonuses for overtricks and doubled contracts*.

As explained above, overtricks beyond the number of tricks contracted for are scored at the same value but are entered above the line.

If the contract has been doubled or redoubled, scoring for tricks is twice or four times the normal amount. So Two Spades doubled and just made counts 120 below the line and game is scored. Overtricks are scored as follows:

    Non-vulnerable, 100 per trick if doubled, 200 if redoubled.
    Vulnerable, 200 and 400, respectively.

In addition, there is a constant bonus of 50 points in respect of doubled or redoubled contracts made, irrespective of vulnerability. So Three Clubs, redoubled, vulnerable, made with an overtrick, scores 240 below the line, 400 above for overtrick and 50 for doubled contract made.

7. *Slam bonuses*. There are special bonuses for bidding and making a small slam, 12 tricks, and a grand slam, 13 tricks. The bonus for a small slam is 500 non-vulnerable, 750 vulnerable; for a grand slam, 1000 non-vulnerable, and 1500 vulnerable.

8. *Honours*. A player who holds four of the five honours (Ace,

King, Queen, Jack, Ten) in the trump suit scores a bonus of 100, and if he has five honours, 150. If at No Trump he has all four Aces, he scores 150.

Bidding

1. *Valuation.* There are two standards by which a hand may be valued: honour tricks and playing tricks. Certain combinations of high cards can be valued in terms of what are known as honour tricks. The following table of honour tricks shows what can be counted for high card combinations:

$$
\begin{aligned}
A\ K &= 2 \text{ honour tricks.} \\
K\ Q\ J &= 1\tfrac{1}{2} \quad ,, \quad ,, \\
A\ Q &= 1\tfrac{1}{2} \quad ,, \quad ,, \\
A &= 1 \quad ,, \quad ,, \\
K\ Q &= 1 \quad ,, \quad ,, \\
K\ x &= \tfrac{1}{2} \quad ,, \quad ,, \\
Q\ J &= \tfrac{1}{2} \quad ,, \quad ,,
\end{aligned}
$$

Not more than 2 H T can be counted in respect of any one suit. A suit such as A K Q J 10 4 will clearly win six tricks in play if the suit is trumps, but if another suit is trumps only the Ace and King are likely to make. Honour tricks are tricks that are likely to make whatever the declaration. They therefore form the basis of opening bids and partnership co-operation.

Another way of assessing the value of honour cards is by means of a point count. The point count most commonly used is as follows:

$$
\begin{aligned}
\text{Ace} &= 4 \text{ points.} \\
\text{King} &= 3 \quad ,, \\
\text{Queen} &= 2 \quad ,, \\
\text{Jack} &= 1 \text{ point.}
\end{aligned}
$$

This point count, as we shall see below, is used mainly as a means of valuing hands for No Trump bids.

2. *Opening Suit bids of One.* To open the bidding, a player should normally have a hand slightly above the average in terms both of honour tricks and playing tricks. These are the generally accepted standards for opening bids of One:

With a good six-card suit, 2 H T

♠ A Q J 9 6 4	♦ 3
♡ K 5 2	♣ 10 6 4

This is a sound opening bid of One Spade.

With a five-card suit, 2½ H T

♠ 3
♡ A Q 8 6 5
◇ K 9 4 2
♣ K 6 3

This is a minimum bid of One Heart.

With a four-card suit, at least 3 H T

♠ A J 8 4
♡ 3
◇ K Q 4 2
♣ A 10 4 3

The best opening bid is One Diamond. One Spade would not be such a good bid, as the hand would then have no sound rebid in face of a response by partner of Two Hearts. In general, when a player opens the bidding, he must always have a sound rebid in face of any such response by partner. If the opening bid contains a five-card or longer suit, the suit can safely be rebid, but when only four-card suits are held, a player must select his opening bid in such a way that he will have a sound rebid in face of any response.

This last consideration apart, a player who has two suits of equal length should normally bid the higher valued; when he has two suits of unequal length, he should normally open the longer suit.

An opening bid in a major suit should not be made on a holding weaker than Q J x x. Minor suit bids are not subject to the same limits. Sometimes a player has no alternative to opening One Club on a three-card suit.

3. *The First Response to Bids of One.* When partner has opened the bidding, responder should pass only if his hand is quite weak.

♠ 8 5 4   ♡ Q 8 3   ◇ K 7 6 2   ♣ 6 4 3

Responder should pass any opening bid; with an extra Jack he would keep the bidding open.

Two responses that show moderate values are One No Trump and a single raise in partner's suit.

♠ 8 4   ♡ J 10 4 3   ◇ Q 7 6   ♣ Q J 3 2

On this hand, the response to One Spade is One No Trump. One Heart could be raised to Two Hearts.

With stronger support for partner's suit, responder can raise to Three or Four.

♠ A 5   ♡ K J 10 3   ◇ Q 7 6 2   ♣ Q 5 3

This is a sound raise of One Heart to Three Hearts. If the hand were slightly stronger, the response would be Four Hearts. A response of Two No Trump shows a balanced hand containing about 11–13 points on the 4-3-2-1 point count described above. A response of Three No Trump shows about 14–16 points.

A simple response in a new suit, such as One Heart over One Diamond, or Two Clubs over One Spade, is a bid of variable strength. A response at the level of One may show quite minimum values, not more than one HT and a biddable suit. On the other hand, it may be the best bid on a powerful hand containing upwards of 3 HT. A suit response at the level of Two shows fair values, generally a five-card suit and not less than 1½ HT.

The strongest response is a jump bid in a new suit, such as Two Hearts over One Diamond, or Three Clubs over One Spade. This response is unconditionally forcing to game; neither partner should pass until game is reached.

♠ 6   ♡ A K 8 4 3   ◇ A 10 7 2   ♣ K 10 7

This hand is worth Two Hearts over One Diamond because, in addition to 3½ HT and a useful suit, it is strong in support of partner's bid; but if the opening bid were One Spade, the response would be simply Two Hearts

4. *The First Rebid by the Opening Bidder.* The opener's rebid depends on the strength of his own hand and on the nature of his partner's response. If partner has made a rather weak response, such as One No Trump or a single raise, then the opener should pass unless he has considerable extra values.

If the response is One No Trump, the opener should pass a balanced hand up to 16 points, and should raise to Two No Trump on 17 to 18 points. In the same way, if partner's response is a suit bid at the level of One, which can be made on quite a weak hand, the opener should rebid One No Trump up to 15 points, Two No Trump on 16 to 18 points.

When the opener has little more than a minimum bid, he can

either repeat his own suit at the level of Two, give a simple raise of his partner's suit, or bid another suit at a low level. Stronger rebids are a jump in the opener's suit and a jump raise of partner's suit. These bids are not forcing, but they invite game unless partner has responded on minimum values.

♠ K 10 6 3   ♡ A K J 9 5 4   ◇ A 8   ♣ 4

You open One Heart, and partner responds Two Diamonds. You have a sound jump to Three Hearts. If partner's response is One Spade, you can go straight to Four Spades.

The strongest rebid is a jump in a new suit; this is forcing to game.

♠ 4   ♡ A K 10 6 3   ◇ A Q J 5   ♣ A J 2

You open One Heart and partner responds Two Clubs; you have such a good fit that you should make a forcing rebid of Three Diamonds, intending to support Clubs later.

5. *No Trump bids and responses.* Opening bids of No Trump, unlike opening suit bids, are affected by vulnerability. These are the general standards for No Trump bids and raises:

Not vulnerable, open One No Trump on 13–15 points; raise to Two No Trump on 10–11 points, to Three No Trump on 12 or more.

Vulnerable, open One No Trump on 16–18 points; raise to Two No Trump on 7–8, to Three on 9 or more.

Some players use a strong No Trump throughout, whether vulnerable or not.

A simple take out of One No Trump into Two of a suit is played as a weakness call by some players, but others treat this response as forcing for one round. This is a matter on which partners have to agree.

An opening bid of Two No Trump shows about 20–22 points irrespective of vulnerability, and partner raises to Three No Trump on 4 to 5 points or so. There is no weakness take out of Two No Trump.

An opening bid of Three No Trump shows a very powerful hand containing about 23 to 25 points. Players who use the Two Club system, however, sometimes use this opening bid of Three No Trump as a tactical measure on a hand whose main feature is a long and solid minor suit. When they have a powerful balanced hand, they bid Two Clubs on the first round.

6. *Opening Bids of more than One.* These are of two kinds: opening forcing bids, either Two of a suit in the Forcing Two system, or Two Clubs in the Two Club system; and opening bids at the range of Three and Four whose main object is to shut out the opponents.

In the Forcing Two system any opening bid of Two is forcing to game. It shows a minimum of 5 H T (occasionally 4½ H T with very strong distribution) and a game-going hand. Partner's weakness ('negative') response is Two No Trump: with upwards of 1 H T he can make a positive response.

In the Two Club system, very strong hands are opened with a conventional bid of Two Clubs. Partner's weakness response is Two Diamonds; then the opener shows his real suit.

Other Two bids in the Two Club system show powerful hands and are often played as forcing for one round.

Opening bids of Three and Four are known as pre-emptive bids. They are made on hands containing a long and strong suit, but little in the way of high cards.

♠ 4   ♡ A Q J 10 7 4 3   ♢ 10 7   ♣ 7 4 2

This is a typical opening bid of Three Hearts. The bid is a fair risk, even vulnerable. With one Heart more, Four Hearts would be a reasonable bid, not vulnerable.

7. *Slam Bidding.* To make slam bidding easier, many conventions have been devised. Most are designed to show first round controls. The simplest way to do this is by means of a 'cue bid' after the trump suit has been agreed.

♠ K Q 10 8 6 4   ♡ A K 5 3   ♢ 2   ♣ A 10

You open One Spade, and partner raises to Three Spades. To investigate slam possibilities, you bid Four Clubs. Since Spades have been agreed as the trump suit, this bid of Four Clubs does not show another suit but is a cue bid; it means normally that you have the Ace of Clubs yourself, and you are inviting partner to show his first round controls. If partner can show the Ace of Diamonds by bidding Four Diamonds, then obviously you are well on the way to a slam.

Certain conventions are used for showing controls wholesale. Of these the most popular is the Blackwood convention. This works as follows:

A bid of Four No Trump is a request to partner to show how many Aces he holds. If partner holds no Aces he responds Five

Clubs; one Ace, Five Diamonds; two Aces, Five Hearts, and so on. It is possible to inquire about Kings in the same way by bidding Five No Trump on the next round. If partner has no King he responds Six Clubs; if one King, Six Diamonds and so on.

The Culbertson Four-Five No Trump convention is more complicated. In this convention the bid of Four No Trump itself guarantees a certain minimum holding, either three Aces or two Aces and the King of a suit bid by the partnership. With two Aces, or one Ace and the King of all bid suits, partner responds Five No Trump. Partner's 'sign-off' is a bid at the range of Five of the lowest valued suit bid by either player. With one Ace, responder makes some intermediate bid at the level of Five or Six.

8. *Defensive bidding and Take-out Doubles*. When opponents have opened the bidding a defensive overcall can be made on less Honour strength than is required for an opening bid.

♠ K Q 10 9 4   ♡ 3   ◇ K J 7 2   ♣ Q 6 4

This is a fair overcall of One Spade, although it would not be a good opening bid.

A jump overcall, Two Hearts over One Diamond, shows a powerful suit and about six playing tricks. The bid is not forcing.

An overcall in opponent's suit, Two Spades over One Spade, is a very strong bid, to which partner must respond. In fact, the bid is often played as forcing to game.

There is an important convention whereby in certain circumstances a double of an opponent's bid at the range of One or Two is not a double of the usual kind, made for penalties, but is a 'take-out' double, requesting partner to show his best suit.

♠ K J 9 3   ♡ A 10 7 4 2   ◇ 3   ♣ A J 4

When an opponent opens One Diamond, you double. Partner must respond by showing his best suit. If he has a fairly good hand, he must make a jump bid. Partner can pass only if his sole strength lies in the opponent's suit.

A take-out double can be distinguished from a penalty double by this test:

If partner has made a bid of any kind, at any time, and in any denomination, then any double by you is a penalty double, made with the expectation of defeating the contract.

If partner has not spoken, or has simply passed, a double of One or Two of a suit is for a take-out.

A double of One No Trump should normally be regarded as a penalty double; nevertheless, the partner of the double may take out the double if he has a weak unbalanced hand.

9. *Bidding Systems.* In the early years of Contract Bridge the game was bedevilled by a multitude of bidding systems. Many players were prevented from taking up the game by the fear that their partners and opponents would be speaking a different language.

The position is now much better. The principles of approach bidding outlined in the preceding sections are accepted by almost all players. The characteristic features of the approach method are the flexible opening bid of One and the One over One principle whereby a simple suit response to an opening bid is treated as forcing for one round.

Players differ nowadays only in their treatment of very strong hands. We have already given an outline of the Forcing Two and Two Club systems. These are some of the better known variants:

The *Acol* system is a variation of approach forcing much favoured by leading players. An opening bid of Two Clubs is forcing to game, Two Diamonds being the weakness response, except that a rebid of Two No Trump by the opener shows about 23 points and can be passed. Other Two bids are forcing for one round, the weakness response being Two No Trump. These Two bids are made on very powerful hands containing not less than eight playing tricks. Emphasis throughout the system is on natural bidding.

The *Baron* system strives for great accuracy in approach bidding. Length of suit is almost the only consideration for opening bids. Changes of suit in the lower rounds are completely forcing. Acol Two Club and Two bids are used.

The *C A B* system is a variation of the ordinary Two Club in which Aces are shown immediately in response to an opening bid of Two Clubs. The Blackwood convention is part of the system; when information about Aces has already been shown by a previous response, Four No Trump is an inquiry for Kings.

The *Vienna* system is a more complicated and artificial method. Opening bids of One Club and One No Trump are both conventional. All moderate hands that have no five-card suit are opened One Club; practically all strong hands, whatever the distribution, are opened One No Trump. The weakest response to One Club is One Diamond, the strongest One No Trump.

The weakness response to the One No Trump opening is Two Clubs.

In the *One Club* system, of which there have been many variations, an opening bid of One Club shows a good hand; the weakness response is One Diamond. These One Club systems have gone out of fashion, but many players use the 'prepared Club', opening One Club on almost all hands that do not contain a five-card suit apart from Clubs. This excessive use of the 'prepared Club' is, however, not favoured by the best players.

The *Lederer Two Clubs* system is another method that has gone out of fashion. In this system the opening Two Club bid shows at least 4½ HT and is forcing for one round only. Other Two bids are made on hands containing at least 3½ HT.

The Play

The play of the cards at Bridge is a very complicated subject. To give an idea of some of the general principles of play, we will analyse two hands, one played at No Trump and one at a suit contract.

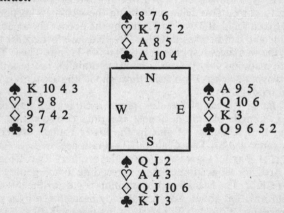

```
                    ♠ 8 7 6
                    ♡ K 7 5 2
                    ◇ A 8 5
                    ♣ A 10 4
                  ┌───────────┐
   ♠ K 10 4 3     │     N     │    ♠ A 9 5
   ♡ J 9 8        │           │    ♡ Q 10 6
   ◇ 9 7 4 2      │  W     E  │    ◇ K 3
   ♣ 8 7          │           │    ♣ Q 9 6 5 2
                  │     S     │
                  └───────────┘
                    ♠ Q J 2
                    ♡ A 4 3
                    ◇ Q J 10 6
                    ♣ K J 3
```

South is declarer at Three No Trump. This is how the play might go:

Trick One: West leads ♠ 3, North plays ♠ 6, East ♠ A, South ♠ 2. At No Trump it is usually best to lead from strength. West leads, by convention, the fourth best card of his longest and strongest suit.

Trick Two: East returns ♠ 9 South plays ♠ J, West ♠ 4, North ♠ 7. West could have won this trick with ♠ K, but he holds up this card so that he can later make a long card in Spades. If he plays the King now, he will never regain the lead to make the 13th Spade.

Trick Three: South leads ◇ Q, losing to East's ◇ K. This is a straightforward finesse; had West held ◇ K, South might have been able to avoid losing a trick in Diamonds.

Trick Four: East returns ♠ 5 to West's King. We see now the advantage of West's hold up play at the second trick.

Trick Five: West leads the good ♠ 10. As everyone has followed to three rounds of Spades, West knows that his last Spade is a master. North discards ♡ 2, East ♣ 2, South ♡ 3.

Trick Six: West exits with a Diamond, won by North's Ace. West plays a Diamond at this point, rather than a Club or a Heart, because there is no danger of a Diamond lead costing a trick.

Tricks Seven and Eight: South makes ◇ Q J. North discards a Heart, East a Heart and a Club. South requires all the last five tricks. He has two A K's and the last trick depends on how he finesses the Clubs. It may seem, on the surface, to be an entirely open question whether South plays East or West for the Queen; but a good player, reviewing all the play to date, would work out that East held originally more Clubs than West; he would, therefore, take the finesse against East.

Now for an example of play at a suit contract.

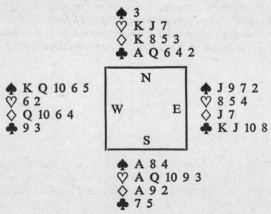

South plays in a contract of Six Hearts.

Trick One: West leads ♠ K, won by South's Ace. The King is the conventional lead from K Q 10.

Trick Two: South leads ♣ 5 and finesses North's ♣ Q, losing to East's ♣ K. Declarer takes this Club finesse immediately. The suit must be developed before dummy's entries are taken out.

Trick Three: East returns ♡ 4, won by North's ♡ 7. It is apparent to the defence that declarer is going to ruff Spades in dummy. This trump lead has a double object. It reduces declarer's opportunity to ruff Spades, and it attacks an entry in dummy that may be needed for the establishment of Clubs.

Trick Four: South leads Ace of Clubs from dummy.

Trick Five: South ruffs a Club with ♡ 9. Declarer is carrying out his plan to establish a long card in Clubs.

Trick Six: South leads a Spade, ruffing with dummy's ♡ J. Declarer cannot afford to draw trumps; he has to use both dummy's trumps for ruffing.

Trick Seven: South ruffs another small Club, establishing the last Club in dummy as a master.

Trick Eight: South ruffs his last Spade with dummy's ♡ K.

Trick Nine: South comes back to hand with the Diamond Ace.

Tricks Ten and Eleven: South plays out his two good trumps, drawing all the trumps against him.

Tricks Twelve and Thirteen: Dummy makes the last two tricks with ♢ K and the established Club.

There follow nine illustrative deals. All are from actual play and most from duplicate matches between teams of four. In duplicate play the same cards are played at two or more tables. A vulnerable game carries a bonus of 500 points; a non-vulnerable game, 300.

I
DAILY TELEGRAPH CUP, 1950

Avoiding a Finesse

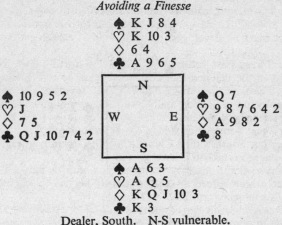

```
                    ♠ K J 8 4
                    ♡ K 10 3
                    ◇ 6 4
                    ♣ A 9 6 5
              ┌─────────────────┐
 ♠ 10 9 5 2   │        N        │   ♠ Q 7
 ♡ J          │                 │   ♡ 9 8 7 6 4 2
 ◇ 7 5        │   W         E   │   ◇ A 9 8 2
 ♣ Q J 10 7 4 2│                 │   ♣ 8
              │        S        │
              └─────────────────┘
                    ♠ A 6 3
                    ♡ A Q 5
                    ◇ K Q J 10 3
                    ♣ K 3
```

Dealer, South.   N-S vulnerable.

SOUTH	WEST	NORTH	EAST
1 ◇	No	1 ♠	No
3 NT	No	4 NT	No
5 ◇	No	5 NT	No
6 NT			

Final Contract: 6 NT by South. ♣ Q led. South made 12 tricks. 990 to N-S.

Comment

The Four No Trump bid in this sequence is not conventional. With 11 points North can visualize a possible slam after his partner's jump to Three No Trump. South is quite willing to co-operate.

West led ♣ Q, declarer won and knocked out ◇ A. East exited with a Heart, and before running off the Diamonds declarer played off three Hearts, ♣ A, noting that East failed, and ♠ A.

When the last Diamond was led, West, playing in front of dummy, had to throw a Spade in order to keep ♣ J. At trick 12 South led a Spade up to the K J. West played the 10, and South knew that West's last card was ♣ J. The Spade finesse could not possibly succeed. So declarer went up with the King and dropped the Queen from East.

II

THE T.B.A. INTER-CITY CHAMPIONSHIP, 1948

Suit-Preference Signal

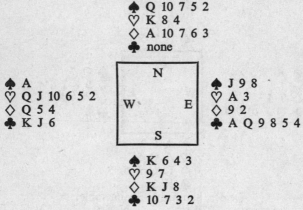

```
                    ♠ Q 10 7 5 2
                    ♡ K 8 4
                    ◇ A 10 7 6 3
                    ♣ none
          ┌─────────────────┐
          │        N        │
♠ A       │                 │   ♠ J 9 8
♡ Q J 10 6 5 2│  W       E  │   ♡ A 3
◇ Q 5 4   │                 │   ◇ 9 2
♣ K J 6   │        S        │   ♣ A Q 9 8 5 4
          └─────────────────┘
                    ♠ K 6 4 3
                    ♡ 9 7
                    ◇ K J 8
                    ♣ 10 7 3 2
```

Dealer, West.　N-S vulnerable.

WEST	NORTH	EAST	SOUTH
1 ♡	1 ♠	2 ♣	2 ♠
3 ♡	3 ♠	4 ♡	

Final Contract: 4 ♡ by West. ♠ 2 led. West made 9 tricks.
50 to N-S.

Comment

This hand is an example of what is known as the suit-preference
signal. North opened ♣ 2—a card that could not be his fourth
best, as he had bid Spades. It was a signal asking his partner to
play the lowest valued suit, Clubs.

West won the Spade lead and played ◇ Q. (He must play
Diamonds before attempting to draw trumps.) South won with
◇ K and made a suit-preference signal in his turn—♣ 2. West
ruffed and, placing partner with an entry in the lower valued
suit, Diamonds, underled ◇ A. South won with ◇ J and gave
his partner another ruff.

North-South were H. Franklin and R. Mercado, of Leeds,
whose team won the Inter-City Championship that year.

III

NORWAY v NORTH OF ENGLAND, 1949

Cutting the Communications

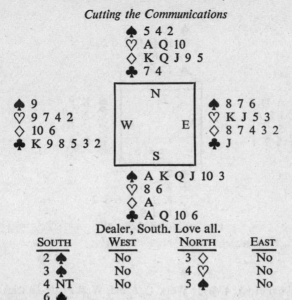

```
                    ♠ 5 4 2
                    ♡ A Q 10
                    ◇ K Q J 9 5
                    ♣ 7 4
                         N
♠ 9                                      ♠ 8 7 6
♡ 9 7 4 2         W         E            ♡ K J 5 3
◇ 10 6                                   ◇ 8 7 4 3 2
♣ K 9 8 5 3 2                            ♣ J
                         S
                    ♠ A K Q J 10 3
                    ♡ 8 6
                    ◇ A
                    ♣ A Q 10 6
```

Dealer, South. Love all.

SOUTH	WEST	NORTH	EAST
2 ♠	No	3 ◇	No
3 ♠	No	4 ♡	No
4 NT	No	5 ♠	No
6 ♠			

Final Contract: 6 ♠ by South. ♡ 2 led. South made 11 tricks. 50 to E-W.

Comment

North-South were playing the Acol system, with the 4–5 No Trump convention. The opening bid of Two Spades showed a powerful hand and was forcing for one round. When North bid Four Hearts he was intending to raise Spades on the next round, having shown that he had a control in Hearts.

West led ♡ 2, the Queen was finessed, and East won. The Norwegian defender now made the brilliant return of a Heart up to the A 10. He placed declarer with one more Heart and, probably, Ace of Diamonds. By the Heart return he killed the entry for the Diamond suit.

Declarer did his best by discarding ◇ A on the third Heart, but when West ruffed the third Diamond the contract was one down.

IV

EUROPEAN CHAMPIONSHIP, 1949—GREAT BRITAIN *v* FRANCE

Loser-on-Loser Elimination

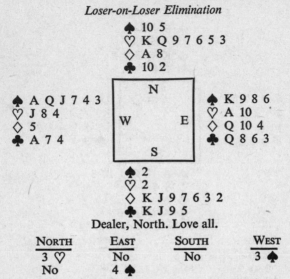

♠ 10 5
♡ K Q 9 7 6 5 3
◇ A 8
♣ 10 2

♠ A Q J 7 4 3
♡ J 8 4
◇ 5
♣ A 7 4

♠ K 9 8 6
♡ A 10
◇ Q 10 4
♣ Q 8 6 3

♠ 2
♡ 2
◇ K J 9 7 6 3 2
♣ K J 9 5

Dealer, North. Love all.

NORTH	EAST	SOUTH	WEST
3 ♡	No	No	3 ♠
No	4 ♠		

Final Contract: 4 ♠ by West. ◇ A led. West made 10 tricks.
420 to E-W.

Comment

North led ◇ A and followed with ◇ 8, declarer ruffing. After
two rounds of trumps declarer led a low Heart. North played
the Queen and dummy the Ace. A Heart was returned; North
won and played a third Heart. West now entered dummy with
a trump and led ◇ Q, discarding a losing Club from his own
hand. South was left on lead, forced either to play away from
♣ K or to concede a ruff and discard.

The British declarer's play was not, in fact, perfect. When
he won with ♡ A he should have played ◇ Q at once, discarding
a Club, for South was marked with a singleton Heart. As it
was, declarer gave North a chance to defeat the contract by
switching to ♣ 10 when he won with ♡ K.

At the other table the defenders played Clubs early and the
French West was one down in the same contract.

V
GOLD CUP, 1950—REESE v HARRISON GRAY

Bidding a Grand Slam

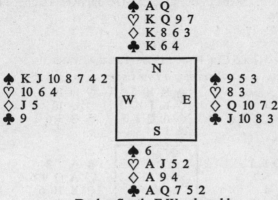

```
              ♠ A Q
              ♡ K Q 9 7
              ◇ K 8 6 3
              ♣ K 6 4
                    N
♠ K J 10 8 7 4 2           ♠ 9 5 3
♡ 10 6 4      W       E    ♡ 8 3
◇ J 5                      ◇ Q 10 7 2
♣ 9              S         ♣ J 10 8 3
              ♠ 6
              ♡ A J 5 2
              ◇ A 9 4
              ♣ A Q 7 5 2
```

Dealer, South. E-W vulnerable.

SOUTH	WEST	NORTH	EAST
1 ♣	No	2 ♡	No
3 ♡	No	3 NT	No
4 NT	No	5 NT	No
6 ◇	No	7 ♡	

Final contract: 7 ♡ by North. ♡ 8 led. North made 13 tricks.
1510 to N-S.

Comment

This is an example of slam bidding by Terence Reese (South) and Boris Schapiro (North).

North's first bid of Two Hearts is a force, and ensures the bidding will not stop below game level. It is therefore unnecessary for South to jump when he makes his second bid (Three Hearts). The response Three No Trump shows that North has a balanced distribution and that his force was not a particularly strong one. South's next bid (Four No Trump) initiates the 4–5 No Trump convention, and, since South has three Aces, the response of Five No Trump shows the fourth Ace and the Kings of both suits bid by the partnership. Now comes South's grand slam try: his bid of Six Diamonds. This means: 'It looks like

Seven to me; bid the grand slam if your trumps are not too bad.'
North's holding of the K Q of Hearts is the deciding factor, and
he duly bids Seven Hearts.

Owing to the bad Club distribution, North had to finesse the
Spade Queen for the thirteenth trick. The opponents stopped in
Six Hearts.

VI

GOLD CUP FINAL, 1950—REESE v EVANS

Penalizing a Low Contract

```
                    ♠ K 10 5
                    ♡ K J 10 3
                    ◇ A Q J 5
                    ♣ J 2
                         N
♠ Q 9 3                           ♠ A 7 2
♡ 7 5 2           W         E      ♡ A Q 9 6 4
◇ 9 4                             ◇ K 10 6
♣ A 9 7 6 3           S            ♣ K Q
                    ♠ J 8 6 4
                    ♡ 8
                    ◇ 8 7 3 2
                    ♣ 10 8 5 4
```

Dealer, East. Game all.

EAST	SOUTH	WEST	NORTH
1 ♡	No	1 NT	Double
Redouble	2 ♣	Double	No
No	2 ◇	No	No
Double	2 ♠	Double	

Final Contract: 2 ♠ doubled by South. ♡ 7 led. South made
5 tricks. 800 to E-W.

Comment

This is an example of the penalization of a low contract in
preference to trying to make game.

North's take-out double is dangerous, since the balance of
the cards must surely be with E-W. East's redouble signals to
West that he is prepared to play for penalties. West duly doubles
South's bid of Two Clubs. South's next bid (Two Diamonds)

is bad. South should redouble: an SOS bid, asking for partner to choose between Spades and Diamonds. East, in his turn, doubles this bid, and South, who has no way of telling that he is leaving a relatively safe spot, plunges into Two Spades. West doubles without waiting for his partner to do so.

West led the ♡ 7. East won with the ♡ Q, and, after cashing ♣ K Q, returned a low Heart. From this point, the defence flowed easily, and declarer was three down.

VII

INTERNATIONAL TRIALS, 1948
A Brilliancy Missed

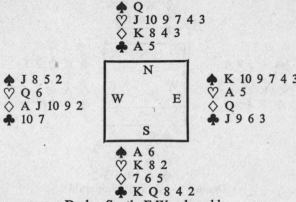

♠ Q
♡ J 10 9 7 4 3
◇ K 8 4 3
♣ A 5

♠ J 8 5 2   ♠ K 10 9 7 4 3
♡ Q 6   ♡ A 5
◇ A J 10 9 2   ◇ Q
♣ 10 7   ♣ J 9 6 3

♠ A 6
♡ K 8 2
◇ 7 6 5
♣ K Q 8 4 2

Dealer, South. E-W vulnerable

SOUTH	WEST	NORTH	EAST
1 ♣	No	1 ♡	1 ♠
2 ♡	2 ♠	4 ♡	

Final Contract: 4 ♡ by North. ◇ Q led. North made 10 tricks. 420 to N-S.

Comment

This was the bidding at both tables in an international trial. As his hand promised some defence, East took a chance of defeating Four Hearts, rather than sacrifice in Four Spades.

East led ◇ Q. West read this as a probable singleton, so he overtook with the Ace and returned the Jack. North covered, and East ruffed with ♡ 5. He switched to a Spade, won in dummy. Declarer came to hand with a Club and led a Heart. A long Club was established by ruffing, and the game was made.

The two East players both missed a chance of immortality. The Diamond return at trick 2 should be ruffed by *Ace of Hearts*! Then West has a trump entry and is able to cash another trick in Diamonds.

VIII

NATIONAL OPEN PAIRS, PHILADELPHIA, 1949

A Bluff that Succeeded

♠ 10 7 3
♡ K 9 8 6 2
♢ J 6 5 4
♣ 5

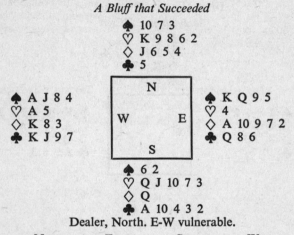

♠ A J 8 4   ♠ K Q 9 5
♡ A 5   ♡ 4
♢ K 8 3   ♢ A 10 9 7 2
♣ K J 9 7   ♣ Q 8 6

♠ 6 2
♡ Q J 10 7 3
♢ Q
♣ A 10 4 3 2

Dealer, North. E-W vulnerable.

NORTH	EAST	SOUTH	WEST
No	1 ♢	2 ♡	2 ♠
Double	Redouble	3 ♣	Double
3 ♠	No	No	3 NT

Final Contract: 3 NT by West. ♡ 6 led. West made 7 tricks. 200 to N-S

Comment

This is an example, by American experts Sam Stayman and Ed Marcus, of modern psychic bidding: 'the art of persuading the other fellow that you hold the cards which, up till then, he thought he held himself.'

South's bid of Two Hearts is meant to show a relatively weak

hand. West now overcalls with Two Spades. North's double, in
view of the previous bidding, just does not make sense: North
relies on his partner to read his bid as nonsensical, and not to
leave it in if East passes.

When the bid comes round to North again, he is sure that the
opponents have game in Spades. He seeks therefore to confuse
the issue still further by bidding the suit himself. Should he be
doubled, there is, of course, an escape into Four Hearts. West,
however, does not double, but bids Three No Trump; and East,
not sure by now who has been fluffing, leaves the Three No
Trump contract alone instead of taking it out into Four Spades.

West could have made Four Spades without difficulty. At
No Trump, North led a Heart, and declarer, taking a·wrong
view of the Diamonds, was two down on his contract.

IX

EUROPEAN CHAMPIONSHIP, 1949—GREAT BRITAIN v SWEDEN

A Bluff that Failed

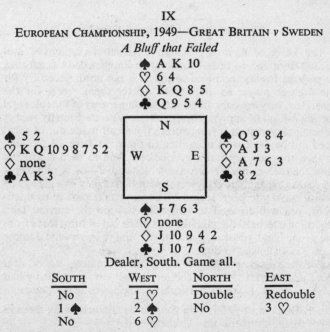

```
                  ♠ A K 10
                  ♡ 6 4
                  ◇ K Q 8 5
                  ♣ Q 9 5 4
                ┌───────────┐
  ♠ 5 2         │     N     │        ♠ Q 9 8 4
  ♡ K Q 10 9 8  │           │        ♡ A J 3
    7 5 2       │  W     E  │        ◇ A 7 6 3
  ◇ none        │           │        ♣ 8 2
  ♣ A K 3       │     S     │
                └───────────┘
                  ♠ J 7 6 3
                  ♡ none
                  ◇ J 10 9 4 2
                  ♣ J 10 7 6
```

Dealer, South. Game all.

SOUTH	WEST	NORTH	EAST
No	1 ♡	Double	Redouble
1 ♠	2 ♠	No	3 ♡
No	6 ♡		

Final Contract: 6 ♡ by West. ♠ A led. West made 11 tricks.
100 to N-S.

Comment

In both 1948 and 1949 Sweden was runner-up to Great Britain in the European Championship. The match between the two teams was of critical importance. On the hand above the Swedish East-West tried to 'pull a fast one', but the British defender kept his head.

West's bid of Two Spades was designed to suggest Spade control and to deter the lead of that suit. After winning the first trick with ♠ A, North might well have hesitated to lead a second Spade, for fear of having it ruffed and establishing the Queen. He saw, however, that if West had in fact a singleton Spade, his King could be ruffed out. So he continued with ♠ K, and West was one down.

In the other room, the British played in Five Hearts, just made.

Contract Bridge: Laws and Etiquette

The Laws of Contract Bridge—internationally agreed and revised from time to time—constitute a complex code which runs to perhaps twenty thousand words. It is not at all necessary for the average player to attempt to master them, since, for the most part, they are concerned with infringements of the rules and the imposition of appropriate penalties. Where a friendly rubber is being played such infringements (*eg* a call made out of turn) need not be dealt with according to the strict letter of the law; in fact, they are normally overlooked. And in card clubs, the laws themselves are always available, and if—as is unlikely— no one at the table is conversant with them, they can always be consulted. If you play 'serious' Bridge, or take part in competitions, you will do well to find out what are the current laws regarding overbids, illegal bids, bids made out of turn, leads from the wrong hand, revokes, and so forth: and to learn what dummy is or is not allowed to do.

For the average player, the *ETIQUETTE* matters a good deal more than the laws. The friendliest rubber can be spoilt by bad table manners. I would particularly emphasize these points:

1. Don't start picking up your cards and arranging them in your hand until the deal is completed.

2. Don't, in arranging your cards, sort them ostentatiously into suits.

CONTRACT BRIDGE SCORING TABLE

	Odd Tricks Bid and Won in	UNDOUBLED	DOUBLED
TRICK POINTS FOR DECLARER	Clubs or Diamonds, each	20	40
	Hearts or Spades, each	30	60
	No-trump { first	40	80
	{ each subsequent	30	60

Redoubling doubles the doubled points for Odd Tricks.
Vulnerability does not affect points for Odd Tricks.
100 Trick Points constitute a Game.

		NOT VULNERABLE	VULNERABLE
PREMIUM POINTS FOR DEFENDERS | DECLARER	**Overtricks**		
	Undoubled each	Trick Value	Trick Value
	Doubled each	100	200
	Undertricks		
	Undoubled, each	50	100
	Doubled { first	100	200
	{ each subsequent	200	300

Redoubling doubles the doubled points for Overtricks and Undertricks.

Making a double contract: where a doubled (or redoubled) contract is made by the declarer, the declaring side score an additional 50 points.

PREMIUM POINTS FOR DECLARER | HOLDER	**Honours in One Hand**	{ All Honours	150
		{ Four Trump Honours	100
		{ Four Aces at No Trump	150
	Slams Bid and Won	{ Little, not vulnerable, 500; vulnerable	750
		{ Grand ,, ,, 1000; ,,	1500
	Rubber Points	{ Two game	700
		{ Three game	500

Unfinished Rubber: The winners of one game score 300 points.
Unfinished Game: A part score in an unfinished game carries a bonus of 50 points.
Doubling and Redoubling do not affect points for Honours, Slams, or Rubber.
Vulnerability does not affect points for Honours.

3. Don't make any comment on your own cards, or on the bids made either by your side or by the adversaries, until the play of the hand is over.

4. Make every effort to bid throughout in a level tone of voice, and—if possible—to express no emotion. There are players who are temperamentally incapable of doing this: the triumphant double, the dubious pass, and so on, will, I suppose, always be with us. It is very difficult for one's partner not to be influenced by such bids.

5. Try to take the same amount of time over every bid—so don't bid too quickly at the beginning. The 'huddle' is sometimes inevitable, but, during the bidding, is much to be deprecated. And if you have hesitated for a long time as to whether to pass or not, and a pass lends itself to obvious inferences, better make the bid and take the consequences. Otherwise you may place your partner in a difficult position.

6. Stick to the accepted formulas for bidding: 'No Bid', 'One Club', 'Two Hearts', 'Three No Trump', 'Double', 'Redouble', and so on. 'No Bid' is preferable to 'Pass', since the latter is often mistaken for a bid in Hearts. And do not say 'I double' or 'I redouble', which often (unconsciously) implies that you are on a very good wicket. In particular, avoid a mistake made by about two players out of five, who say 'Double' or 'I double', meaning 'business', but 'Double One Heart' or 'Double Two No Trump' when the double is for a take-out.

7. You may ask for the bidding sequence to be repeated any time before the auction closes, but do not ask for it to be repeated because you think your partner has missed something.

8. As in bidding, so in play: try to play your cards at a uniform rate, and not—if you can possibly help it—to 'huddle'. To play either too quickly or too slowly may give information to your partner. There are players who think it 'smart' to play with extra deliberation where a finesse may be taken against them and they do not hold the relevant card. But this practice is tantamount to cheating. If you have inadvertently been slow in playing, and declarer may draw a wrong inference, it is better to say outright that your hesitation had nothing to do with that particular trick.

9. You may ask which player played which card to a trick, but, again, don't do so for your partner's benefit.

10. Don't play any card with exaggerated emphasis, *eg* a high card designed to ask for a lead.

11. When dummy, don't help declarer by playing your own cards, even though there is only one of a suit.

12. Post mortems are a nuisance unless everyone wants them, and post mortems which take the form of criticism of one's partner are not likely to improve your chances of winning.

It should be clearly understood that neither the Laws nor the etiquette of Bridge are designed as a defence against cheating. Any pair of players who have a modicum of intelligence can cheat with comparative impunity. In Bridge, as in all partnership games, the integrity of everyone at the table is assumed as a matter of course.

DUPLICATE BRIDGE

THE ILLUSTRATIVE hands already presented are taken from team-of-four duplicate matches. In these matches the same hands are played in two rooms, the members of each team sitting North-South in one room, and East-West in the other. The element of luck is thus, to a large extent, eliminated, since—taking the two rooms together—each team has held the same cards.

The result of a team-of-four match is assessed on a prescribed number of hands, which may be anything from thirty-two upwards. Each hand is a separate event, the vulnerability position and the dealer being prescribed beforehand. Thus, at Board 1, South is assumed to be the dealer, and neither side vulnerable; at Board 2, West is the dealer, and North-South are vulnerable; and so on. Where 'aggregate scoring' is being played, the scoring is as at rubber Bridge, except that there are no rubber points. A non-vulnerable game bid and made scores 300 points; a vulnerable game bid and made, 500 points; a part-score bid and made, 50 points. But in the more serious matches, scoring is by what are called International Match Points: this method of scoring eliminates big 'swings', which may otherwise have an exaggerated effect upon the result of the match.

Duplicate competitions—one should strictly say multiplicate competitions—between pairs are also a popular feature of Bridge tournaments. Here the same hands are played at anything up to twenty or thirty tables, and the movement of players can be so organized that each pair meets each of the others. There are a number of recognized 'movements', the intricacies of which are only known to tournament directors. Scoring can be either by an aggregation of points, or—in the more serious competitions—may be based on a scale of 'match points'.

Participation in tournament Bridge is an excellent method of improving one's game, but a detailed explanation of its organization and mechanics lies outside the scope of this book.

BOOBY

(Contract Bridge for three players)

BOOBY IS a game which I invented during World War II. I frequently found myself working late in Fleet Street with only two other card players in the party. So we thoroughly explored the possibilities of card games for three.

Our favourite game, perhaps, was Black Maria, of which much is said later in this book. But we also experimented with a number of forms of three-handed Bridge.

We began by playing the familiar three-handed game in which four hands are dealt, one of which is dummy's. The other three players then bid against one another, and whoever secures the contract plays with dummy as partner. This game, however, is a pure gamble, since dummy may have the strongest, or the weakest, hand of the four.

We next tried the same game with varying numbers of dummy's cards exposed. There is some improvement here, but not very much, and we found Booby much more satisfying as a game which not only calls for a high degree of skill, but also provides first-rate entertainment.

In this game seventeen cards are dealt (face downwards) to each player, and the remaining card is thrown (face downwards) into dummy. Now each player contributes four of his cards to the dummy hand—again, of course, without exposing any of them. The selection of these four cards for dummy is one of the most interesting features of the game. For, in discarding, one must try to envisage (*a*) what kind of a dummy one is likely to have if one secures the declaration oneself, and (*b*) how—while perhaps rendering assistance to oneself—one can best make dummy comparatively useless from the point of view of other players.

The tactical situation is complicated by the fact that in Booby there is a Nullos call. Nullos is a No Trump contract where one's aim is, not to win tricks, but to lose them; *eg*, to make a contract of One Nullo, one must take no more than six tricks; to make a contract of Two Nullos, not more than five tricks; and so on. Scoring is as in Contract Bridge, with Nullos, at thirty points a trick, ranking above Hearts and below Spades. There follow six illustrative hands, originally published in the *Evening News*. These should suffice to show what a fascinating game Booby is.

The scoring should present no difficulty. It is, as I have said, on Contract Bridge lines, a player who has won a game becoming vulnerable. When a player has won two games, he scores rubber points in the ordinary way; the three scores are then totalled, and each player settles with each of the others at whatever stakes have been agreed.

I

The players were Tom Brown, Charlie Jones and Joe Smith, and these were the cards as Brown distributed them:

To Smith: ♠ Q 10 7 2   ♡ K J 9 6 5 3   ◇ 10 9 5 4   ♣ A J 6
To Jones: ♠ J 5 3   ♡ A 10 7 2   ◇ Q 8 6 3   ♣ K Q 9 8 5 3
To Brown: ♠ A K 9 8 6 4   ♡ Q 8 4   ◇ A J 7 2   ♣ 10 7 4 2

The remaining card (Dummy's) was thus the ◇ K.
Each player now studied his hand with a view to discarding four cards.

Smith threw out his four Diamonds: ◇ 10 9 5 4.

Jones also threw his four Diamonds (a curious coincidence): ◇ Q 8 6 3.

Brown has no such simple discard. After some hesitation, he threw ♡ Q 8 and ♣ 10 7. He was bearing in mind the possibility of Nullos as an alternative to his Spades.

Now came the bidding. Brown (as Dealer) bid first. With a view to 'testing the market' he opened with One Spade. Smith overcalled with One No Trump, and Jones bid Two Nullos. Brown now bid Two Spades; Smith cautiously passed; Jones bid Three Nullos. After a protracted huddle, Brown bid Three Spades, and Smith, not surprisingly, doubled. Jones passed and Smith, as Declarer, turned up Dummy with its Spade void and its nine Diamonds.

'A nasty jar,' was his comment. 'I almost bid Four Spades. I felt sure that both you fellows would have contributed something in my suit.'

Here is the layout for the play:

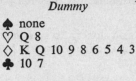

Dummy

♠ none
♡ Q 8
◇ K Q 10 9 8 6 5 4 3
♣ 10 7

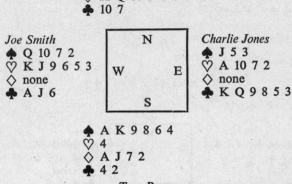

Joe Smith
♠ Q 10 7 2
♡ K J 9 6 5 3
◇ none
♣ A J 6

Charlie Jones
♠ J 5 3
♡ A 10 7 2
◇ none
♣ K Q 9 8 5 3

♠ A K 9 8 6 4
♡ 4
◇ A J 7 2
♣ 4 2

Tom Brown

Brown was most unlucky (as his comment suggests) to find all seven outstanding Spades against him, though their 4–3 distribution saved him from serious disaster. He was set one trick, which is, I think, inevitable whatever the line of defence adopted.

Here is the play:

Trick	W	N	E	S
	Smith	*Dummy*	*Jones*	*Brown*
1	♣ A	♣ 7	♣ 9	♣ 4
2	♣ J	♣ 10	♣ Q	♣ 2
3	♣ 6	◇ 3	♣ K	♡ 4
4	♠ 10	◇ 4	♣ 8	♠ 8
5	♡ 6	♡ 8	♡ A	♠ 4
6	♠ 2	◇ 5	♠ 3	♠ A
7	♡ 7	♡ Q	♡ J	♡ K
8	♠ Q	◇ 6	♡ 2	♠ 6

and, whatever West's lead, South must make the remaining tricks. The score on this deal is thus 100 points each to Smith and Jones.

'It's interesting,' said Jones, 'to speculate as to what would have happened had I taken my courage in both hands and made a game call in Nullos.'

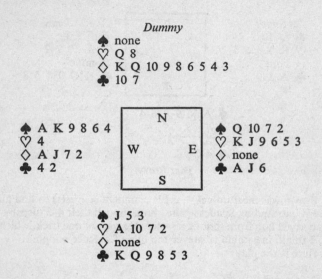

Dummy
♠ none
♡ Q 8
◇ K Q 10 9 8 6 5 4 3
♣ 10 7

♠ A K 9 8 6 4   ♠ Q 10 7 2
♡ 4   ♡ K J 9 6 5 3
◇ A J 7 2   ◇ none
♣ 4 2   ♣ A J 6

♠ J 5 3
♡ A 10 7 2
◇ none
♣ K Q 9 8 5 3

The layout of the cards would have been as above, and readers will find it interesting to speculate how Joe Smith (sitting South) would have fared. To make his contract, he must take not more than three tricks. There are many possible lines of defence, and it must be remembered that the defenders (East and West) cannot see each other's cards.

II

Charlie Jones and Joe Smith are playing again. Bill Robinson (advised by Tom Brown) is playing for the first time.

Joe, sitting South, dealt thus:

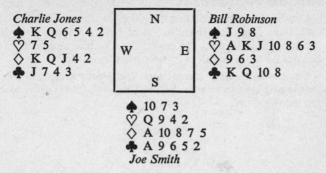

Charlie Jones
♠ K Q 6 5 4 2
♡ 7 5
◇ K Q J 4 2
♣ J 7 4 3

Bill Robinson
♠ J 9 8
♡ A K J 10 8 6 3
◇ 9 6 3
♣ K Q 10 8

♠ 10 7 3
♡ Q 9 4 2
◇ A 10 8 7 5
♣ A 9 6 5 2
Joe Smith

The remaining card—the ♠ A—he dealt face downwards to the centre of the table. This card, it will be recalled, is the nucleus of the Dummy hand.

Each player now contributed (face downwards) four more cards for Dummy.

Joe threw ♠ 10 7 ♡ Q 9.
Charlie threw ♡ 7 5 ♣ J 7.
Bill (advised by Tom Brown) threw ♠ 8 ◇ 9 6 3.

This left them with the following hands:

Joe: ♠ 3 ♡ 4 2 ◇ A 10 8 7 5 ♣ A 9 6 5 2.
Charlie: ♠ K Q 6 5 4 2 ♡ none ◇ K Q J 4 2 ♣ 4 3.
Bill: ♠ J 9 ♡ A K J 10 8 6 3 ◇ none ♣ K Q 10 8.

The bidding of these hands did not take very long.

Joe, after some hesitation, passed. He has good defensive values against a game call in Nullos or a suit, but poor chances of making any game himself. If he bids, then, he runs the risk of losing more points than he can expect to score.

'Ca' canny, eh?' grinned Charlie Jones. 'Well, I'm out for game. Four Spades.'

Bill Robinson indicated the Heart suit. 'Do I bid?'

'Yes,' answered Brown.

'Five Hearts, then,' proclaimed Robinson.

'Double,' said Joe promptly. With his two Aces, and a strong hand announced by Charlie, there should—he thought—be every chance of three tricks.

Charlie was contemplating Five Spades. But the Double—an intimation from Joe that the latter held a winner or two—decided him against it. He passed the Double; and, of course, Bill passed too. His call is by no means 'cast iron'.

Charlie Jones now moved into the North seat, the layout for the play being as under. Before Dummy's hand was exposed, Joe led the ◇ A.

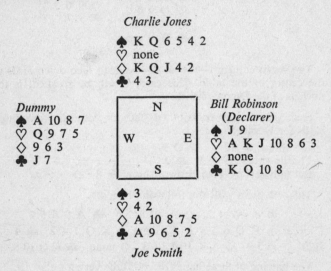

Charlie Jones

♠ K Q 6 5 4 2
♡ none
◇ K Q J 4 2
♣ 4 3

Dummy
♠ A 10 8 7
♡ Q 9 7 5
◇ 9 6 3
♣ J 7

Bill Robinson
(Declarer)
♠ J 9
♡ A K J 10 8 6 3
◇ none
♣ K Q 10 8

♠ 3
♡ 4 2
◇ A 10 8 7 5
♣ A 9 6 5 2

Joe Smith

Before playing to the first trick, Bill carefully studied the position. Then he laid down his cards. 'Nothing in the play,' he said. 'I ruff that Ace right away and draw trumps. I concede one Spade trick and one Club.'

'True bill,' said Charlie Jones resignedly. He jotted down the score. 'Five Hearts doubled. That's 300 points to you, Bill, against each of us. What would have happened, I wonder, if I'd bid Five Spades?'

The cards were laid out. Had Charlie bid Five Spades (which Joe Smith, undoubtedly, would have doubled) the position would have been as follows:

Bill Robinson

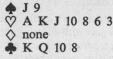

♠ J 9
♡ A K J 10 8 6 3
◇ none
♣ K Q 10 8

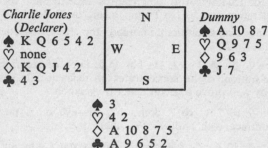

Charlie Jones
(Declarer)
♠ K Q 6 5 4 2
♡ none
◇ K Q J 4 2
♣ 4 3

Dummy
♠ A 10 8 7
♡ Q 9 7 5
◇ 9 6 3
♣ J 7

♠ 3
♡ 4 2
◇ A 10 8 7 5
♣ A 9 6 5 2

Joe Smith

'I should have been one down,' said Charlie. 'I lose—almost certainly—two Club tricks and one Diamond. 100 points to each of you—that's 200 in all—instead of 300, plus the value of Bill's game. A bad business.'

Joe turned to Tom Brown. 'Any criticisms?'

'Yes,' said Tom. 'Your double, Joe, was poor. It deterred Charlie from bidding Five Spades, and you lost, in consequence, a great many more points than he did. But that, if you like, is an *ex post facto* criticism. The real case against your double lies in the fact that you hadn't adequate strength. Two Aces? Pooh! Bill's almost sure to have voided at least one suit.'

III

Brown, Jones and Smith are the players. Joe Smith deals:

Brown: ♠ K 9 5 3   ♡ A 9 6 5   ◇ K J 10 9 6 3   ♣ J 5 3.
Jones: ♠ A Q J 8 7 4 2   ♡ 10 7 3   ◇ Q 7 5 2   ♣ K 10 7.
Smith: ♠ 10 6   ♡ K Q J 8 4 2   ◇ 8 4   ♣ A Q 9 8 6 4 2.

The remaining card (the ◇ A) Smith dealt, face downwards, to Dummy.

Now each player discarded four cards (face downwards) to complete the Dummy hand.

At this game one does not simply discard worthless cards, because one hopes to secure the Dummy oneself. At the same time, one must keep a strong hand oneself, because someone else *may* get the Dummy. Also, one needs to bear in mind that the final declaration may be No Trump, a suit, or Nullos.

With these considerations in mind, the three discarded as follows:

Brown: ♡ 5 ♣ J 5 3. He has little hope of securing the final declaration, so he concentrates on defence. His void in Clubs may well prove a useful defensive weapon.

Jones: ♡ 10 7 3 ♣ 7. Jones has his eye on a possible Spade contract, with Nullos as an alternative.

Smith: ♠ 10 6 ◇ 8 4. Smith, with seven Clubs and six Hearts each suit including the 4 2, has a possible Nullo call. On the other hand, Dummy is not likely to be too helpful in this respect; Smith, however, can also go a long way in Hearts.

After discarding for Dummy, the three hands were:

Smith (dealer): ♡ K Q J 8 4 2 ♣ A Q 9 8 6 4 2.

Brown: ♠ K 9 5 3 ♡ A 9 6 ◇ K J 10 9 6 3.

Jones: ♠ A Q J 8 7 4 2 ◇ Q 7 5 2 ♣ K 10.

The declarations are based on these holdings, *plus* each player's knowledge of what he himself has contributed to Dummy.

Smith opened the bidding with Four Hearts, which, on balance, seemed to him a better contract than Four Nullos. Scoring is on a Contract basis; hence a player who has reasonable chances of game should make a game call right away. Otherwise the bidding may 'die on him'.

Brown passed. He can't possibly compete with a game call.

Jones bid Four Spades. His hand barely warrants the venture. 'But,' he thinks, 'it is highly probable that the others have contributed unwanted Spades to Dummy.'

Smith now tried Five Clubs. There are arguments both for and against this call. If he is to get the final contract, he wants to keep his second suit dark. On the other hand, if Jones goes to Five Spades, an exact knowledge of Smith's holding may enable Brown to double.

Brown again passed and so did Jones. Dummy's hand was now exposed, the layout for the play being as follows:

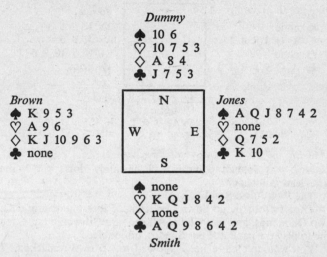

Dummy
- ♠ 10 6
- ♡ 10 7 5 3
- ◇ A 8 4
- ♣ J 7 5 3

Brown
- ♠ K 9 5 3
- ♡ A 9 6
- ◇ K J 10 9 6 3
- ♣ none

Jones
- ♠ A Q J 8 7 4 2
- ♡ none
- ◇ Q 7 5 2
- ♣ K 10

Smith
- ♠ none
- ♡ K Q J 8 4 2
- ◇ none
- ♣ A Q 9 8 6 4 2

'H'm,' said Smith to himself, 'things might be worse. As I'd hoped, there are both Hearts and Clubs in Dummy.'

He had no difficulty in making his contract—and, indeed, there is, I think, no play which will defeat it.

Brown's opening lead was the ♠ 3. Jones played the ♠ A, which was ruffed by the Declarer.

Smith, with eleven trumps in his own hand and Dummy's, now led out the ♣ A. When the ♣ K failed to drop he laid down his cards.

'I concede the ♣ K and ♡ A,' said Smith. 'Just home.' He chalked up 100 points and game.

'Nicely judged,' said Tom Brown. 'And there's nothing that we could have done either. How would your Four Spade call have fared, Charlie?'

'Not too well, I'm afraid,' said Jones. 'Let's just see what would have happened.' He rearranged the four hands as under:

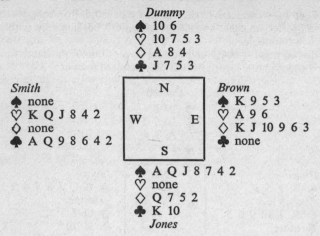

Dummy
♠ 10 6
♡ 10 7 5 3
◇ A 8 4
♣ J 7 5 3

Smith
♠ none
♡ K Q J 8 4 2
◇ none
♣ A Q 9 8 6 4 2

N
W   E
S

Brown
♠ K 9 5 3
♡ A 9 6
◇ K J 10 9 6 3
♣ none

♠ A Q J 8 7 4 2
♡ none
◇ Q 7 5 2
♣ K 10
Jones

'No,' was Jones's comment. 'I certainly don't get home. The lead is—what?'

'The ♡ K,' said Smith.

'Then I probably go down two tricks. I lose one trump trick, two Diamonds, and two Clubs. All the same, it would have paid me to play the hand at Four Spades, undoubled.'

'You wouldn't have been allowed to,' Brown remarked. 'If Joe doesn't overcall, I double.'

'In that case,' said Jones, 'the gamble wouldn't have paid me. I suspected that my call was a poor one.'

IV

The players are Brown, Smith and Robinson, and Robinson deals the cards:

Tom Brown's hand: ♠ A 7 5 3   ♡ 10 5 4 2   ◇ J 9 8 4 3 2
          ♣ J 4 2

Joe Smith's hand: ♠ K Q J 10 8 6 2   ♡ Q J 3   ◇ K Q 10
          ♣ 10 8 6 3

Bill Robinson's hand: ♠ 9 4   ♡ K 9 8 7 6   ◇ A 7 6 5
          ♣ A K Q 9 7 5

The remaining card (the ♡ A) was dealt face downwards for Dummy.

The players now inspected their cards: each had to contribute four for Dummy. Tom, who had decided to call Nullos, threw his four Hearts; Joe, with a Spade call in mind, threw his Clubs; Bill discarded his Spades and the ◇ 6 5. Bill had no intention of bidding. As dealer he had the right to call first, and passed.

'Four Nullos,' said Tom Brown promptly. Four Nullos is a game call. Declarer, playing in partnership with Dummy, contracts to win not more than three tricks.

Joe considered his hand carefully. Dare he risk Four Spades, which is the next call above Four Nullos? He decided not to do so. 'Pass,' he said, and Bill, of course, passed also.

Tom now took his seat opposite Dummy, and Joe, on his left, led the ♠ K. Tom laid out the Dummy cards. The four hands were as follows:

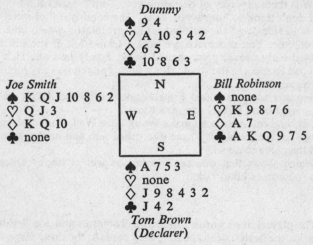

Dummy
♠ 9 4
♡ A 10 5 4 2
◇ 6 5
♣ 10 8 6 3

Joe Smith
♠ K Q J 10 8 6 2
♡ Q J 3
◇ K Q 10
♣ none

Bill Robinson
♠ none
♡ K 9 8 7 6
◇ A 7
♣ A K Q 9 7 5

♠ A 7 5 3
♡ none
◇ J 9 8 4 3 2
♣ J 4 2
Tom Brown
(Declarer)

To trick 1, Tom played the ♠ 9 from Dummy. Bill discarded the ◇ A, and Tom won with the ♠ A. There are no trumps in a Nullos call: it resembles somewhat a Misère call at Solo.

To trick 2, Tom led the ◇ 2. Joe put up the ◇ K; the ◇ 6 was played from Dummy and the ◇ 7 by Bill. Joe was now in something of a quandary.

After some thought, he led the ◇ Q. His idea was to try to cut off Dummy's hand from Tom's. He could still force Tom to win with a Spade trick, and, if Bill could make him win a Heart and a Club, the contract would be defeated.

The ♦ 5 was played from Dummy; Bill threw the ♣ A and Tom the ♦ J.

Joe could not lead his third Diamond because Tom could have discarded Dummy's ♥ A. He therefore next led the ♥ Q.

The ♥ 10 was played from Dummy. Bill played the ♥ 9 and Tom, after a little thought, the ♣ J. The ♥ J followed from Joe. This time Tom won with Dummy's ♥ A, and, discarding his own ♠ 7, next led Dummy's ♠ 4. This he overtook with his ♠ 5.

Joe played the ♠ 2 and Tom had now won his three tricks. But he was clearly 'home'. He threw the lead to Joe with a small Diamond, and no play by the adversaries can compel him to take another trick.

'Was there any way of defeating you, Tom?' asked Bill.

'I don't think so,' answered Tom. 'The hand is full of pitfalls for both sides, and to work out all its possibilities would take a lot of time. You can make me take a Club trick, if the suit is tackled early enough; but then, I think, I only lose one Heart and one Spade. On the whole, Joe's line of attack was as promising as any.'

'I ought to have called Four Spades,' said Joe. 'With that Dummy, I don't think I can miss them.'

Bill laughed. 'And I can make Five Clubs. Well, Tom deserves his game. We could both have overcalled him and neither of us had the pluck to do so.'

Which shows that one can't expect to win at Booby unless one sometimes takes risks!

V

The players are Charlie Jones, Bill Robinson and Joe Smith. Charlie, the dealer, dealt the following cards to the three players:

To Bill: ♠ 9 5 ♥ A K Q 7 4 ♦ 10 3 ♣ K J 9 8 7 5 4 2
To Joe: ♠ A Q J 7 4 ♥ 10 9 5 2 ♦ A 9 8 7 5 4 ♣ 6 3
To himself: ♠ K 10 8 6 3 2 ♥ J 8 6 3 ♦ Q J 6 2 ♣ A Q 10

The remaining card (the ♦ K) he dealt (face downwards) for Dummy.

Each player now threw four cards (also face downwards) to complete Dummy's hand.

Bill, with a ready-made Two-suiter (Hearts and Clubs), threw his Spades and Diamonds.

Joe threw his four Hearts. His hand is not a very good one, but the creation of a void improves it from the point of view of defence.

Charlie also threw his Hearts. He had decided to call One No Trump. The discard of the Hearts gives him (should he secure the contract) three fairish suits in his own hand and a possible Heart 'stopper' in Dummy.

As dealer, Charlie had the first bid. He duly called One No Trump, and Bill promptly bid Four Hearts. At Booby, if one has hope of game, one should, of course, make a game-going call at once. Otherwise—since one has no partner—one may be left in a part-score contract.

Joe, after a little consideration, doubled. Charlie's bid might have been pure 'spoof', but, on balance, there seemed to Joe to be every chance of defeating the contract. Charlie passed the double and Bill now switched to Five Clubs. For all Bill could tell, Joe might be sitting over him with six or even more Hearts; Five Clubs, therefore, seemed now the better contract.

Joe cheerfully doubled this call also, and Five Clubs, doubled, was the final declaration.

Bill now moved to the seat opposite the Dummy, and, as soon as Joe had led the ◊ A, turned up the Dummy cards:

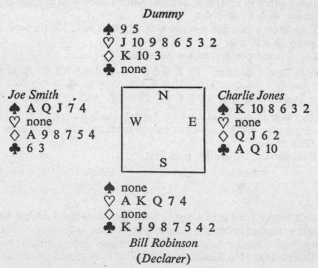

Dummy

♠ 9 5
♡ J 10 9 8 6 5 3 2
◊ K 10 3
♣ none

Joe Smith
♠ A Q J 7 4
♡ none
◊ A 9 8 7 5 4
♣ 6 3

Charlie Jones
♠ K 10 8 6 3 2
♡ none
◊ Q J 6 2
♣ A Q 10

♠ none
♡ A K Q 7 4
◊ none
♣ K J 9 8 7 5 4 2

Bill Robinson
(*Declarer*)

Bill's chagrin when he saw the Dummy can be imagined. There sat every one of the eight missing Hearts! With Hearts as trumps, he could not have failed to make the whole of the 13 tricks.

That would have given him 540 points and a game; whereas, at his call of Five Clubs, he inevitably went down one trick—100 points to each of his opponents.

VI

Tom Brown distributed the cards as under:

To Charlie Jones: ♠ Q 10 8 4   ♡ K 9 6 4   ◇ K J 9 8 7 5 4
♣ K 5
To Joe Smith: ♠ 6 3 2   ♡ A J 10 7 5 3 2   ◇ 6 3   ♣ A 9 7 4 2
To himself: ♠ A K J 9 7 5   ♡ Q 8   ◇ A Q 10 2   ♣ J 10 8 6 3

This left the ♣ Q which was dealt (face downwards) for Dummy.

Discarding the Dummy: Each player had an interesting problem. Charlie, with little hope of securing the final contract, decided to 'jam the works' if possible, by voiding one of his suits. He threw ♠ Q 10 8 4.

Joe has an attractive assortment of cards. He can aim at a contract either in Hearts or Nullos. After a good deal of thought, he threw ♠ 6 3   ♣ 9 4.

Tom Brown had his eye on a Spade contract. He threw for Dummy ♣ J 10 8 6.

This left the players' hands as under:

Charlie Jones: ♠ none   ♡ K 9 6 4   ◇ K J 9 8 7 5 4   ♣ K 5
Joe Smith: ♠ 2   ♡ A J 10 7 5 3 2   ◇ 6 3   ♣ A 7 2
Tom Brown: ♠ A K J 9 7 5   ♡ Q 8   ◇ A Q 10 2   ♣ 3

On these hands bidding now began. Each player, it will be remembered, only knows at this stage what his own contribution to Dummy is.

Tom Brown, as dealer, bids first.

Brown	Jones	Smith
1 ♠	1 NT	4 Nullos
No	No	

This bidding is fairly simple. Tom Brown decides to try for a part-score in Spades. His hand does not justify a more strenuous effort.

Charlie's One No Trump is a 'spoof' call, designed to confuse the issue. If he is doubled, he will fall back on a Two Diamonds bid.

Joe goes all out for a game in Nullos. He is taking a big chance, of course, but he has thrown some useful cards into Dummy. Neither opponent feels justified in doubling.

Tom Brown led the ♡ Q, and Dummy's hand was now exposed:

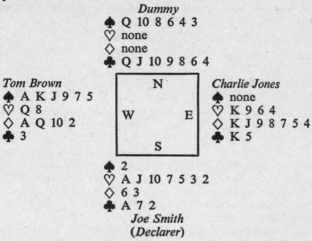

Dummy
♠ Q 10 8 6 4 3
♡ none
♢ none
♣ Q J 10 9 8 6 4

Tom Brown
♠ A K J 9 7 5
♡ Q 8
♢ A Q 10 2
♣ 3

N
W E
S

Charlie Jones
♠ none
♡ K 9 6 4
♢ K J 9 8 7 5 4
♣ K 5

♠ 2
♡ A J 10 7 5 3 2
♢ 6 3
♣ A 7 2
Joe Smith
(*Declarer*)

Joe grinned when he saw his Dummy. To make his Four Nullos contract, he must take not more than three tricks. This, surely, should not be difficult.

Tom, however, had his own ideas. This is how the play went:

Trick	W	N	E	S
1	♡ Q	♣ Q	♡ K	♡ J
2	♡ 8	♣ J	♡ 4	♡ 3
3	♠ A	♠ Q	♣ K	♢ 6
4	♠ K	♠ 10	♣ 5	♣ A
5	♠ J	♠ 8	♡ 9	♣ 7
6	♠ 9	♠ 6	♡ 6	♡ A
7	♠ 7	♠ 4	♢ K	♡ 10
8	♠ 5	♠ 3	♢ J	♡ 7
9	♢ A	♣ 10	♢ 9	♢ 3

Now Tom led the ♣ 3, and, of course, Joe Smith had to take the last four tricks.

Joe was crestfallen. 'I muddled that, Tom,' he said. 'I ought to have made my contract easily.'

'Of course,' said Tom. 'But you lost your opportunity of taking the initiative. You should have won the first (or second) trick with the ♡ A and then led out the ♣ A and another Club. That way you kill my exit card and you'd only have lost two tricks.'

SOLO WHIST

SOLO WHIST is something of a Cinderella in the great family of 'trump and partnership' games. Very little has been written about it. Its strategy and tactics, fascinating as they are, have never been explored as have those of Contract Bridge. I have tried to do something, in the space available in this book, to make good this deficiency.

Solo Whist is an extraordinarily good game: it is just as difficult as Bridge; it has what is obviously the advantage—from the point of view of its social appeal—that each deal is a separate event; it has the further advantage (as many think) that it is in part a partnership game and in part a game in which each player is operating independently. In circles where it is played with intelligence and with an understanding of its finer points, it has a very strong hold; indeed, many good Solo players look down almost with contempt upon the more highly regimented and, as they think, less flexible game of Bridge.

How Solo Whist is Played

Solo Whist is normally played by four persons with the full pack of fifty-two cards. It also makes a good game for five, each player in turn standing out for one deal. In what follows, I shall assume that four players are participating.

1. The Deal

The pack is shuffled and cut and one card turned up to each player. The lowest card deals, the Ace for this purpose ranking as lowest. It is convenient, further, to rank the suits in their Bridge order: Clubs (lowest), Diamonds, Hearts, Spades.[1]

The pack having been shuffled and cut to the dealer by the

[1] Solo Whist differs from Contract Bridge in that there is no universally accepted code of rules. It may well be, therefore, that what follows differs from the practice which obtains in some schools, and there is obviously no reason why schools which prefer to do so should not conform to rules of their own. But there is a very complete code of rules to be found in A. S. Wilks's book on *Solo Whist and Auction Solo*, and in this section I follow this authority throughout.

player on his right, he deals out the cards three at a time, face downwards, to each player, beginning with the player on his left. This leaves four cards, which are dealt out singly, the last card being turned up to indicate the trump suit.

At the conclusion of the hand, the deal passes to the player on the dealer's left.

2. The Tricks

The cards having been dealt, the players look at their hands. Each player's objective is to secure that number of tricks which has been agreed beforehand, either singly or in partnership with another player. Whether, in the end, one player will be playing against the other three, or two players against the other two, depends upon the calling, shortly to be explained. Before discussing the calling, however, it should be explained what constitutes a trick. When the final call has been determined, the player to the dealer's left will lead to the first trick and each of the other players must follow if he can do so. Where everyone can follow to the suit led, the trick is won (as in all games of the Whist family) by the highest card played (Ace high). If a player has no card of the suit led, he can either discard from another suit or trump; if one or more players trump, the highest trump played takes the trick.

The winner of a trick leads to the next one, and this process continues until the fate of the caller is determined. In some calls, as we shall see, it will be necessary to play out all thirteen tricks; in others, there is no point in doing so.

3. The Calls

Each player in turn is entitled to take part in the calling, the first caller being the Eldest Hand, *ie* the player to the dealer's left. Calls rank in a predetermined order, a call which is low in the scale can thus be overcalled by one which is higher. Moreover, a player who has called, and has been overcalled by another player, may amend his first call to one which is yet higher in the scale. But a player who has passed is not allowed to make a subsequent call.

A 'call' is an announcement by a player of his willingness to attempt to take a specified number of tricks—in one case in partnership with another player; in the remaining cases, against the other three players combined.

The calls, beginning with the lowest, are as follows:

(i) *Proposal and Acceptance* (frequently known as 'Prop' and 'Cop'). A player who Proposes expresses his willingness to attempt to take eight of the thirteen tricks in partnership with any of the other three. In this call the suit of the turned-up card is the trump suit, and whoever Proposes is thus announcing that, given a suitable partner, his hand is worth about four tricks, having regard to the suit turned up as trumps.

Note that *any* subsequent caller can Accept (unless, of course, there has been an intervening call). Partners do not have to be alternate players, as at Whist or Bridge, but may play next after one another.

Note that the first caller (Eldest Hand) may Accept another player's Proposal even if he has passed. This is the only exception to the rule mentioned above, that once a player has passed he cannot make another call. If a player Proposes and none of the others Accepts, he can amend his call, if he wishes, to anything higher; otherwise the hand is turned in.

(ii) *Solo*. This ranks next above Proposal and Acceptance and is an intimation by a player of his willingness to attempt to take five (or more) tricks, with the suit of the turned-up card as trumps.

A call of Solo, as explained, supersedes a Proposal and Acceptance, and, similarly, with each of the subsequent calls in the table.

(iii) *Misère*, which ranks next above Solo, is an intimation by a player that he will attempt to *lose* all thirteen tricks against the combined efforts of the other three to make him take one. At Misère there is no trump suit.

(iv) *Abondance*. This is an intimation that the caller will attempt to take nine of the thirteen tricks—the trump suit, however, being a suit named by himself. When calling Abondance, a player may not state what his proposed trump suit is. He announces it *after his call has been ratified, ie* when the other three players have passed.

(v) *Abondance in Trumps*. Where one player has called Abondance, another player may overcall with an Abondance in the trump suit indicated by the turned-up card. In this case, he says at once 'Abondance in the Trump Suit', and the suit which the previous player was proposing to make trumps is, of course, not disclosed. A player does not immediately announce his Abondance as an Abondance in Trumps unless there has been a previous Abondance call.

The object of these somewhat complicated rules regarding the announcement of trump suits is to prejudice as little as possible another player who may subsequently call Misère Ouverte.

(vi) *Misère Ouverte.* This very rare call is the same as a Misère, *ie* the player making it undertakes not to win a single trick, but, after the completion of the first trick, the caller must place his remaining twelve cards face upwards on the table.

(vii) *Abondance Declarée.* This is the highest call and no call can be made over it. (*NB:* There is not, as many players seem to think, a call of Abondance Declarée in the trump suit.) Abondance Declarée is, in effect, an undertaking to take all thirteen tricks, and it differs in two respects from an ordinary Abondance:

(*a*) there is no trump suit;
(*b*) the lead to the first trick is made, not, as in the case of every other declaration, by the player to the dealer's left, but by the caller himself.

Thus, a player holding such a hand as: ♠ A K Q J 10 9 7 3, ♡ A K Q, ◇ None,' ♣ A K, has a cast-iron Abondance Declarée, and as soon as he has made his call can lay his hand down and claim the stakes.

To make perfectly clear the above rules in regard to calling, a few examples of possible calling situations follow.

In each case, South is dealer (the players being named by their geographical positions) and West, therefore, is the Eldest Hand, and not only calls first, but (save in the one case of Abondance Declarée) leads to the first trick.

(i) *Proposal and Acceptance*
  West: Pass.
  North: I Propose.
  East: I Accept.
  South: Pass.
  West: (West, having passed, can say nothing.)

North and East have now undertaken to take eight tricks against South and West, with the suit of the turned-up card as trumps.

NB: As soon as a call has been ratified, the dealer takes the turned-up card back into his hand.

  (ii) *Proposal and Acceptance after an initial pass by Eldest Hand*

        West: Pass.
        North: I Propose.
        East: Pass.
        South: Pass.
        West: I Accept.

West and North have now undertaken to take eight tricks playing against South and East.

  (iii) *Initial Proposal amended to a Solo*

        West: Pass.
        North: I Propose.
        East: Pass.
        South: Pass.
        West : Pass.
        North: Solo.

North has now undertaken to win five of the thirteen tricks, with the suit of the turned-up card as trumps, playing against the other three.

  (iv) *Competitive bidding (a)*

        West: I Propose.
        North: Pass.
        East: I Accept.
        South: Solo.
        West: Pass.
        North: Pass.
        East: Misère.
        South: Pass.
        West: Pass.

East has now undertaken not to win a single trick playing without any trump suit against the other three.

(v) *Abondance*

> West: Pass.
> North: Solo.
> East: Abondance.
> South: Pass.
> West: Pass.
> North: Pass.

East's Abondance having been ratified, he now announces his trump suit before West leads to the first trick.

(vi) *Competitive bidding* (*b*)

> West: Solo.
> North: Misère.
> East: Pass.
> South: Abondance.
> West: Abondance in Trumps.
> North: Pass.
> East: Pass.
> South: Pass.

West has now undertaken to take nine tricks against the other three players, the trump suit being that indicated by the turned-up card.

(vii) *Competitive bidding* (*c*)

> West: Solo.
> North: Misère.
> East: Abondance.
> South: Pass.
> West: Abondance in Trumps.
> North: Misère Ouverte.
> East: Abondance Declarée.

East has now undertaken to take all thirteen tricks at a no trump declaration, he himself leading to the first trick.

Note. The above calling is improbable but by no means impossible. Each call in itself gives information to the other players as to the character of the caller's hand, and this information enables West, North and East in turn to amend their first calls.

4. The Stakes

Each deal at Solo Whist constitutes a separate game and stakes are paid in respect of it. The score can, if desired, be kept on paper in the form of 'plus and minus' account, but, more usually, the stakes are settled in cash or counters at the conclusion of each deal.

The stakes themselves are purely a matter for arrangement between the players, and a normal basis would be the following:

Proposal and Acceptance—one unit (a unit, or course, may be anything: 2p, 10p, or what you will). On this basis the Proposer and Accepter each receive one unit from their adversaries if they succeed in making eight tricks with (as a rule) one-quarter unit in respect of each trick made over eight. Thus if the unit stake is 10p, Proposer and Accepter, making eleven tricks, would each receive 17½p. Similarly, if they fail to make eight tricks, they pay one unit each, with a quarter unit for every trick above six made by their opponents. Thus, if they make only five tricks, each pays 15p .

Solo—one unit (accruing to or paid by the caller), with a quarter unit in respect of each overtrick or undertrick. Thus, a player calling Solo, and making seven tricks, receives (if 10p is the unit) 15p from each player, or 45p in all. While, if he fails by one trick, *ie* if he makes only four tricks, he pays 10p to each of the others or 30p in all.

Misère—two units, *ie* a player calling Misère, and making his call, receives (if 10p is the unit), 20p from each player; if he fails he pays 20p to each player.

At Misère, there is no question of overtricks or undertricks. Thus, as soon as the caller takes a trick, there is no object in playing the hand out further.

Abondance and Abondance in Trumps—three units, with one-half units in respect of any overtricks or undertricks. Here (with a 10p unit) a player calling Abondance and making ten tricks, would receive 35p from each of the other players; if he takes only eight tricks, he pays 30p to each of the others.

Misère Ouverte—four units.

Abondance Declarée—six units.

In both these cases, as in Misère there is no question of overtricks or undertricks, the deal coming to an end as soon as the call is defeated.

Some Critical Solo Deals and how they should be called

(1) *Misère Ouverte*

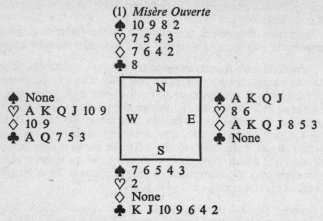

♠ 10 9 8 2
♡ 7 5 4 3
◇ 7 6 4 2
♣ 8

♠ None
♡ A K Q J 10 9
◇ 10 9
♣ A Q 7 5 3

♠ A K Q J
♡ 8 6
◇ A K Q J 8 5 3
♣ None

♠ 7 6 5 4 3
♡ 2
◇ None
♣ K J 10 9 6 4 2

South dealt, and the ♡ 2 was turned up to indicate the trump suit.

How should the hands have been called?

The actual calling was:

> *West:* Solo.
> *North:* Misère.
> *East:* Abondance.
> *South:* Misère Ouverte.

West led the ◇ 10 and South made his Misère Ouverte, the play going as follows:

Trick	W	N	E	S
1	◇ 10	◇ 7	◇ J	♣ K
2	♡ 9	♡ 7	♡ 8	♡ 2
3	◇ 9	◇ 6	◇ 8	♣ J
4	♡ A	♡ 5	♡ 6	♠ 7
5	♡ K	♡ 4	♠ A	♠ 6
6	♡ Q	♡ 3	♠ K	♠ 5
7	♡ J	♣ 8	♠ Q	♠ 4

There is now no play which will defeat South's call.

By a different attack, however, the Misère Ouverte can be broken. West had the right idea, but East missed it. East, when he saw South's hand, decided that the attack must be in Spades and that, therefore, he must get Spade discards on West's Hearts. South saw the danger and, having first got rid of two high Clubs, proceeded to discard his own Spades. In any case, once North had thrown the ♣ 8, there was no means of putting him in. East failed to envisage that West might be void in Spades.

Here is the play that defeats South:

Trick	W	N	E	S
1	◇ 10	◇ 7	◇ J	♣ K
2	◇ 9	◇ 6	◇ Q	♣ J
3	♡ A	◇ 4	◇ 3	♣ 10
4	♣ A	♣ 8	♠ A	♣ 6
5	♣ 7	any	any	♣ 4
6	♣ 5	any	any	♣ 2
7	♣ 3	any	any	♣ 9

How far are the calls made open to criticism? West's Solo is correct, since he can hardly hope to make the three Club tricks needed for a Royal Abondance; North's Misère is (to my mind) over-optimistic; East's Abondance is a 'cinch'. What of South's daring Misère Ouverte? The balance of opinion, among players whom I have consulted, seems to be in favour of calling it; but personally I would not take the risk. A suit of five with the 2 missing, is too formidable an obstacle altogether. And (as I have shown) even the Club suit is not foolproof.

(2) *Abondance in Trumps*

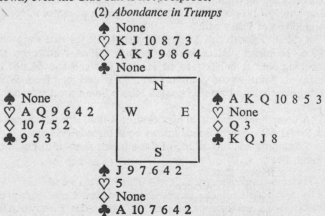

```
              ♠ None
              ♡ K J 10 8 7 3
              ◇ A K J 9 8 6 4
              ♣ None
                     N
 ♠ None                        ♠ A K Q 10 8 5 3
 ♡ A Q 9 6 4 2   W       E     ♡ None
 ◇ 10 7 5 2                    ◇ Q 3
 ♣ 9 5 3                       ♣ K Q J 8
                     S
              ♠ J 9 7 6 4 2
              ♡ 5
              ◇ None
              ♣ A 10 7 6 4 2
```

The ♠ 9 is turned up to indicate the trump suit.

1. West should pass. He will, of course, seriously consider a Misère. But his Club suit is not good, his Diamond suit has a 'hole' in it (the ◇ 4 and ◇ 3 are both missing), and he has to negotiate the difficulty of a sound initial lead.

I should judge that he has by no means an even chance of bringing off a Misère call successfully.

2. North has an odds-on Abondance call. Working on the balance of probabilities, he reckons one Diamond loser (he can, of course, lose more than one Diamond trick, but would be very unlucky to do so), and two Heart losers. And, with ordinary luck, he should have no difficulty in bringing in the rest of the Hearts. Thus his expectation is ten tricks, which fully justifies the call.

As the cards lie, North would just make an Abondance call against West's best opening lead of a Club. He is forced twice in that suit, and the trumps are also obstreperous, but at the critical point in play West only has Hearts left. By 'trumps' of course, is meant Diamonds.

3. East can overcall North with an Abondance in the trump suit. He reckons that (again, with ordinary luck) he should not lose more than one trump trick; it is actually about 3 to 1 on that he will not lose any at all.

There is a good chance of his making three Club tricks, which gives him the nine tricks he needs. Of course, as the cards lie—the six outstanding trumps massed in South's hand—the Abondance is a hopeless proposition. That fact, however, does not affect the soundness of East's call.

4. Should South call Misère Ouverte? But for one snag—his ♡ 5—he has a perfect Misère Ouverte call. As, however, the opening lead is unlikely to be Hearts, this call should not be essayed. South would get home on a Diamond lead from West, but any other lead would be fatal. Hence South must reluctantly pass.

A contributory factor in his decision is that, if East has called a Royal Abondance, South knows he is already on velvet.

To summarize, the calling of these hands should, in my judgment, be:

> *West:* Pass.
> *North:* Abondance.
> *East:* Abondance in trumps.
> *South:* Pass.

(3) *A Cast-iron Abondance*

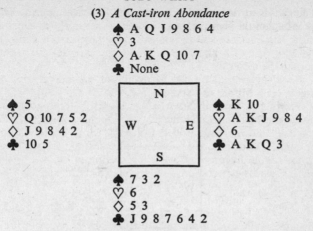

♠ A Q J 9 8 6 4
♡ 3
♢ A K Q 10 7
♣ None

♠ 5
♡ Q 10 7 5 2
♢ J 9 8 4 2
♣ 10 5

N
W   E
S

♠ K 10
♡ A K J 9 8 4
♢ 6
♣ A K Q 3

♠ 7 3 2
♡ 6
♢ 5 3
♣ J 9 8 7 6 4 2

South deals. The ♣ 9 is turned up to indicate the trump suit. *How should the four hands be called?*

My answers would be as follows:

1. West should pass. Apart from his Clubs, he has the makings of a Misère hand, but it is long odds against his getting away with a Misère call where he holds the 10 and 5 of a suit.

2. North has obviously a good Abondance call with the Spade suit as trumps. He is not likely to lose more than three tricks (as the cards lie he will probably lose four) but, anyway, there is a good margin of safety.

3. Over North's call, East can say nothing. I doubt if he could attempt a call even if Hearts were trumps. He has five probable losers.

4. Now we come to the *clou* of the hand; should South attempt Misère Ouverte? I have consulted several players about this hand and opinions are very evenly divided. My own somewhat conservative calling principles, however, incline me to answer the question in the negative. Misère Ouverte, against good players, is a serious proposition, and when all is said and done, three of South's suits are vulnerable. At Double Dummy he can be defeated out of hand by the lead of ♡ 2. Admittedly West is more likely to lead the ♠ 5, but this does not help South at all; as soon as his hand goes down his weaknesses are exposed; Clubs will be led out by East, enabling North to show

his single Heart and, in due course, the ♡ 4 will appear. The best calling of the hand is thus:

W	N	E	S
Pass	Abondance	Pass	Pass

(4) *Misère*

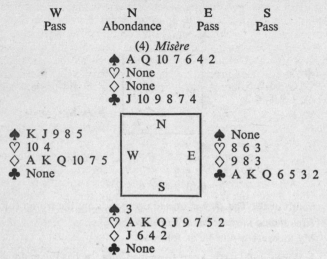

♠ A Q 10 7 6 4 2
♡ None
◊ None
♣ J 10 9 8 7 4

♠ K J 9 8 5
♡ 10 4
◊ A K Q 10 7 5
♣ None

♠ None
♡ 8 6 3
◊ 9 8 3
♣ A K Q 6 5 3 2

♠ 3
♡ A K Q J 9 7 5 2
◊ J 6 4 2
♣ None

South deals and turns up the ♠ 3 to indicate the trump suit. *How should the four hands be called?*

This is a very puzzling deal. My answer to it would be as follows:

West should Propose. There are players who would attempt Solo on West's hand, but, in spite of his five trumps and his nice suit of Diamonds, a Solo call seems to me extraordinarily dangerous.

His distribution (6 5 2 0) suggests that the deal is a freak. In that case the suit may well be trumped almost at once by one of the other players, and if the trump distribution is unbalanced, West, who by no means commands the trump suit, will find that he cannot bring the Diamonds in. As few as four trumps in one hand may easily wreck his chances (to say nothing of the seven which, in fact, are held by North). Hence he should play for safety and be content with a Proposal.

North should call Solo. He has no second suit comparable to West's Diamonds, but his trumps are a very different proposition from West's in that (1) he has seven of them as against five, and (2) he controls at least the first round of the suit. It is very unlikely that more than four trumps are held by any one player— the more so as West has proposed and one trump at least is in South's hand. If, then, the adverse trump distribution is no worse than 3 3 0, North is virtually certain of his five tricks.

Actually, of course, the distribution from North's point of view is just as bad as it could be, but, even as the cards lie, North, if he plays properly, cannot fail to make five tricks. In fact, I doubt if there is any line of play which will prevent his making six.

East's hand is what might be called a near-Misère. But it would be madness to attempt to call, and East must pass, no doubt reluctantly.

South. Now we come to South, who will give serious consideration, not only to Misère, but to Misère Ouverte. (Abondance is out of the question in spite of the solid Heart suit; there is no possible ninth trick). I do not, myself, think that South should attempt Misère Ouverte. His Knave of Diamonds is a dangerous feature and still more dangerous is the absence of both the Four and Three of Hearts. Indeed, he cannot be sure, on his holding, that a Misère call will succeed. Nevertheless, he should attempt it.

In fact, the call of Misère can be defeated, though I do not think this result would be likely in practice.

(5) *Abondance*

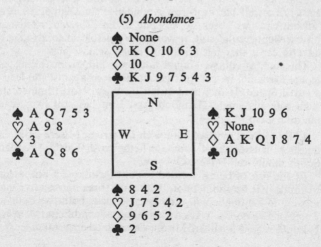

```
                    ♠ None
                    ♡ K Q 10 6 3
                    ◇ 10                        •
                    ♣ K J 9 7 5 4 3

                         ┌─────────┐
                         │    N    │
♠ A Q 7 5 3              │         │       ♠ K J 10 9 6
♡ A 9 8                  │ W     E │       ♡ None
◇ 3                      │         │       ◇ A K Q J 8 7 4
♣ A Q 8 6                │    S    │       ♣ 10
                         └─────────┘

                    ♠ 8 4 2
                    ♡ J 7 5 4 2
                    ◇ 9 6 5 2
                    ♣ 2
```

South is dealer.

The ♣ 2 is turned up to indicate the trump suit.

How should the four hands be called?

My answers would be these:

1. West can reasonably Propose. In collaboration with the average accepting hand, his cards should be worth at least five tricks. A proposal on four probable tricks is permissible, provided it is buttressed by strength in trumps, and West's trumps are adequate.

2. North, with seven trumps, will smile when he hears West's proposal. Should he accept, or call Solo? I think, undoubtedly, the latter.

It is, of course, just possible that West has five of the outstanding trumps (he cannot have more, since it is known that one is in South's hand) and, in that case, North might fail to get home. But the chances are against this, and except against trump concentration, North should succeed in making his Solo; but he will not succeed as the cards lie, unless he plays carefully.

Left in with his Solo call, he might well be forced with Spades at the first trick, and he would just scrape home with four trump tricks and one established Heart. The play is an exercise in what Bridge players call the use of 'tempos'.

3. In actual play, however, the question will not arise, as East has an all but cast-iron Abondance (in Diamonds). I say 'all but cast-iron' because, in spite of East's seven trumps and his excellent second suit, it would be possible so to arrange the adverse cards that five tricks are made against him.

This fact, of course, should not deter him from calling, and as the cards lie, he can just get home, even against the lead of a small Spade. If this card is led by West, North immediately ruffs with his single Diamond, and East has still two Spades and one Club to lose.

4. This brings me to South with his strong Misère hand. The question at issue is, of course, whether over East's Abondance South should call Misère Ouverte.

At the risk of being accused of 'ultra caution', I am inclined to think that he should not. There are three consecutive cards missing in his Spade suit, and he also lacks both the Four and Three of Diamonds. With a hand thus vulnerable in two places, I should regard a call of Misère Ouverte as a mistake.

The final call, then, is Abondance by East, with Diamonds as trumps.

(6) *A Headache for Everybody*

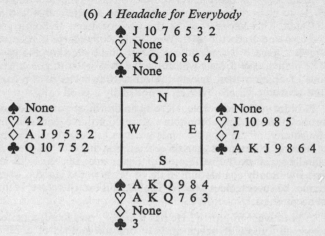

♠ J 10 7 6 5 3 2
♡ None
◇ K Q 10 8 6 4
♣ None

♠ None
♡ 4 2
◇ A J 9 5 3 2
♣ Q 10 7 5 2

N
W   E
S

♠ None
♡ J 10 9 8 5
◇ 7
♣ A K J 9 8 6 4

♠ A K Q 9 8 4
♡ A K Q 7 6 3
◇ None
♣ 3

South is dealer and the ♣ 3 is turned up to indicate the trump suit.

How should the four hands be called?

This is a particularly interesting deal since there is—or can be—a problem in each one of the four hands.

1. West has two possible calls: Solo and Misère. Let us consider Misère first, since, obviously, if there is a reasonable chance of making this call, it should be chosen in preference to Solo.

The hand is a promising one, but it has its weaknesses. In the first place, West will have to lead, which, at Misère, is generally a disadvantage; in the second place, neither of the long suits can properly be called a safe one.

In Diamonds there is a nasty gap between the 9 and the 5, so that a player holding 8 7 6 4 will be able to defeat the call; in Clubs there is a far more serious defect—both 4 and 3 are missing. This means that if both those cards are in one hand, West is almost certain to be defeated.

The chances are certainly that these two Clubs—the ♣ 4 and ♣ 3—are not both in one hand; it is difficult to calculate this chance, because the Solo deal (three cards at a time) offsets the mathematical odds.

Moreover it is possible for these two cards—the ♣ 4 and the ♣ 3—to be in different hands and for the Misère call still to be defeated. This happens to be the position here. If South gets the lead and leads the ♣ 3, West is in a quandary. If he plays the ♣ 2, East will win and can defeat him by leading the ♣ 4; if he plays the ♣ 5, East will throw the ♣ 4 under it. I am therefore of opinion that, taking the other drawbacks of the hand into account, Misère by West is not really a good call.

Now let us consider Solo. Here again one must give an adverse verdict. West could just about scratch up five tricks if the distribution of the adverse cards were as favourable as possible to himself, *ie* not more than three trumps in any one hand and an equally satisfactory distribution of Diamonds. But the odds are actually heavily against him; Solo by West would stand a worse chance of success than Misère. The conclusion, therefore, is that West must pass.

2. Now what of North? He has that very rare hand, a perfect two-suiter, and with seven cards of one suit and six of another one always expects to be able to do something. Nevertheless, on analysis, it will be seen that North must pass. Suppose he calls Abondance (the only call he is in a position to consider), making Spades the trump suit.

The most favourable distribution of the adverse trumps is two trumps in each hand. But the odds against such a distribution are considerable: we can put them down as at least six to one against. North must, therefore, assume that one hand holds at least three trumps and there is not a very good chance even of this. But suppose no other player has more than three trumps. North will probably be forced at trick 1 and must then lead out a trump. He is similarly forced at trick 3 and again at trick 5. By the time he has cleared the adverse trumps he will only have one trump left and he still has to bring in the Diamonds—a virtual impossibility. Thus, his promising-looking hand is seen to be worthless.

3. We pass then to East, whose hand is a good deal more promising than North's in that, while the subsidiary suit (Hearts) is inferior to North's Diamonds, East's Clubs are much better than North's Spades. East, then, will consider an Abondance in the trump suit.

With seven trumps headed by Ace King, he can reasonably assume that he will not lose more than one trump trick, but that means that he must make three tricks in the Heart suit. This, with reasonable luck, he should be able to do; it is on the whole unlikely that the other six Hearts will be so distributed that the A K Q all make separately. In my opinion, then, East should bid his Royal Abondance.

Of course, if he were left with this call, he would be massacred out of hand as the cards lie. West has all but one of the outstanding trumps and South has all the high Hearts. That, however, is neither here nor there.

4. Over East's Abondance in trumps, South cannot reasonably make a call; Abondance Declarée would be impossible in view of his Club loser, apart from the fact that no player could expect both the Spade and Heart suits to break favourably. Suppose, however, that East decides to pass, South has a reasonable call. He can attempt Abondance with either Spades or Hearts as trumps—there is nothing to choose between them. A six trump Abondance, however, is no 'sitter'. In spite of his good second suit, South is likely to be defeated if five trumps are held in one hand against him. For example, as the cards lie, he could not possibly make his call.

This deal illustrates admirably the chances and excitements of Solo. At first blush everyone seems to have something rather good in his hand; but, actually, there is disaster lurking round the corner for whoever has the temerity to make a call.

Illustrative Hands

In the play of these hands four relatively experienced players participate: Tom Brown, Joe Smith, Charlie Jones and Bill Robinson. Newcomers to this game will, I hope, find the players' comments instructive.

I

PROP AND COP

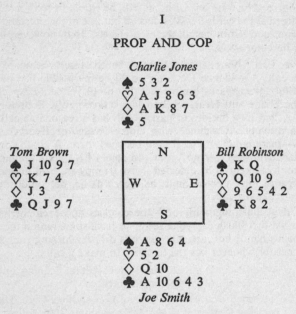

Charlie Jones
♠ 5 3 2
♡ A J 8 6 3
♢ A K 8 7
♣ 5

Tom Brown
♠ J 10 9 7
♡ K 7 4
♢ J 3
♣ Q J 9 7

Bill Robinson
♠ K Q
♡ Q 10 9
♢ 9 6 5 4 2
♣ K 8 2

♠ A 8 6 4
♡ 5 2
♢ Q 10
♣ A 10 6 4 3
Joe Smith

Joe, sitting South, dealt, and to indicate the trump suit turned up the ♠ A. Tom Brown passed; Charlie, who was feeling somewhat above himself, proposed; Bill Robinson passed; and Joe, not unnaturally, accepted with some alacrity. On his holding, eight tricks at least should certainly be 'in the bag'.

Nevertheless, the call flopped.

Tom Brown made the workmanlike lead of the ♠ J. Bill played the ♠ Q and Joe won with the ♠ A. The latter (misreading the trump situation) decided to continue the suit. He led the ♠ 4 and Tom's ♠ 9 was overtaken by Bill's ♠ K.

Bill was in some difficulty with his lead. He selected the ♣ 2, after some hesitation; Joe played low; and Tom's ♣ J took the trick. Tom now played out the ♠ 10, drawing Charlie's last trump, and then led the ♣ 7, on which Charlie discarded the ◇ 7. Bill's ♣ K was taken by Joe's ♣ A, and Joe led out the ◇ Q.

The ◇ Q held the trick (the score now being three tricks all) and was followed by the ◇ 10. Charlie won this trick with the ◇ K and led out next the ◇ A.

Tom ruffed with his last trump and—since he held the Club tenace over Joe—broke new ground by leading the ♡ 4.

Joe had discarded a Heart on the ◇ A, so Charlie put up the ♡ A and, having now only Hearts in his hand, played out the ♡ 3. Bill's ♡ 9 was ruffed by Joe, who had now only Clubs left; and the last three tricks were taken by Tom with the ♣ Q 9 and ♡ K. Joe and Charlie were two tricks 'shy'.

'My fault,' said Charlie. 'Sorry, Joe. I wasn't really strong enough to propose.'

Tom Brown was setting out the cards. 'I agree about that, Charlie,' he said. 'But, do you know, you can make your eight tricks if you find the right line of attack? I won't say that it's clearly indicated, but it's a perfectly feasible one.'

This is the play by which, against the lead of the ♠ A, the Prop and Cop contract can be made.

The first trick falls to Joe's ♠ A. The latter does not now continue trumps, since that (as Tom's lead suggests) is to his adversaries' advantage. Instead, he tackles Clubs, leading out the ♣ A, then the ♣ 3, which Charlie ruffs.

Charlie has now to put Joe in to lead him another Club. He therefore tries the ◇ K and, when Joe plays the ◇ 10, follows up the ◇ K with a small Diamond.

Joe wins with the ◇ Q and gives Charlie another Club ruff. Joe and Charlie have now won six tricks. At trick 7, Charlie leads the ◇ A and Joe discards a Heart. Tom ruffs, but, in doing so, establishes one more trump trick for Joe; and, with this and the ♡ A, the Prop and Cop call just gets home.

'Very pretty,' said Joe, when Tom had finished demonstrating all this. 'I think, Charlie, I'm more to blame than you are. I ought to have smelt a rat when old Tom led that Knave of trumps.'

II

DISASTER

Charlie Jones

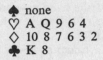

♠ none
♡ A Q 9 6 4
◇ 10 8 7 6 3 2
♣ K 8

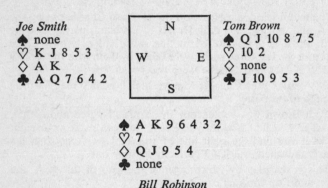

Joe Smith
♠ none
♡ K J 8 5 3
◇ A K
♣ A Q 7 6 4 2

Tom Brown
♠ Q J 10 8 7 5
♡ 10 2
◇ none
♣ J 10 9 5 3

♠ A K 9 6 4 3 2
♡ 7
◇ Q J 9 5 4
♣ none

Bill Robinson

Bill, sitting South, dealt and turned up the ♡ 7 to indicate the trump suit.

Joe called a confident Solo and, as no one else could call anything, was permitted to play it. Charlie, it must be admitted, smiled faintly to himself as he contemplated his array of trumps.

Joe considered his Solo fairly safe with his three 'quick tricks', one Spade ruff at least, and one or more tricks in trumps. As he did not command the trump suit, he decided to open with his Diamonds, and to let the trump lead come from elsewhere.

To trick 1, therefore, he led the ◇ A. The first shock was administered when Tom Brown trumped with the ♡ 2. The latter now led the ♠ Q; Bill played low; Joe, grinning, put up the ♡ 3—and had the mortification of seeing this over-ruffed with Charlie's ♡ 4. 'Dear me,' murmured Joe. 'Things don't seem to be going according to plan.'

To trick 3 Charlie led a small Diamond, and Tom played his second trump. 'Rum game, Solo,' commented Tom. He led the ♠ J, Bill, as before, playing low.

Joe was in a quandary. It seemed useless not to try to check the flow of Spades; so, hoping for the best, he put up the ♡ 8. Charlie, however, produced the ♡ 9 and once again led a Diamond.

This time, of course, Joe did contrive to win the trick. Tom discarded a small Club and Joe trumped with his ♡ 5. He was now left with his six Clubs and the losing tenace of trumps.

After long thought, he led out the ♣ A. And now came 'the unkindest cut of all'. Bill pounced on this Ace with his solitary trump and led the ♠ A. Joe, in desperation, played the ♡ J; Charlie won with the ♡ Q and led out the ♡ A; with the fall of his ♡ K, Joe's last hopes were extinguished. His promised Solo call was defeated by four tricks.

'I suppose I played badly, Tom,' Joe said, as he handed out counters to the other three.

Tom considered. 'Maybe,' he said. 'You played recklessly, Joe, that's certain. You might, at the finish, have saved a trick or so by discarding losers on the Spades. And, as it happens, you'd certainly have done better if you'd attacked at once in trumps.'

Brown set out the cards again, and had no difficulty in showing that, if Joe begins by leading trumps, he can make three tricks against the best defence. 'That,' said Tom, 'is your maximum, I think. It was a brute of a hand to play. And, as it happened, you fell for whatever misfortune was going.'

III

EXPERT DEFENCE

'I'll make it Abondance,' said Tom Brown. He had dealt the cards shown below:

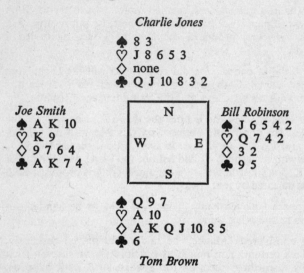

Charlie Jones
- ♠ 8 3
- ♡ J 8 6 5 3
- ◇ none
- ♣ Q J 10 8 3 2

Joe Smith
- ♠ A K 10
- ♡ K 9
- ◇ 9 7 6 4
- ♣ A K 7 4

Bill Robinson
- ♠ J 6 5 4 2
- ♡ Q 7 4 2
- ◇ 3 2
- ♣ 9 5

Tom Brown
- ♠ Q 9 7
- ♡ A 10
- ◇ A K Q J 10 8 5
- ♣ 6

The card turned up was the ♣ 6. Joe opened the ball by proposing; Charlie passed; Bill called Misère. Tom, with eight virtually certain tricks, carefully weighed his chances. Could he hope to make the ♠ Q, and with it a ninth trick? The chances were slender, obviously; but Joe had proposed, which suggested to Tom that Joe might well have strength in Spades. If so, and if Spades were opened, the ♠ Q would stand a sporting chance. So, as already stated, he took his courage in both hands and cheerfully called Abondance.

Tom, however, is not the hero of this story. Diamonds having been announced as trumps, Joe led the ♣ K. This held the trick, and the ♣ A followed, trumped, of course, by Tom. The latter now proceeded to lead out trumps, watching carefully his opponents' discards. With six tricks played, this was the position:

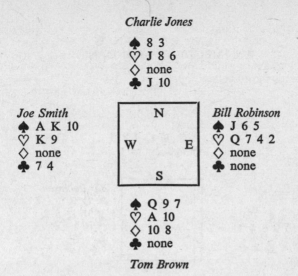

Charlie Jones

♠ 8 3
♡ J 8 6
◇ none
♣ J 10

Joe Smith
♠ A K 10
♡ K 9
◇ none
♣ 7 4

Bill Robinson
♠ J 6 5
♡ Q 7 4 2
◇ none
♣ none

♠ Q 9 7
♡ A 10
◇ 10 8
♣ none

Tom Brown

Tom pondered; things were not shaping well. If he now played the ♡ A, followed by a losing Heart, he would inevitably be forced with a trump and must lead away from his ♠ Q.

The only hope was to continue to lead trumps, so he led the ◇ 10 and then the ◇ 8; Joe discarded Clubs; Charlie, Spades; Bill, Hearts. 'H'm,' said Tom to himself, 'there's only the one chance left now. If Joe holds—as seems to be probable—the guarded ♡ K and three Spades headed by the Ace, King, I can just scrape home by putting him in with a Heart.' Tom, therefore, led the ♡ A.

Unfortunately for Tom, Joe also had been thinking things over. The latter had been much puzzled as to what card to play to the eighth trick; had he thrown the ♠ 10 instead of the ♣ 7 he would, as the cards lie, have made certain of defeating Tom's call. Now, at the eleventh hour, he grasped Tom's plan of campaign, and realized that there was just one chance of defeating it. When Tom played the ♡ A, therefore, Joe nonchalantly discarded the ♡ K. Bill's ♡ Q took the next trick and a Spade lead through Tom's guarded ♠ Q gave the last three tricks to his adversaries.

IV

AN IMPUDENT ABONDANCE

Joe Smith

♠ 10 6 4
♡ A
◇ A K Q J 8 5
♣ 4 3 2

Charlie Jones
♠ 8 7
♡ J 9 4
◇ 10 9 6 4 2
♣ 8 7 5

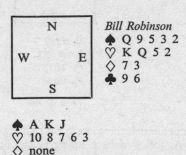

Bill Robinson
♠ Q 9 5 3 2
♡ K Q 5 2
◇ 7 3
♣ 9 6

♠ A K J
♡ 10 8 7 6 3
◇ none
♣ A K Q J 10

Tom Brown

Bill Robinson, sitting East, dealt and the ♡ Q was turned up to indicate the trump suit. Tom Brown studied his hand quizzically. Then he said: 'We don't get too much fun nowadays. I'll venture an Abondance.'

No one else had anything to say and Tom, announcing Hearts as trumps, led out the ♡ 3.

Joe's ♡ A, of course, took the first trick, and the ◇ A was led. Tom ruffed with the ♡ 6 and played the ♡ 7.

Charlie won this trick with the ♡ 9, Joe discarding a Club while Bill played the ♡ 5. Charlie led a Diamond; Tom ruffed with the ♡ 8 and played his last trump, the ♡ 10. When Bill won this trick with the ♡ Q, the position was as follows:

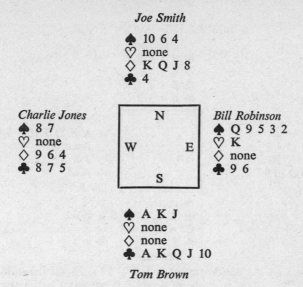

Joe Smith

♠ 10 6 4
♡ none
◇ K Q J 8
♣ 4

Charlie Jones
♠ 8 7
♡ none
◇ 9 6 4
♣ 8 7 5

N
W   E
S

Bill Robinson
♠ Q 9 5 3 2
♡ K
◇ none
♣ 9 6

♠ A K J
♡ none
◇ none
♣ A K Q J 10

Tom Brown

Tom's adversaries had won three tricks, and the ♡ K in Bill's hand gave them a certain fourth. But can the call be defeated? The answer is: No, not at this stage. Bill made things as easy as possible for Tom by leading the ♠ Q—he can now lay his cards on the table, conceding one trick to the ♡ K—but no other lead is any better. If Bill leads a small Spade, Tom must play the ♠ J and hope for the best; if Bill leads a Club, Tom wins and continues the suit.

Tom's impudent call—did it deserve to succeed? I expect opinions will differ—can only be defeated by a Double Dummy play. If, at trick 3, Bill overtakes the ♡ 9 with his ♡ Q, he unblocks Charlie's ♡ J; Diamonds can then be continued at trick 6 and Tom is heavily routed.

Note that if Tom selects Clubs as his trump suit he has next to no chance of making his call. With a solid and a ragged suit of equal length, the ragged suit should be selected for trumps; for then one can use losers for ruffing with, instead of squandering one's winners.

V
A MISPLAYED ABONDANCE

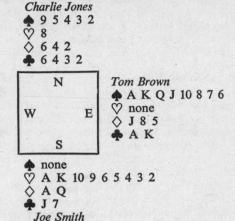

Charlie Jones
♠ 9 5 4 3 2
♡ 8
♢ 6 4 2
♣ 6 4 3 2

Bill Robinson
♠ none
♡ Q J 7
♢ K 10 9 7 3
♣ Q 10 9 8 5

Tom Brown
♠ A K Q J 10 8 7 6
♡ none
♢ J 8 5
♣ A K

♠ none
♡ A K 10 9 6 5 4 3 2
♢ A Q
♣ J 7
Joe Smith

Joe, who was dealer, turned up the ♡ 9 to indicate the trump suit. The calling is fairly obvious. Bill passed; Charlie tried Misère (but for the ♡ 8, he has a perfect Misère Ouverte) and Tom, with his ten certain tricks, called a confident Abondance.

He was overcalled, to his disappointment, by Joe, who, with eight virtually certain trump tricks and the ♢ A as well, had little doubt that his venture would succeed.

Bill led the ♣ 10—his hand is not too easy a one to lead from —and Tom won the first trick with the ♣ K. Tom did not now play out his ♣ A, but, showing his usual flair for a card situation, led the ♠ A.

Joe ruffed with the ♡ 2 and Bill promptly over-ruffed with the ♡ 7. Now Bill led the ♣ 9 and again Tom won the trick. When Tom led the ♠ K, Joe realized that his call was in peril. After much cogitation, he won the trick with the ♡ K and led out the ♡ A. But no miracle occurred; Joe, who had already lost three tricks, was obliged to concede one Heart and one Diamond and was defeated by one trick.

'Could I have got home there, Tom?' he asked.

Tom nodded.

'How, Tom? By putting a higher trump on your first Spade?'

'No, not that way,' said Tom.

'By discarding a Diamond on your second Spade?'

'No,' said Tom.

'Then I'm completely flummoxed,' said Joe.

'But it's simple enough, Joe,' said Tom. 'You get home by discarding your ◇ Q—or, for that matter, your ♣ J—on my first Spade. The whole point of this hand is that you must lose three tricks anyway—barring, that is, a lead of Diamonds up to your A Q.

'Very well, then; lose those three tricks as quickly as you like; then, unless there are four trumps to the Q J in one hand, you can only lose one more. When you played your small trump, Joe, you gave us an extra trick. And you could not recover your lost ground at trick 4, because the lead was again coming through your trump strength; Bill's ♡ Q was unguarded by his over-ruff, but when he put me in to lead another Spade it became none the less a potential trick.'

'I get you, Tom,' said Joe. 'And I see, too, that the real crux of this hand was your refusal to play out your ♣ A at trick 2. You wanted an entry card so that you could lead through my hand twice.'

VI

ABONDANCE IN TRUMPS

Joe Smith
♠ Q 7 4 3 2
♡ none
◇ 9 6 4 2
♣ A 6 4 2

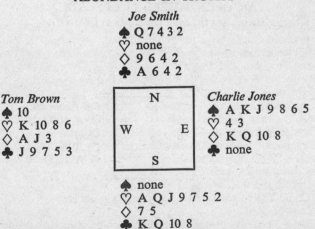

Tom Brown
♠ 10
♡ K 10 8 6
◇ A J 3
♣ J 9 7 5 3

Charlie Jones
♠ A K J 9 8 6 5
♡ 4 3
◇ K Q 10 8
♣ none

♠ none
♡ A Q J 9 7 5 2
◇ 7 5
♣ K Q 10 8
Bill Robinson

Bill Robinson, sitting South, dealt, and turned up the ♡ 9 to indicate the trump suit.

Tom Brown opened the calling with a Proposal. Joe Smith ventured Misère.

'Oh no, you don't, Joe,' said Charlie. 'I'm trying an Abondance.' And: 'Oh no, *you* don't,' said Bill. 'Mine's an Abondance in trumps.'

Tom Brown passed. Joe looked long and wistfully at his hand. Barring his ♣ A, he has a perfect Misère Ouverte. And, if a Heart is led, he gets rid of that ♣ A at once.

But what hope is there of a Heart lead when one of his opponents has called Abondance in trumps after a Proposal from another one? Humanly speaking, no hope at all.

Joe, therefore, very sensibly passed, as did Charlie; and Bill Robinson was left to play his Royal Abondance.

The attempt, of course, was doomed from the start. Indeed, Bill was defeated by three tricks. He lost two trump tricks, two Diamonds and three Clubs.

'Rash, Bill; very rash!' said Tom Brown. 'Not like you at all. What real hope had you of your Royal Abondance with a Proposal to the left of you?'

'I'm asking myself that very question,' said Bill Robinson.

VII
AN OPEN MISÈRE IS DEFEATED

Charlie, sitting South, dealt the cards as follows:

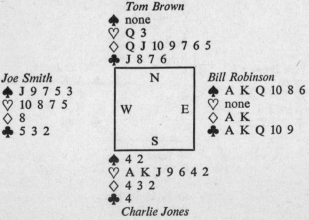

Tom Brown
♠ none
♡ Q 3
◇ Q J 10 9 7 6 5
♣ J 8 7 6

Joe Smith
♠ J 9 7 5 3
♡ 10 8 7 5
◇ 8
♣ 5 3 2

Bill Robinson
♠ A K Q 10 8 6
♡ none
◇ A K
♣ A K Q 10 9

♠ 4 2
♡ A K J 9 6 4 2
◇ 4 3 2
♣ 4
Charlie Jones

The ◇ 4 was turned up to indicate the trump suit.

Joe, of course, passed, and Tom, with five virtually certain tricks, called Solo.

Bill thought long and hard. Dare he venture an Abondance Declarée? He finally decided that the call was not worth risking—he would need a favourable break in two suits—and contented himself with Abondance.

'Misère Ouverte,' said Charlie promptly. Again Bill Robinson considered his 'rock-crusher' of a hand. In view of his holding, a Misère Ouverte call must stand a good chance of getting home. Even so, he could hardly hope for a 3 2 2 break in Spades, *and* a 3 3 2 break in Clubs. 'Pass,' said Bill resignedly.

The Misère Ouverte failed! Joe led the ♠ J (the ◇ 8 seemed useless in view of Tom's call of Solo), and excellent teamwork by Charlie's three adversaries brought about his downfall:

Trick	W	N	E	S
1	♠ J	♣ J	♠ Q	♠ 4
2	◇ 8	◇ 5	◇ A	◇ 4
3	♠ 3	◇ 6	◇ K	◇ 3
4	♠ 9	♣ 8	♠ 8	♠ 2
5	♡ 10	♡ Q	♣ A	♡ J
6	♠ 5	◇ Q	♣ K	◇ 2
7	♡ 7	♡ 3	♣ Q	♡ 4
8	♡ 8	♣ 7	♣ 10	♡ 6
9	♡ 5	♣ 6	♣ 9	♡ 2
10	♣ 2			♣ 4

'We all did our bit,' said Tom. '*And* we had to be lucky. You found a very good lead, Joe. If you lead a Heart, we don't break him, because you can never get me in to play the Diamond at trick 6. Or, if I conserve my entry by playing the ♡ 3 first, I haven't any exit card.'

VIII

TEAM WORK AGAINST AN OPEN MISÈRE

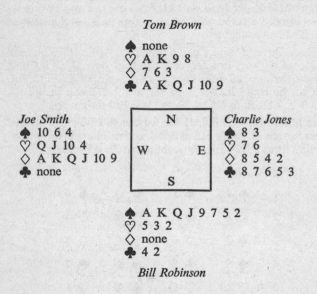

Tom Brown

♠ none
♡ A K 9 8
◇ 7 6 3
♣ A K Q J 10 9

Joe Smith
♠ 10 6 4
♡ Q J 10 4
◇ A K Q J 10 9
♣ none

Charlie Jones
♠ 8 3
♡ 7 6
◇ 8 5 4 2
♣ 8 7 6 5 3

♠ A K Q J 9 7 5 2
♡ 5 3 2
◇ none
♣ 4 2

Bill Robinson

Bill Robinson dealt, turned up the ♠ Q, and, after three passes, called Misère Ouverte.

Joe led the ♠ 10. He did not like the look of his hand, with its rigid block of winning Diamonds. His best plan, clearly, was to open a suit in which Bill was presumably well stocked with cards.

Tom, after some consideration, played the ♡ A. Charlie contributed the ♠ 8 and Bill played the ♠ 9, then, with a grin, put his hand down. 'Make what you can of that,' he said.

This was a somewhat truculent observation, as one player might easily have held the ♠ 4 3. In that case, there is no hope of making the Misère Ouverte. Bill had banked on one of these cards dropping when the suit was led the first time.

'Bill, I'm surprised at you,' said Tom Brown, in accents of mock reproach.

Joe, meanwhile, was reviewing the situation. Charlie Jones, he could deduce, had only one Spade left—the ♠ 3. To continue the suit, therefore, would be fatal. The lead of the ♠ 3 must come from Charlie. But how could Charlie be given the lead?

After some thought, Joe played the ♡ Q. Now it was Tom Brown's turn to think. With four high Hearts in his own hand, it was quite likely that Charlie could not be given the lead in this suit. Tom therefore won the trick with the ♡ K—Charlie dropping the ♡ 7—and played the ◇ 7.

Charlie promptly put up the ◇ 8, and Tom, who had inferred the Spade position, said to himself: 'that's that.' His hopes were disappointed.

Bill, with a grin, threw the ♠ A, and Joe took the trick with the ◇ 9 and went into another huddle.

This was Joe's analysis of the position: 'Why has Tom not continued with the Hearts? Because Charlie has thrown the ♡ 7. That is his highest Heart; at best, therefore, he has the ♡ 6 left.

'That ♡ 6 may be his only card of entry. For Tom's lead of Diamonds—in which the caller is void—suggests that, for reasons best known to himself, he does not find a Club lead encouraging. Maybe he has the Club suit blocked, just as I have the Diamonds.

'The fact that the 7 is Tom's highest Diamond suggests that he is over-stocked in Clubs. At any rate, he is clearly asking that I should not continue Hearts. So, since I have no Clubs, I can only go on with Diamonds and hope for the best.'

So Joe played the ◇ A—thus showing his solid holding in the suit—followed by the ◇ K.

Tom and Charlie followed suit, while Bill, of course, shed the ♠ K and ♠ Q. When, on Joe's leading the ◇ Q, Tom threw the ♡ 9, Joe knew he was on the right track.

'It's a race against time, so to speak,' said Joe to himself, as Bill discarded the ♠ J. 'But I think we just get home.'

This was the position after trick 6:

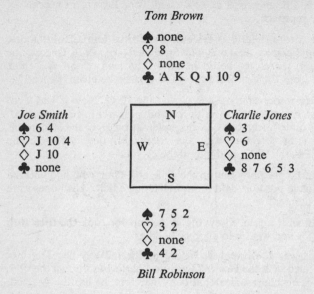

Tom Brown

♠ none
♡ 8
◇ none
♣ A K Q J 10 9

Joe Smith
♠ 6 4
♡ J 10 4
◇ J 10
♣ none

N
W   E
S

Charlie Jones
♠ 3
♡ 6
◇ none
♣ 8 7 6 5 3

♠ 7 5 2
♡ 3 2
◇ none
♣ 4 2

Bill Robinson

Joe led the ◇ J, Tom played the ♡ 8, and Charlie—on whose discard this time everything depended—correctly played the ♣ 8. For Charlie, to whom it was evident that neither of his partners held a Club lower than his, this discard was simple enough.

But Joe did not know what Charlie knew; it was with genuine relief that he saw the Club discarded.

Bill, struggling in vain in the toils, discarded the ♠ 7.

Now came the crucial play: the lead by Joe of the ♡ 4. Tom threw the ♣ A and Charlie won with the ♡ 6. Now at last came the ♠ 3. Bill played the ♠ 2, hoping against hope that Joe had only the ♠ 6 left; but Joe won with the ♠ 6 and triumphantly led the ♠ 4 to defeat Bill's call.

'Well played, all!' was Joe's comment. 'You couldn't have done better if you'd been able to see through the backs of the cards.'

'That's exactly what teamwork means,' said Tom Brown.

IX

OPEN MISÈRE FAILS AGAIN

Tom dealt, turning up the ♣ 2. The four hands were as follows:

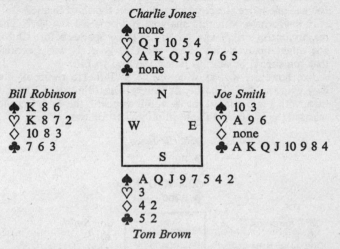

Charlie Jones
♠ none
♡ Q J 10 5 4
◇ A K Q J 9 7 6 5
♣ none

Bill Robinson
♠ K 8 6
♡ K 8 7 2
◇ 10 8 3
♣ 7 6 3

N
W   E
S

Joe Smith
♠ 10 3
♡ A 9 6
◇ none
♣ A K Q J 10 9 8 4

♠ A Q J 9 7 5 4 2
♡ 3
◇ 4 2
♣ 5 2

Tom Brown

In the calling, as will at once be obvious, three players participated. Bill can only pass and hope to be on the winning side; but Charlie has a 'cast-iron' Abondance in Diamonds, and Joe an equally safe Abondance in the trump suit.

Both these calls were confidently made. And both callers had the disappointment of hearing Tom announce 'Misère Ouverte'.

'I don't want to swank, boys,' Tom added, 'but this time I think it's in the bag.'

'Maybe,' said Bill. He thought for some seconds before deciding on his opening lead and eventually selected the ◇ 10. Charlie played the ◇ J; Joe discarded the ♡ A; Tom contributed the ◇ 4 and laid down his cards. It was, of course, now clear to the others that his Achilles heel was the ♡ 3.

To trick 2, Charlie played the ◇ 5. It was clear that he must disembarrass himself of the lead. Joe threw the ♡ 9 and Bill won with the ◇ 8. Bill decided that now his safest course was to try out the Spade situation. He led the ♠ K; and, when

Charlie threw the ♠ Q, the chance of defeating the call became brighter.

Bill could count Charlie's Diamonds and, since Joe must have held eight Clubs to justify his call, Bill was morally certain that Charlie's remaining cards were Hearts. 'Two more discards on Spades,' he said to himself, 'and two discards on Clubs. And Joe has one more Heart which will go on the third Spade.'

In conformity with this analysis, Bill now led the ♣ 7. The reason for this switch was that, if he played Spades before Clubs, Joe might inadvertently block the Club suit. It was essential that Joe should be able to return the lead to Bill.

Joe, however, was as wide awake as Bill. He overtook the ♣ 7 with the ♣ 8 (Charlie, of course, discarding the ♡ J) and then, with a grin, played the ♣ 4. Bill won with the ♣ 6, Charlie released the ♡ 10, and the position was as follows:

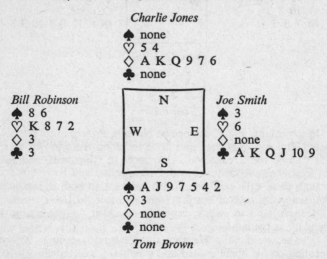

Charlie Jones

♠ none
♡ 5 4
◇ A K Q 9 7 6
♣ none

Bill Robinson
♠ 8 6
♡ K 8 7 2
◇ 3
♣ 3

Joe Smith
♠ 3
♡ 6
◇ none
♣ A K Q J 10 9

♠ A J 9 7 5 4 2
♡ 3
◇ none
♣ none

Tom Brown

Bill led out his Spades, Charlie throwing his remaining Hearts, and Joe the ♠ 3 and ♡ 6, and at trick 8 the lead of the ♡ 2 administered the *coup de grâce*.

'You chaps,' said Tom, 'are getting altogether too good. I've never seen prettier teamwork. Each of you, at some stage or other, had to find the right thing to do, and each of you—confound you!—did it.'

X

AN OPEN MISÈRE SUCCEEDS

Joe Smith

♠ K 9 7 6 5
♡ Q J
◇ K 10 7
♣ J 10 9

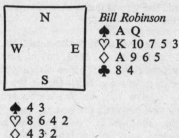

Charlie Jones
♠ J 10 8 2
♡ A 9
◇ Q J 8
♣ A K Q 3

Bill Robinson
♠ A Q
♡ K 10 7 5 3
◇ A 9 6 5
♣ 8 4

♠ 4 3
♡ 8 6 4 2
◇ 4 3 2
♣ 7 6 5 2

Tom Brown

Tom Brown was the dealer, and the ♡ 6 was turned up to indicate trumps.

Charlie Jones Proposed, Joe Smith passed and Bill Robinson accepted Charlie's Proposal. Tom Brown looked at his hand quizzically. 'I'll try Misère Ouverte,' he said.

Charlie led the ♣ A, Joe played the ♣ J and Bill the ♣ 8; Tom contributed the ♣ 7, and laid down his cards. 'There you are,' he said. 'As vulnerable as they make 'em. Have a stab at sinking it.'

Charlie considered. 'Clearly,' he said to himself, 'the weak spot of Tom's hand is the 4, 3 of Spades. If I can induce Spade discards from the others, my ♠ 2 does the trick.'

Charlie, therefore, led out his remaining Clubs. Bill duly discarded the ♠ A Q and Joe the ♠ K.

Charlie now switched to the ♡ A, and four rounds of the

suit were played. But by this time it was evident that Tom's call could not be beaten. 'It's no go,' said Charlie. 'Our cards are too evenly distributed. As they lie, Tom, that call of yours is cast-iron.'

Tom was setting out the four hands. 'Like to bet on that, Charlie?'

'No,' said Charlie. 'I know you too well, Tom. But if we can defeat your call—well, I'd like to see how it's done.'

'Right,' said Tom. 'I'll show you. This is the point, Charlie: you made the wrong guess in thinking that the danger to me lay in Spades.'

Tom proceeded to play the cards. 'Your Club lead, Charlie, was all right. But at trick 2, having seen my hand, you should have thought things out more carefully. Superficially, the Spade plan looks promising. But—this is the point you overlooked—you and I have only six Spades between us. That means that the other two players have seven. Three of these can be discarded on Clubs. But how are you going to get four more discards? Only a quite freakish distribution of the red suits would render such a thing possible.'

'Joe might have been void in Hearts,' said Charlie.

'Oh, come!' retorted Tom. 'How could he be? If Joe has no Hearts, Bill has seven—in which case, he calls Solo. And, similarly, if Joe has no Diamonds, Joe accepts your Proposal. No, Charlie: the calling should have made it clear that there was no hope of disposing of all the Spades.'

'I never thought of that,' admitted Charlie. 'You're implying, I suppose, that you should have been attacked in Clubs?'

'Precisely,' said Tom. 'This is the way to defeat me. Having weighed up the position, you switch to Hearts at trick 2. You lead the ♡ A, Joe plays the ♡ Q, and Bill, say, the ♡ 7.

'Now you play the ♡ 9; Bill's ♡ K wins the trick and Bill continues the suit. You, Charlie, discard—say—Diamonds; Joe, of course, throws his two remaining Clubs. And, after four rounds of Hearts, this is the position:

Joe Smith
♠ K 9 7 6 5
♡ none
◇ K 10 7
♣ none

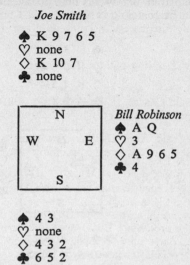

Charlie Jones
♠ J 10 8 2
♡ none
◇ 8
♣ K Q 3

Bill Robinson
♠ A Q
♡ 3
◇ A 9 6 5
♣ 4

♠ 4 3
♡ none
◇ 4 3 2
♣ 6 5 2

Tom Brown

'And now,' said Tom, 'I'm done for. Bill leads the ♣ 4, and that's the end of the story.'

General Misère

(GENERAL MISÈRE—AN 'UNOFFICIAL' VARIATION—IS PLAYED IN SOME SOLO SCHOOLS)

The losing player—who pays to the other three a stake equivalent to that which obtains for Solo—is the player who wins the last trick. It is a matter of indifference which players have won the other tricks.

The play has great possibilities; in essentials it is similar to that of Black Maria.

The deal which I give is not a particularly thrilling one, nor was it played by very expert players, but it illustrates the tactics of this interesting Solo variant:

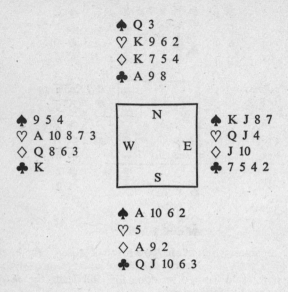

```
                    ♠ Q 3
                    ♡ K 9 6 2
                    ◇ K 7 5 4
                    ♣ A 9 8

    ♠ 9 5 4            N            ♠ K J 8 7
    ♡ A 10 8 7 3                    ♡ Q J 4
    ◇ Q 8 6 3     W        E        ◇ J 10
    ♣ K                            ♣ 7 5 4 2
                      S

                    ♠ A 10 6 2
                    ♡ 5
                    ◇ A 9 2
                    ♣ Q J 10 6 3
```

South deals. The ◇ 9 is turned up.

All four players pass. The deal is now played out as a General Misère, with, of course, no trump suit.

THE PLAY

Note that East is doomed from the start; he gets no opportunity—until it is too late—of leading his quite hopeless Spade suit. Even if, at trick 11, South leads the ◇ 2, the last trick must fall to one of East's Spades.

West is quite right to open Hearts, and South to insist on playing out the Clubs. As at Black Maria, a long suit of which the 2 is not held is always fraught with danger.

Trick	W	N	E	S
1	♡ A	♡ 9	♡ Q	♡ 5
2	♡ 10	♡ K	♡ J	♣ Q
3	♣ K	♣ A	♣ 7	♣ J
4	♠ 9	♣ 9	♣ 5	♣ 10
5	♡ 8	♣ 8	♣ 4	♣ 6
6	◇ Q	◇ K	◇ 10	◇ A
7	♡ 7	♡ 6	♣ 2	♣ 3
8	◇ 8	◇ 7	◇ J	◇ 9
9	♡ 3	♡ 2	♡ 4	♠ 10
10	♠ 5	♠ Q	♠ K	♠ A
11	♠ 4	♠ 3	♠ J	♠ 6
12	◇ 6	◇ 5	♠ 8	♠ 2
13	◇ 3	◇ 4	♠ 7	◇ 2

Competitive Misère

This is an amusing alternative to a General Misère. The loser is the player who takes most tricks, and he pays each of the others.

Here is an illustrative deal:

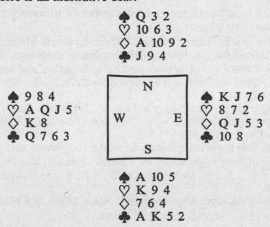

```
                    ♠ Q 3 2
                    ♡ 10 6 3
                    ◇ A 10 9 2
                    ♣ J 9 4

                 ┌─────────┐
                 │    N    │
  ♠ 9 8 4        │         │        ♠ K J 7 6
  ♡ A Q J 5      │ W     E │        ♡ 8 7 2
  ◇ K 8          │         │        ◇ Q J 5 3
  ♣ Q 7 6 3      │    S    │        ♣ 10 8
                 └─────────┘

                    ♠ A 10 5
                    ♡ K 9 4
                    ◇ 7 6 4
                    ♣ A K 5 2
```

South has dealt, and has turned up the ◇ 7. No player can find a call, and it is decided to play the deal as a Competitive Misère.

Here is the play in detail:

Trick	W	N	E	S
1	♠ 9	♠ 3	♠ 7	♠ 5
2	♠ 8	♠ 2	♠ 6	♠ A
3	♠ 4	♠ Q	♠ J	♠ 10
4	◇ 8	◇ 10	◇ 5	◇ 6
5	◇ K	◇ 9	◇ 3	◇ 7
6	♣ 7	♣ 4	♣ 10	♣ 5
7	♣ Q	♣ J	♣ 8	♣ K
8	♡ A	◇ 2	◇ J	◇ 4
9	♡ Q	◇ A	◇ Q	♣ A
10	♡ J	♡ 3	♡ 2	♡ 4
11	♣ 6	♣ 9	♡ 7	♣ 2
12	♡ 5	♡ 6	♡ 8	♡ K
13	♣ 3	♡ 10	♠ K	♡ 9

North, having taken the greatest number of tricks (5), pays each of the other players.

The play is very interesting. It is difficult to decide whether to lead an intermediate card of a suit, hoping to drop high ones and so save one's own low ones, or to play for safety and lead a low card. This hand bristles with difficulties and opportunities for critical decisions.

Even at trick 12, South is in a dilemma. He knows that there are two outstanding Hearts—the ♡ 10 and ♡ 5—and that West has one of them. But which?

If West has the ♡ 10, South will take four tricks and will become joint loser with North. He decides (correctly) that West's Heart is the ♡ 5, and by playing the ♡ K he is able to lose the last trick.

The game has some resemblances to Black Maria and Hearts.

Solo for Three

There are several ways in which Solo can be adapted to the requirements of three players. Here are two of them:

I

The simplest game, perhaps, is that arrived at by removing one complete suit (*eg* the Spades). This leaves a pack of thirty-nine cards, dealt out (in threes) in the ordinary way. Thus the deal might be as follows:

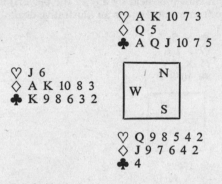

```
                    ♡ A K 10 7 3
                    ◇ Q 5
                    ♣ A Q J 10 7 5

  ♡ J 6              ┌───────────┐
  ◇ A K 10 8 3       │      N    │
  ♣ K 9 8 6 3 2      │ W         │
                     │        S  │
                     └───────────┘

                    ♡ Q 9 8 5 4 2
                    ◇ J 9 7 6 4 2
                    ♣ 4
```

South (dealer) turns up ◇ 7 which indicates the trump suit. The order of calls is:

> *Solo.*
> *Abondance.*
> *Abondance in the Trump Suit.*
> *Misère.*
> *Abondance declarèe.*
> *Misère Ouverte.*

It will be noted that in this game Misère overcalls Abondance, as Misère against only two opponents is more difficult to make. On the deal set out above the calls would be:

> *West:* Pass.
> *North:* Pass.
> *South:* Misère.

The Misère hand looks a good one, but may conceivably be defeated, nevertheless.

In some schools it is permissible, if all players pass, to have a second round of calls, including a six-trick Solo in some suit other than trumps.

II

A second variant (more interesting, I think) is played with a pack of forty cards, the 2's, 3's and 4's having been removed. In this case the fortieth card (not held by any of the players) is turned up to mark the trump suit. Here is an illustrative deal:

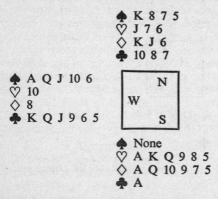

♠ K 8 7 5
♡ J 7 6
◇ K J 6
♣ 10 8 7

♠ A Q J 10 6
♡ 10
◇ 8
♣ K Q J 9 6 5

♠ None
♡ A K Q 9 8 5
◇ A Q 10 9 7 5
♣ A

The remaining card is turned up by the dealer (South) to indicate the trump suit. This is the ♠ 9.

The calling here would be:

> *West:* Solo.
>
> *North:* Pass.
>
> *South:* Abondance.

South will choose Hearts as his trump suit, and will, of course, have no difficulty in making his call.

PIQUET

PIQUET is, in a sense, the aristocrat of card games for two. Its polished technique and its 'Frenchified' terminology bear witness to its courtly origin. It is, moreover, one of the best games ever devised.

Let us begin with an epitome of its rules, to be followed by an illustrative 'partie'.

Piquet is played with a pack of thirty-two cards, *ie* an ordinary pack from which the 2's, 3's, 4's, 5's and 6's have been removed. A 'partie' or game consists of six deals. The object of each player is to score as many points as possible. The scores are recorded at the end of each deal. If, at the end of the six deals, each player has scored 100 points, the player with the better score subtracts the other player's score from his own; he wins by the *difference* between the scores plus an additional 100 points. If one or both players fail to reach 100 points, the player with the higher score wins by the *sum* of the scores, plus an additional 100 points. In this case the player who loses is said to have been 'rubiconed'. (Metaphorically speaking, he has failed to get over the 'Rubicon'.)

Examples of scoring. A is playing B.
1. A scores 139; B, 105.   A wins by 34 + 100 = 134.
2. A scores 426; B, 79.   A wins by 505 + 100 = 605.
3. A scores 96; B, 95.   A wins by 191 + 100 = 291.

Obviously, then, a player's first tactical objective is at all costs to get over the 'Rubicon'.

For this reason, the player who secures choice of deal should always elect to deal first. This gives him, normally, a wider range of options for the critical sixth hand.

The Mechanics of the Game

These are simple.

1. The players cut for deal. The player drawing the higher card (Ace high) has the option of dealing first. (He should always elect to do so.) In each deal, the dealer is *Younger Hand*; his opponent, who discards and plays first, is *Elder Hand*.

2. Younger Hand shuffles the cards; Elder Hand cuts. Younger Hand now deals twelve cards, face downwards, to each

player. He can either deal in 3's (three cards to Elder Hand, then three to himself, and so on); or he can deal 2, 3, 2, 3, 2. Whichever deals he adopts must be followed by his opponent, when the latter in his turn becomes Younger Hand.

3. The remainder of the cards (eight in number) are placed face downwards between the players. These cards constitute the *talon* or stock.

4. Each player looks at his hand. Elder Hand discards a certain number of his cards, taking into his hand an equivalent number from the stock. He *must* discard one card; he *may* (and usually will) discard as many as five. In discarding he has two objects in view: (*a*) to score as much as possible in hand; (*b*) to take what tricks he can in play. He announces the number of cards that he is taking. He places his discard face downwards beside him; he may refer to these cards during the play.

5. Younger Hand now discards in his turn. He need not take any cards; he *may* take as many as are left after Elder Hand has discarded. Thus, if Elder Hand takes only two cards, Younger Hand *may* take six. He, like Elder Hand, may consult his discards.

6. If any cards are not taken from the stock, these may be exposed (at Younger Hand's option) after Elder Hand has led to the first trick.

7. Elder Hand now 'declares' his hand. The *scoring features* at Piquet are as follows:

(i) *Point*. The player with most cards of one suit scores as many points as he has cards in that suit; *eg* a 'point of six' scores six. If both players have the same number of cards in their respective longest suits, the point with the higher pip value is scored. For this purpose, an Ace counts 11; court cards 10 each. If there is an equality of pips, neither player scores.

(ii) *Sequence*. Three or more cards of a suit in sequence. The following sequences score:

Tierce	(3 cards in sequence)	..	3
Quart	(4 ,, ,, ,,)	..	4
Quint	(5 ,, ,, ,,)	..	15
Sixième	(6 ,, ,, ,,)	..	16
Septième	(7 ,, ,, ,,)	..	17
Huitième	(8 ,, ,, ,,)	..	18

The player with the better sequence scores: (*a*) in respect of his higher sequence; (*b*) in respect of any other sequences which he holds. If each player's best sequence contains the same number of cards, the better sequence is determined by its highest card. If the player's best sequences are equal, neither player can score in respect of any sequence.

(iii) *Quatorze or Trio*. Four Aces, Kings, Queens, Knaves or 10's constitute a *Quatorze* and score 14. Three Aces, Kings, Queens, Knaves or 10's constitute a *Trio* and score 3. Four Aces rank above four Kings; and so on down to four 10's. Four 10's rank above three Aces. The player with the best Quatorze (or Trio) can score in respect of any other Quatorzes or Trios held.

Note. Only one player can score in respect of each class of feature—Point, Sequence, Quatorze or Trio. For the method of reckoning (by verbally repeating the score) see the illustrative hands which follow.

Certain other scores will be discussed after the play has been explained.

8. THE PLAY. Elder Hand having declared, he leads a card to the first trick. Younger Hand declares before playing to this trick.

In play, there is no trump suit. The second player must follow suit, if he can, to the card led by the first player. The highest card of the suit led wins the trick; the winner of a trick leads to the next one.

POINTS SCORED IN PLAY

In respect of each card led to a trick 1
  ,,   ,,   ,,   ,, trick won to which the adversary has led 1
  ,,   ,,   ,, the last trick (additional) 1
  ,,   ,,   ,, 'the cards' (*ie* winning more than 6 tricks) .. 10

9. ADDITIONAL SCORES IN RESPECT OF CERTAIN SPECIAL COMBINATIONS

(i) *Carte Blanche*. A player who is dealt a hand without King, Queen or Knave in it may claim 10 for Carte Blanche. To prove that he holds Carte Blanche, he counts his cards rapidly *face upwards* on the table.

(ii) *Repique*. A player who scores 30 in hand where his adversary has not scored at all scores 60 extra for a Repique.

Note (*a*) Carte Blanche debars a Repique or Pique by the adversary.

(*b*) Equality in respect of Point or Sequence debars a Repique or Pique by either player.

(c) The fact that Younger Hand does not declare until Elder Hand has led to the first trick does not debar the former from scoring a Repique.

(iii) *Pique*. Elder Hand, scoring 30 *in hand and play*, where Younger Hand has nothing to declare, and has not claimed equality in Point or Sequence, scores 30 extra for a Pique.

(iv) *Capot*. A player winning all twelve tricks scores 40 for a Capot instead of 10 for the cards.

An Illustrative Partie

Let A and B be the players. They first cut for choice of deal. A cuts, let us say, the ♠ Q and B cuts the ♣ J. The former is the higher card, and A elects to deal. (The dealer has this advantage: he becomes Elder Hand for the 6th deal. He is then in the more favourable position should 'playing to the score' be indicated.)

FIRST DEAL

A deals to B: ♠ K   ♡ A 9 8   ◇ J 7   ♣ A K J 10 9 7.
A deals to himself: ♠ A J 10 9 8   ♡ K Q   ◇ A Q 10 8   ♣ Q.

DISCARDING AND TAKING-IN CARDS

B (Elder Hand) discards: ♠ K   ♡ 9 8   ◇ J 7. B has already 7 tricks good 'against the cards', so there is no point in his keeping the ♠ K. He must go 'all out' to draw Clubs and at least one Queen.

He takes in ♠ Q 7   ♡ 7   ◇ 9   ♣ 8.

A (Younger Hand) discards: ◇ A 10 8. This is an extremely difficult hand to discard from and many would not agree with the discard of the ◇ A. But A has a chance of a Repique. If he can draw the ♠ Q or ♠ 7 his Quint may well be good and the ♠ Q, in addition, will give A a Quatorze. Hence he must not disturb his Spades or Queens. Nor can he afford to throw the ♡ K, since Hearts may be B's suit. Less risk is involved in throwing the ◇ A.

A's draw is disappointing. He takes in ♡ J 10   ◇ K.

THE HANDS ARE NOW

B (Elder Hand): ♠ Q 7   ♡ A 7   ◇ 9   ♣ A K J 10 9 8 7.
A (Younger Hand): ♠ A J 10 9 8   ♡ K Q J 10   ◇ K Q ♣ Q.

DECLARATIONS

(For this first deal I will set out the appropriate conversation.)
B: 'Point of seven.'
A: 'Good.'

B: 'Seven. And Quint to the Knave.'

A: 'Good.'

B: 'Twenty-two.' (Leading the ♣ A.) 'Twenty-three.'

A: (Playing the ♣ Q.) 'Three Queens. Three.'

THE PLAY CONTINUES

B: (Playing his remaining Clubs.) 'Twenty-four, twenty-five, twenty-six, twenty-seven, twenty-eight, twenty-nine.'

A: (Playing ♠ J 10 9 6 ♡ J 10.) 'Three.'

B: (Leading ♠ Q.) 'Thirty.'

A: (Playing ♠ A.) 'Four.' (Leading ♡ K.) 'Five.'

B: (Playing ♡ A.) 'Thirty-one.' (Playing ♠ 7.) 'Thirty-two.'

A: (Throwing ◇ Q.) 'Five.'

B: (Playing ◇ 9.) 'Thirty-three. And the cards, forty-three.'

A: (Taking last two tricks.) 'Six, Eight.'

RECAPITULATION OF THE SCORE

The score is 43 to 8 in favour of B and it is made up as follows:

B:					
Point of seven	..	..	..	7	
Quint	.. .. ..	..	..	15	(Both in hand)
Nine winners	..	..	..	9	
Two losers led out	..	..	2	
'The cards' (majority of tricks)		..	10	(All in play)
		Total	..	43	

A:					
Three Queens	..	..	..	3	(In hand)
Three winners	..	..	..	3	
One loser led out	..	..	1	
Last trick ..	..	..	..	1	(All in play)
		Total	..	8	

SECOND DEAL

B now becomes Younger Hand and deals the cards as under:

To A: ♠ 7 ♡ J 10 9 8 ◇ J 7 ♣ A 10 9 8 7.
To himself: ♠ A Q 8 ♡ A K 7 ◇ A K Q 10 8 ♣ K.

DISCARDING AND TAKING-IN CARDS

A (Elder Hand) discards ♠ 7 ♡ 10 9 8 ◇ 7. He takes in ♠ K 9 ♡ Q ◇ 9 ♣ J. Poor as his hand was to begin with,

A's holding is now not so bad. The ♠ J would have given him a Repique.

B (Younger Hand) discards: ♠ Q 8   ♡ 7. (These three cards 'discard themselves'.) He takes in ♠ J 10   ♣ Q.

THE HANDS ARE NOW

A (Elder Hand): ♠ K 9   ♡ Q J   ◇ J 9   ♣ A J 10 9 8 7.
B (Younger Hand): ♠ A J 10   ♡ A K   ◇ A K Q 10 8   ♣ K Q.

DECLARATIONS

A: Point of Six and Quint	..	..	21
B: Three Aces: three Kings	..	..	6

			Score to	
The Play				
Trick	A	B	A	B
1	♣ A	♣ Q	1	—
2	♣ J	♣ K	1	1
3	◇ 9	◇ A	—	1
4	◇ J	◇ K	—	1
5	♣ 7	◇ Q	—	1
6	♣ 8	◇ 10	—	1
7	♣ 9	◇ 8	—	1
8	♠ 9	♠ A	—	1
9	♠ K	♠ J	1	1
10	♣ 10	♡ K	1	—
11	♡ Q	♡ A	1	1
12	♡ J	♠ 10	—	2
	The Cards	..	..	—	10

Total scores in play: A 5, B 21.

Hence the score for the second deal is:

A: 21 + 5 = 26.
B: 6 + 21 = 27.

The score at the end of two deals is:

A: 8 + 26 = 34.
B: 43 + 27 = 70.

THIRD DEAL

A deals to B: ♠ K Q 10 7   ♡ A K Q 9 8 7   ◇ None   ♣ K Q.
A deals to himself: ♠ J 9 8   ♡ J 10   ◇ 10 9 8 7   ♣ A J 10.

DISCARDING AND TAKING-IN CARDS

B (Elder Hand) has a horrible hand to discard from because
(1) with no Diamonds and no Knaves (*ie* a potential Repique
against him) he must take in five cards, but (2) he cannot, if he
throws five cards, keep all his Hearts and a trio. Something must
be sacrificed. In my judgment B must throw one Heart and keep
three Kings.

He discards, then, ♠ Q 10 7   ♡ 7   ♣ Q.

He takes in ♠ A   ♢ A   ♣ 9 8 7—realizing at once that the
worst has happened and that Younger Hand probably holds a
Repique.

A (Younger Hand) has an unpromising array of cards, but
realizes at once that the Diamonds and Knaves probably
constitute his best chance. He therefore throws ♠ 9 8 ♡ 10 (it is
a nice question whether to throw ♡ 10 or ♣ 10) and takes in
♢ K Q J.

The hands are now:

B (Elder Hand): ♠ A K ♡ A K Q 9 8 ♢ A ♣ K 9 8 7.
A (Younger Hand): ♠ J ♡ J ♢ K Q J 10 9 8 7 ♣ A J 10.

DECLARATIONS

B : 'Point of Five.'
A: 'Not good.'
B: 'Tierce major.'
A: 'Not good.'
B: 'Three Aces.'
A: 'Not good.'
B (resignedly): 'Nothing.' He now leads, and A, before playing
to this first trick, declares:

Point of Seven (Diamonds)	.. ..	7
Septième (sequence of seven)	.. ..	17
'Fourteen' Knaves	.. .. ..	14
Repique	.. ..	60
		—
		98

A Repique is scored when a player has 30 in his own hand,
provided that his opponent has nothing, has not scored for Carte
Blanche, and has not declared equality in Point or Sequence.

THE PLAY   *Score to*

Trick	B	A	B	A
1	♡ A	♡ J	1	—
2	♡ K	♠ J	1	—
3	♡ Q	◇ 7	1	—
4	♡ 9	◇ 8	1	—
5	♡ 8	◇ 9	1	—
6	♣ 9	♣ 10	1	1
7	◇ A	◇ K	1	1
8	♠ A	♣ J	1	—
9	♠ K	◇ 10	1	—
10	♣ 8	♣ A	1	1
11	♣ 7	◇ Q	—	1
12	♣ K	◇ J	—	2
	The Cards	.. ..	10	—

Total scores in play: B 20; A 6.

Score for third deal:

> A: 98 + 6 = 104.
> B: 0 + 20 = 20.

Score at the end of three deals:

> A: 34 + 104 = 138.
> B: 70 + 20 = 90.

A's Repique has put him well ahead, as he has still two 'Elder Hands' to come.

FOURTH DEAL

B now becomes Younger Hand. He deals:

To A: ♠ A 10 8 7   ♡ 9 8 7   ◇ A 10 9   ♣ 10 9.
To Himself: ♠ K Q   ♡ A K Q   ◇ Q J   ♣ A K Q J 7.

DISCARDING AND TAKING-IN CARDS

As soon as A sees his hand, and before discarding, he claims *Carte Blanche*, scoring 10. Carte Blanche is a hand containing no King, Queen or Knave. To establish his claim, A plays his cards rapidly in front of him, face upwards, and counting 'One, two, three . . . twelve'.

A now discards ♡ 9 8 7   ♣ 10 9. He is Elder Hand, and his

best chance is to concentrate on the suits of which he holds the Aces.

He takes in ♣ J ♡ J ◇ K 7 ♣ 8.

B discards ♡ A ◇ J ♣ 7.

This discard gives him a chance of two Quatorzes—Kings and Queens—and a good chance of at least dividing the cards.

He takes in ♠ 9 ♡ 10 ◇ 8.

The hands are now:

A (Elder Hand): ♠ A J 10 8 7 ♡ J ◇ A K 10 9 7 ♣ 8.

B (Younger Hand): ♠ K Q 9 ♡ K Q 10 ◇ Q 8 ♣ A K Q J.

THE DECLARATIONS

A:	Point of Five	..	..	..	5
					—
B:	Quart in Clubs	..	..	..	4
	'Fourteen' Queens	..	..	..	14
	Three Kings ..	..	..	..	3
					—
					21

The play is simple. A takes five Diamond tricks and the ♠ A and B takes the remainder. Cards divided.

Points Scored:

A (six tricks and one loser led out)   7

B (six tricks, including the last) ..   7

Score for fourth deal:

A: 10 (Carte Blanche) + 5 + 7 = 22

B: ..   ..   ..   21 + 7 = 28

Score at the end of four deals:

A: 138 + 22 = 160.

B: 90 + 28 = 118.

Each player is 'over the Rubicon', with two more deals to play.

FIFTH DEAL

A (Younger Hand) deals as under:

To B: ♠ A K J 9 7 ♡ K 10 8 7 ◇ K Q ♣ J.

To himself: ♠ Q ♡ A Q J 9 ◇ J 8 7 ♣ A Q 9 7.

DISCARDING AND TAKING-IN CARDS

B's discard is very easy. His five useless cards—♡ 10 8 7 ◇ Q ♠ J—discard themselves; this leaves him with five Spades and a trio (and chance of a Quatorze) of Kings.

B takes in ♠ 10 8 ◇ A ♣ 10 8.

A's discard is more difficult. After considering various possibilities, he throws all three Diamonds in the hope of getting a winning point in either Hearts or Clubs. He takes in the three remaining cards, ◇ 10 9 ♣ K.

The hands are now:

B (Elder Hand): ♠ A K J 10 9 8 7 ♡ K ◇ A K ♣ 10 8.
A (Younger Hand): ♠ Q ♡ A Q J 9 ◇ 10 9 ♣ A K Q 9 7.

NOTE. In drawing the ◇ 10 9 after throwing ◇ J 8 7, A has had bad luck. These three Diamonds, could he have them back now in exchange for, say ♡ Q J 9, would be worth 48 points; since B would not score either Quint or Pique and A would score a Tierce Major. But such unavoidable misadventures are all part of the game.

DECLARATIONS

B: Point of seven   7
        Quint   15
        Three Kings   3

(B's score is now 25. As A has scored nothing, B now plays out his winning Spades, which brings his score to 30 odd. This means he scores an extra 30 for a Pique.)

A: 0

THE PLAY

This is straightforward. B plays out 9 winners (9) and one loser (1) and takes 10 for the cards.

A takes the last 3 tricks (4).

SCORES FOR THE FIFTH DEAL

A: In hand   0
      In play   4
                                        —
                                        4

B: In hand   25
      In play   20
      Pique   30
                                        —
                                        75

Scores at the end of the fifth deal:

A: 160 + 4 = 164.
B: 118 + 75 = 193.

There is now one more deal to be played. A (original dealer) becomes Elder Hand. Scoring has been high, but B has a promising lead; all the same, 'anything can happen'.

SIXTH DEAL

B becomes Younger Hand and deals:
To A: ♠ A 10 ♡ A K Q J 10 ◇ K J ♣ A K Q.
To himself: ♠ Q J 9 7 ♡ 8 ◇ Q 10 9 8 7 ♣ 10 8.

DISCARDING AND TAKING-IN CARDS

A, with a Quint Major that is good 'against the cards', three Aces, and three Kings, is in something of a quandary. If he keeps both Aces and Kings, he has only three cards from which to complete either Quatorze; if he throws two Kings he will have five chances of the fourth Ace, but he may have the maddening experience of drawing the now unwanted King.

In the end he decides to throw three cards only, as, unless B produces a six-card Point, he will have a Pique in any case. So A throws ♠ 10 ◇ J ♣ Q and to his delight draws ♠ K ♡ 9 ◇ A. This means that this last deal has brought him one of the largest hands it is possible to hold.

B, with disaster staring him in the face, throws ♠ 9 7 ♡ 8 ♣ 10 8, hoping to draw, say, ◇ J and an Ace and King. But he draws ♠ 8 ♡ 7 ♣ J 9 7. A, by the way, had exercised his privilege of inspecting the first two of these cards, being cards he could have taken into his hand.

The hands are now:

A (Elder Hand): ♠ A K ♡ A K Q J 10 9 ◇ A K ♣ A K.
B (Younger Hand): ♠ Q J 8 ♡ 7 ◇ Q 10 9 8 7 ♣ J 9 7.

DECLARATIONS

A puts down his hand. He scores:

Point of six	..	..	..	6
Sixième	..	..	..	16
'Fourteen' Aces	..	..	..	14
'Fourteen' Kings	..	..	..	14
Repique	..	..	..	60
All the cards	..	..	..	13
Capot (as tricks)	..	..	..	40

163

B, of course, scores nothing, and the final scores for the Partie are:

$$A: 164 + 163 = 327$$
$$B: 193 + 0 = 193$$

$$134$$

A wins by $134 + 100 = 234$ points.

I trust that this very representative Partie will, at any rate, have made clear the technique and scoring of Piquet. Its strategy and tactics are, however, worth continuous study.

Duplicate Piquet

AN INSTRUCTIVE EXPERIMENT

Piquet is a first-rate game; and the Browns and Smiths, who were spending the weekend together, had a first-rate idea. 'Let us,' said Mr Brown, 'make this into a team game. My wife and I, Smith, will play a *partie* against your wife and you. All we want is two packs of cards.

'For the first deal you (shall we say?) are Elder Hand. The cards are shuffled and cut ready for dealing; then, before they are dealt, some fifth person will arrange the cards similarly in the second pack. Now precisely the same deal is played at two tables. At the second one my wife is Elder Hand. Then, if you, as Elder Hand, score, say, 42 to my 9, while my wife—playing the same cards—scores only 28 to your wife's 15, you win on that deal by 20. And so it goes on for six deals.'

'The same idea,' said Smith, 'as in duplicate Bridge?'

'Precisely. Except that Piquet, being ordinarily a two-handed game, can be played in duplicate by just the four of us.'

Here is a record of this interesting *partie*.

TABLE 1.—Brown (Younger Hand) *v* Smith (Elder Hand).

TABLE 2.—Mrs Smith (Younger Hand) *v* Mrs Brown (Elder Hand).

FIRST DEAL

Elder Hand's cards: ♠ A Q 9 7 ♡ Q 10 9 ◇ J 10 8 ♣ A K.
Younger Hand's cards: ♠ 10 8 ♡ A K 8 ◇ A K Q 7 ♣ J 10 9.
Talon: ♣ 7 ♠ J ♣ Q ♠ K ♣ 8 ♡ 7 ♡ J ◇ 9.

(In each case the cards of the Talon, or Stock, are given in the order in which they will be drawn.)

At Table 1 Smith discarded ♠ 9 7 ♢ J 10 8. Thus his hand, after drawing cards, was: ♠ A K Q J ♡ Q 10 9 ♢ None ♣ A K Q 8 7.

Brown discarded ♠ 8 ♡ 8 ♢ 7. His hand was: ♠ 10 ♡ A K J 7 ♢ A K Q 9 ♣ J 10 9.

SCORE. Smith scored for point of five, quart major, tierce major and three Queens—15. In play he took the first nine tricks.

Smith 35. Brown 4.

At Table 2 Mrs Brown discarded ♡ 10 9 ♢ J 10 8. Her hand was thus: ♠ A K Q J 9 7 ♡ Q ♢ None ♣ A K Q 8 7.

Mrs Smith discarded ♠ 10 8 ♡ 8. Her hand was: ♠ None ♡ A K J 7 ♢ A K Q 9 7 ♣ J 10 9.

SCORE. Mrs Brown scored point of six, quart major and tierce major—'sinking' her three Queens—13. In play she led out her eleven winners, and Mrs Smith, put to the discard, kept the ♢ A for trick 12. Mrs Brown now scored Pique and Capot.

Mrs Smith 0. Mrs Brown 96.

Combined scores for First Deal: Smiths 35; Browns 100.

'By no means a sensational deal,' remarked Smith, 'yet already there are 65 points between us. Who says there is no scope for skill in Piquet?'

SECOND DEAL

(Brown and Mrs Smith now become Elder Hand.)

Elder Hand: ♠ Q J 9 7 ♡ Q 9 7 ♢ K J 10 ♣ A Q.

Younger Hand: ♠ A K 10 ♡ A J ♢ Q 9 8 7 ♣ K 10 9.

Talon: ♡ K ♢ A ♣ J ♡ 8 ♠ 8 ♣ 7 ♣ 8 ♡ 10.

At Table 1 Brown discarded ♠ J 9 7 ♡ 9 7. His hand was, therefore: ♠ Q 8 ♡ K Q 8 ♢ A K J 10 ♣ A Q J.

Smith discarded ♠ 10 ♡ J ♣ 9. His hand was: ♠ A K ♡ A 10 ♢ Q 9 8 7 ♣ K 10 8 7.

SCORE. Brown: Point of 4 and three Queens—7. Smith: Tierce in Diamonds—3.

The play was tricky. Brown scored 13 (and the cards) to 9.

Smith 12. Brown 30.

At Table 2 Mrs Smith discarded the same cards as Brown. Her hand was thus as above.

Mrs Brown discarded ♢ 9 8 7. Her hand was: ♠ A K 10 ♡ A J 10 ♢ Q ♣ K 10 9 8 7.

SCORE. Mrs Smith: Three Queens—3. Mrs Brown: Point of 5 and Quart—9.

In play Mrs Smith scored 9 (and the cards) to 7.

Mrs Smith 22. Mrs Brown 16.

Combined scores for Deal 2: Smiths 34; Browns 46.

'Again we have been out-manœuvred,' observed Smith. 'Mrs Brown showed judgment in scrapping those three little Diamonds.'

THIRD DEAL

Elder Hand: ♠ Q 8 ♡ K J 10 9 ◇ 9 8 ♣ K J 8 7.

Younger Hand: ♠ K J 9 ♡ Q 7 ◇ A K J 10 7 ♣ 10 9.

Talon: ♠ A ♣ A ♡ A ♠ 10 ♡ 8 ♡ 7 ◇ Q ♣ Q.

At Table 1 Smith discarded ♠ 8 ♣ 8 7 ◇ 9 8. His hand was thus: ♠ A Q 10 ♡ A K J 10 9 8 ◇ None ♣ A K J.

Brown discarded ♠ 9 ♣ 10 9. His hand was: ♠ K J 7 ♡ Q 7 ◇ A K Q J 10 7 ♣ Q.

SCORE. Smith: Three Aces—3. (Points are equal.) Brown: Quint Major—15.

Smith took the first ten tricks and the cards.

Smith 24. Brown 18.

At Table 2 Mrs Brown discarded the same cards as Smith. Her hand was thus as above.

Mrs Smith discarded ♣ 10 9 ◇ 7. Her hand was: ♠ K J 9 7 ♡ Q 7 ◇ A K Q J 10 ♣ Q.

SCORE. Mrs Brown: Point of 6 and three Aces—9. Mrs Smith: Quint Major—15.

Mrs Brown took 10 tricks and the cards.

Mrs Smith 18. Mrs Brown 30.

Combined scores for Deal 3: Smiths 42; Browns 48.

'That fatal discard of the ◇ 7!' said Smith.

FOURTH DEAL

TABLE 1.—Brown is Elder Hand.

TABLE 2.—Mrs Smith is Elder Hand.

Elder Hand: ♠ 9 8 7 ♡ K J 9 ◇ Q J 10 8 ♣ K 9.

Younger Hand: ♠ A Q 10 ♡ A Q 8 7 ◇ K 9 7 ♣ 10 7.

Talon: ◇ A ♣ J ♣ Q ♣ 8 ♡ 10 ♠ J ♣ A ♠ K.

At Table 1 Brown discarded ♠ 9 8 7 ♡ 9 ♣ 9. His hand was thus: ♠ None ♡ K J 10 ◇ A Q J 10 8 ♣ K Q J 8.

Smith discarded ♡ 8 7 ◇ 7. His hand was thus: ♠ A K Q J 10 ♡ A Q ◇ K 9 ♣ A 10 7.

SCORE. Brown: 0. Smith: Point and quint, three Aces—23. In play, Smith scored 11 (and the cards) to 5.

Smith 44. Brown 5.

At Table 2 Mrs Smith made the same discard as Brown. Mrs Brown made the same discard as Smith.

SCORE. Mrs Smith: 5. Mrs Brown: 44.

(This was the only hand of the six on which discards and play were identical.)

Combined scores for Deal 4: Smiths 49. Browns 49.

FIFTH DEAL

Elder Hand: ♠ J 10 9 8 ♡ A ◇ Q J 10 8 ♣ J 10 9.
Younger Hand: ♠ None ♡ K Q J 9 8 7 ◇ A K 9 ♣ A K Q.
Talon: ♠ Q ♣ 7 ♠ K ◇ 7 ♣ 8 ♡ 10 ♠ A ♠ 7.

At Table 1 Smith discarded ♣ J 10 9 8 ◇ 8. His hand was thus: ♠ K Q ♡ A ◇ Q J 10 7 ♣ J 10 9 8 7.

Brown discarded ♣ K Q ◇ 9. (With one suit missing, he goes all out for Hearts.) His hand was ♠ A 7 ♡ K Q J 10 9 8 7 ◇ A K ♣ A.

SCORE. Smith: 0. Brown: Point and septième, three Aces—27. In play Smith led the ◇ Q. Brown scored 13 (and the cards) to 5.

Smith 5. Brown 50.

At Table 2 Mrs Brown discarded ◇ Q 10 8 ♣ 10 9. Her hand was ♠ K Q J 10 9 8 ♡ A ◇ J 7 ♣ J 8 7.

Mrs Smith discarded ♡ 8 7 ◇ 9. Her hand was ♠ A 7 ♡ K Q J 10 9 ◇ A K ♣ A K Q.

SCORE. Mrs Brown: Point and sixième—22. Mrs Smith: three Aces and three Kings—6. In play Mrs Brown led ♠ K and the cards were divided. Each player scored 8.

Mrs Smith 14. Mrs Brown 30.

Combined scores for Deal 5: Smiths 19; Browns 80.

'Once again,' Smith justly commented, 'we have succumbed to superior tactics.'

SIXTH DEAL

Elder Hand: ♠ A K Q 9 ♡ J ◇ A K Q 8 7 ♣ A K.
Younger Hand: ♠ 10 8 ♡ A Q 9 8 7 ◇ None ♣ Q 10 9 8 7.
Talon: ♡ K ♡ 10 ◇ 10 ◇ 9 ◇ J ♠ 7 ♠ J ♣ 7.

At Table 1 Brown discarded ♠ K Q 9 ♡ J ♣ K. ('One can't keep everything,' said Brown to himself. 'I must go for Diamonds and the fourth Ace.') His hand was: ♠ A ♡ K 10 ◇ A K Q J 10 9 8 7 ♣ A.

Smith discarded ♠ 8 ♣ 8 7. His hand was : ♠ J 10 7 ♡ A Q 9 8 7 ◇ None ♣ Q J 10 9.

SCORE. Brown: Point and huitième, three Aces—29. Smith 0.

In play Brown took the first 10 tricks, scoring the cards and a Pique.

Smith 3. Brown 80.

At Table 2 Mrs Smith discarded ♠ 9 ♡ J ◇ 8 7, leaving one card. Her hand was: ♠ A K Q ♡ K 10 ◇ A K Q 10 9 ♣ A K.

Mrs Brown discarded ♠ 8 ♡ 9 8 7. Her hand was: ♠ J 10 7 ♡ A Q ◇ J ♣ Q J 10 9 8 7.

SCORE. Mrs Smith: 'Fourteen' Kings, three Aces—17. Mrs Brown: Point and sixième—22. In play Mrs Smith took 10 tricks and the cards.

Mrs Smith 38. Mrs Brown 25.

Combined scores for Deal 6: Smiths 41; Browns 105.

SCORE FOR THE PARTIE

			Smiths	Browns
1st deal	..	..	35	100
2nd deal	..	..	34	46
3rd deal	..	..	42	48
4th deal	..	..	49	49
5th deal	..	..	19	80
6th deal	..	..	41	105
			220	428

The Browns, who throughout played superior Piquet, thus won by 208 points. Note that Brown, scoring 187 to 123, defeated Smith over six hands by 64 (ie 164 at ordinary Piquet scoring), while Mrs Brown, *holding the same cards as the defeated Smith*, scored 241 points to Mrs Smith's 97—at ordinary scoring 438 points, as Mrs Smith is rubiconed. Thus the difference in result on these not very sensational deals is 602 points. 'A very instructive experiment,' said Smith.

Piquet

PROBLEMS IN DISCARDING AND PLAY

I

It is the first deal of a partie.

1. Elder Hand is dealt: ♠ A K J ♡ Q J 10 8 ◇ K J 9 ♣ A Q.

Younger Hand is dealt: ♠ 10 9 8 ♡ K 7 ◇ A Q 8 7 ♣ J 9 8.

Before reading further, ask yourself: What cards should be discarded by each player?

2. The eight cards of the stock, in their order of availability, are: ♣ 10 ♡ 9 ♠ Q ♣ 7 ◇ 10 ♡ A ♣ K ♠ 7.

What should be the result of the deal?

My answers are as follows:

1. Elder Hand has an extremely awkward hand to discard from. His best suit (♡ Q J 10 8) is the poorest from the point of view of high cards, and there are no definite indications as to what he should keep otherwise—he has two Aces, two Kings, and two Queens! His best bet, in my opinion, is to keep the Hearts, Aces and Queens, *ie* to throw ♠ K J ◇ K J 9. A novice cannot bring himself to sacrifice high cards in this way; but they are less useful than those retained, and it is unlikely that Younger Hand will be dangerous in either of these suits.

With Elder Hand's scrappy collection he should not consider throwing fewer than five cards.

2. Younger Hand has also a difficult discard. I think he should throw his three Spades in the hope that something will materialize in one of the other suits. I prefer throwing the Spades to throwing the Clubs, because the three cards in the latter suit are more likely to constitute a guard; and this consideration outweighs the fact that the three Spades are in sequence.

3. After the cards have been exchanged the hands are:

Elder Hand: ♠ A Q ♡ Q J 10 9 8 ◇ 10 ♣ A Q 10 7.
Younger Hand: ♠ 7 ♡ A K 7 ◇ A Q 8 7 ♣ K J 9 8.

POINTS SCORED IN HAND

Elder Hand:

Point of 5 ..	..	..	5
Quint ..	..	..	15
Three Queens	..	..	3
Three Tens	..	..	3
			—
			26
			—
Younger Hand		.. ..	0

PLAY

Tricks	Elder Hand	Younger Hand
1	♡ Q	♡ K
2	◇ 10	◇ A
3	♣ 7	◇ Q
4	♣ 10	◇ 8
5	♡ 8	◇ 7
6	♡ 9	♡ A
7	♡ 10	♡ 7
8	♡ J	♠ 7
9	♠ A	♣ 8
10	♠ Q	♣ 9
11	♣ Q	♣ K
12	♣ A	♣ J

NOTE. The play of this deal is very interesting. If, at trick 6, Younger Hand leads a Spade or Club, he may only divide the cards, because he can be forced to lead away from his minor tenace in Clubs. By 'cashing' the ♡ A, and hanging on to the guarded ♣ K, Younger Hand makes certain of a seventh trick. (Why certain? Because Elder Hand has declared the ♣ Q.) At trick 12, Elder Hand leads the ♣ Q, thus getting one point extra at trick 11.

SCORES IN PLAY

         Elder Hand 8; Younger Hand 19.

TOTAL SCORE FOR THE DEAL

         Elder Hand: 26 + 8 = 34.
         Younger Hand: 0 + 19 = 19.

Both players have made the most of their opportunities.

II

It is the first deal of the partie.

1. Younger Hand deals the cards as under:

To Elder Hand: ♠ A Q   ♡ A Q J 9   ◇ 8   ♣ Q J 9 8 7.
To Younger Hand: ♠ K J 10 9 8   ♡ K   ◇ Q J 10 7   ♣ A K.

First Problem: What cards should be discarded by each player?

2. The cards in the stock, in their order of availability, are:
♣ 10 ◇ K ♡ 8 ♡ 7 ♡ 10 ♠ 7 ◇ A ◇ 9.

Second Problem: How should the hand be played and what are the players' final scores?

My answer would be as follows:

FIRST PROBLEM

Elder Hand: The most obvious feature of Elder Hand's cards is his holding in Clubs; if he can take in the ♣ 10, he will have a Sixième in this suit, which, unless Younger Hand holds all the top Diamonds, will be good.

What are the chances of drawing the ♣ 10? They are 3–1 against. Hence, what looks at first blush the most promising discard, ie ♠ Q   ♡ Q J 9   ◇ 8, becomes, on examination, a rather unpromising one. I say 'unpromising' because, even if the ♣ 10 is drawn, Elder Hand will only have a moderately good chance of the cards.

Is there a better alternative? I think there is. This is to discard the ♣ J 9 8 7 and the ◇ 8, which gives Elder Hand a good chance of four Queens, a much better chance of the cards (since he has only to take in the ♡ K to be sure of them), and by no means a bad chance of a winning sequence. If Elder Hand can secure either the ♡ K or the ♡ 10, and a high Diamond, his score should be a very satisfactory one. I suggest, then, that he throws ◇ 8 ♣ J 9 8 7.

Younger Hand: Younger Hand is also in some difficulty. As with Elder Hand, one card (♠ Q) will give him a Sixième; moreover, he has three Kings which clearly he should keep. He cannot, however, keep both the Spades and the Kings without unguarding Diamonds.

Now, normally speaking, I think it bad play for Younger Hand to unguard a suit. But, in this case, I do not regard unguarding the Diamonds as a heinous offence, for Younger Hand holds four of them, including the Q J 10, and it is most unlikely that Elder Hand will be putting his money on ◇ A K 9 8. On the other hand, Elder Hand may well be attacking in Clubs and the ♣ A K should be kept. I suggest, therefore, that Younger Hand throws ◇ Q 10 7.

Note that the discard of the ◇ Q should be preferred to that of the ◇ J since Younger Hand holds one Knave already, and there is no harm in his giving himself a better chance of a Trio.

SECOND PROBLEM

With these discards the hands, after cards have been drawn, are:

Elder Hand: ♠ A Q ♡ A Q J 10 9 8 7 ◇ K ♣ Q 10.
Younger Hand: ♠ K J 10 9 8 7 ♡ K ◇ A J 9 ♣ A K.

(Elder Hand has had all the luck of the draw.)

THE SCORE

Elder Hand declares Point of Seven, Sixième—23.
Younger Hand declares three Kings—3.

THE PLAY

Elder Hand runs his seven winning Hearts, and then leads one of his losers, and Younger Hand must lead up to his tenace in Spades at the eleventh trick.

Elder Hand scores 21 and Younger Hand 4, making the total scores for the partie: Elder Hand, 44; Younger Hand, 7.

III

It is the first deal of a partie. Younger Hand deals the cards as under:

Elder Hand: ♠ K Q J ♡ Q 9 8 7 ◇ A Q J ♣ Q J.
Younger Hand: ♠ A 10 ♡ K 10 ◇ K 10 ♣ A K 10 9 8 7.

What cards should each player discard?

The eight cards of the stock in order of availability are:

♡ J ♠ 9 ♠ 7 ♠ 8 ♡ A ◇ 8 ◇ 7 ◇ 9

What should be the result of the deal?

These would be my answers:

DISCARDING

Elder Hand must, obviously, keep his Quatorze, and, since he has nothing else of much value, must discard five cards in all. If he keeps his Knaves with his Queens, he has a chance of a second Quatorze, but little chance of either Point or Sequence. This idea, then, should be rejected.

In my judgment the Heart suit is too 'thin' to justify the un-guarding of other suits, and Elder Hand therefore should keep his Spades and the ◇ A, hoping that more Spades will material-ize. If he can take in the ♠ A 10 he will have a fair chance of a Repique; if, in addition, he takes in one Club the Repique will be good against the cards.

His discard, then, is: ♡ 9 8 7 ◇ J ♣ J.

Younger Hand is in a horrid dilemma. He has 'fourteen' Tens (*not* good against the cards) and a Club suit which, he knows, *is* good. He has a Repique if he can take in the ♣ J and a Queen. On the other hand, he must keep his suits guarded since, if he fails to do so, there is a potential Capot against him. The chance of his Repique is very remote and should be reckoned at its true value.

In my opinion, then, Younger Hand should adopt the unusual course of throwing no cards at all. It is useless to throw the ♣ 7 in the hope of collecting the ♣ J; the exchange leaves Younger Hand exactly where he is; while if there are Queens or Knaves among the last three cards they may just as well remain there.

Younger Hand, then, announces 'No cards'.

The hands after Elder Hand has drawn are:

Elder Hand: ♠ K Q J 9 8 7 ♡ A Q J ◇ A Q ♣ Q.
Younger Hand: ♠ A 10 ♡ K 10 ◇ K 10 ♣ A K 10 9 8 7.

DECLARATIONS

Elder Hand scores for his Quatorze of Queens—14.

Younger Hand scores Point and Quart (in Clubs)—10.

PLAY

Play is simple, the sequence of tricks being shown in the diagram below.

Elder Hand scores 7, making 21 in all.

Younger Hand scores 18, making 28 in all.

Tricks	Elder Hand	Younger Hand
1	♠ K	♠ A
2	♣ Q	♣ A
3	◇ Q	♣ K
4	♡ J	♣ 10
5	♡ Q	♣ 9
6	♠ 7	♣ 8
7	♠ 8	♣ 7
8	♠ J	♠ 10
9	♠ Q	◇ 10
10	♠ 9	◇ K
11	♡ A	♡ 10
12	◇ A	♡ K

IV

It is the opening deal of a partie.

1. Younger Hand deals the cards as follows:

To Elder Hand: ♠ K Q 10 ♡ A 9 8 ◇ J 9 7 ♣ Q J 9.

To Younger Hand: ♠ A 9 8 7 ♡ K Q J 7 ◇ K 10 ♣ K 8.
What should be the players' discards?

2. The cards of the 'stock', in the order of their accessibility, are:

♡ 10 ◇ 8 ♣ 7 ♣ A ♠ J ◇ A ♣ 10 ◇ Q.

How should the hand be played? And with what result?
These would be my answers:

DISCARDS

Elder Hand's discard is fairly obvious. With nothing much to go for, he keeps his ♡ A and the best two suits, which give him the best chance of a sequence.

His discard, therefore, is: ♡ 9 8 ◇ J 9 7.

Younger Hand has a more difficult problem. He *must* retain guards to the ◇ K and ♣ K. Should he keep his Spades intact, or his Hearts? If the former, he must unguard the ♡ K; on the other hand, if he can draw in the ♠ K he will stand a good chance of the cards. Or should he keep the ♠ A and the Hearts—when, if he draws the ♡ A, his chance of the cards will be even better?

I think, on a balance of considerations, his best discard is the Tierce minor in Spades.

DECLARATIONS AND PLAY

After cards have been drawn, the hands are:

Elder Hand: ♠ K Q J 10 ♡ A 10 ◇ 8 ♣ A Q J 9 7.
Younger Hand: ♠ A ♡ K Q J 7 ◇ A K Q 10 ♣ K 10 8.

DECLARATIONS

Elder Hand: Point of 5, Quart major in Spades: 9.
Younger Hand: Three Kings: 3.

THE PLAY

Elder Hand leads ♠ K.

Younger Hand wins and leads out his Diamonds. On the Diamonds Elder Hand must discard *three of his Clubs*. If he throws the apparently worthless ♡ 10 (as a beginner well might do), Younger Hand will win the cards. For Younger Hand will next lead a Heart, and now Elder Hand can only take three Spade tricks and two Aces.

As it is, to trick 6 Younger Hand leads a Heart, Elder Hand wins and, after cashing his Spades, *leads back* the ♡ 10. Younger Hand, compelled to keep his ♣ K guarded, will have parted with two of his Hearts, and must lose the last two tricks to the ♣ A and ♣ Q.

The cards are thus divided, scores in play being:

Elder Hand: 9.
Younger Hand: 8.
Total score for the deal: Elder Hand 18; Younger Hand 11.

V

It is the first deal of a partie. Younger Hand deals the cards as under:

To Elder Hand: ♠ Q 10 9 8 ♡ A K J ◇ Q J 10 7 ♣ A.
To Younger Hand: ♠ A J 7 ♡ Q 10 9 7 ◇ K 9 ♣ K J 10.
What cards should be discarded by each player?

The eight cards of the 'stock', in sequence from the top, are:

♣ 9   ♠ K   ♣ 8   ◇ 8   ♡ 8   ♣ 7   ♣ Q   ◇ A.

What should be the result of the deal?
My answers are as follows:

DISCARDS

Elder Hand must choose, for his Point, between Spades and Diamonds. He cannot afford not to throw five cards. I think he must keep Spades—as giving him the better chance of a Quint—together with ♡ A K and ♣ A, his only certain tricks. His discard, therefore, is: ♡ J ◇ Q J 10 7.

Younger Hand has a very scrappy selection. His best feature is the ♣ K J 10, and he should keep these cards intact. But also he must keep every suit guarded, and he can just manage to do this. His discard is: ♠ J 7 ♡ 7.

THE PLAY

The hands, after cards have been taken in from the stock, are:

Elder Hand: ♠ K Q 10 9 8 ♡ A K 8 ◇ 8 ♣ A 9 8.
Younger Hand: ♠ A ♡ Q 10 9 ◇ A K 9 ♣ K Q J 10 7.

DECLARATIONS

Elder Hand: 'Point of Five.'

Younger Hand: 'How many?'

Elder Hand: '47.'

Younger Hand: 'Equal.'

Elder Hand: 'Then I score nothing. Your sequence is better than mine.'

Elder Hand now leads ♠ K to the first trick.

Younger Hand: 'Quart in Clubs—four.'

[Note the exceptionally low scoring from hand. Equal points; neither player has a Trio. Younger Hand scores 4 in all and Elder Hand nothing.]

Tricks	Elder Hand	Younger Hand
1	♠ K	♠ A
2	♣ A	♣ K
3	♠ Q	◇ 9
4	♠ 10	♣ 7
5	♠ 9	♣ 10
6	♠ 8	♣ J
7	♡ A	♡ 9
8	♡ K	♡ 10
9	♡ 8	♡ Q
10	♣ 8	♣ Q
11	◇ 8	◇ A
12	♣ 9	◇ K

Elder hand scores 1 when he leads to trick 1, 1 each in respect of tricks 2–8, 1 when he leads to trick 9, and 10 for the cards: total, 19.

Younger Hand scores 1 for trick 1, 1 when he leads to trick 2, 1 each for tricks 9, 10, 11, and 2 for trick 12: total, 7.

Hence the result of the deal is:

Elder Hand: 19.

Younger Hand: 11.

These scores are well below the average.

VI

It is the first deal of a partie and Younger Hand deals cards as follows:

To Elder Hand: ♠ K J 10 9 8 7 ♡ A K Q J ◇ A ♣ J.
To Younger Hand: ♠ Q ♡ 10 ◇ K Q J 10 8 ♣ A K 10 9 7.

What should be their respective discards?

When you have made up your mind about discards, consider the following:

The eight cards of the stock, in their order of availability, are:

♡ 9 ♡ 8 ♡ 7 ♣ 8 ◇ 7 ♣ Q ♠ A ◇ 9

What should be the result of the deal?

My answers are:

DISCARDS

Elder Hand has rather an awkward choice. There is nothing in his hand which is good 'against the cards' and therefore he must take full advantage of his privilege of exchanging five cards.

Now the most valuable element in his hand is his Quint in Spades, and therefore this must be retained, whatever other cards are thrown. The Diamond Ace also must certainly be retained, since Younger Hand may be very strong in this suit, so that the choice of the last card to be kept lies between the Heart Ace and the Spade King.

In my opinion, Elder Hand should keep the Heart Ace. If he takes in the Spade Queen (but not the Spade Ace), his Spade suit will only be stopped once by Younger Hand, and if he fails to take in the Spade Queen, his suit will be stopped twice by Younger Hand, whether he discards the Spade King or no. Retaining the Heart Ace gives him a second certain trick and may give him three or four Aces.

The disadvantage in throwing the Spade King is, of course, that Elder Hand may find himself with an inferior sequence, but here, on a balance of considerations, he must be content to take a chance. His discard, therefore, is ♠ K ♡ K Q J ♣ J.

This is a maddening type of hand from which to discard, since it is, on the whole, more likely than not that Elder Hand's final selection of cards will not be as good as those with which he starts.

Younger Hand has, to my mind, a fairly simple discard to make. In the first place, he must keep his single Spade and his single Heart to give himself the best chance of stopping these two suits. The question, then, is whether he should go for Diamonds or for Clubs, and the answer, quite obviously, is that he should go for Diamonds, in which suit he already has a Quart. Ignoring, then, the fact that he is scrapping his chance of four 10's, he should throw ♣ 10 9 7.

DECLARATION AND PLAY

After taking in cards, the hands are:

Elder Hand: ♠ J 10 9 8 7 ♡ A 9 8 7 ◇ A 7 ♣ 8.
Younger Hand: ♠ A Q ♡ 10 ◇ K Q J 10 9 8 ♣ A K Q.

This is, of course, a singularly unlucky affair from Elder Hand's point of view. There are only two cards of any value in the stock, both of which are drawn by Younger Hand, and Elder Hand, further, has the disappointing knowledge that if he had scrapped his Quint in Spades and stuck to his Quart Major in Hearts, he would, at any rate, have had the better Point and the cards. As it is, he scores nothing.

DECLARATIONS

Elder Hand scores nothing.

Younger Hand scores Point (6) and Sequence (16) in Diamonds, Tierce Major in Clubs (3) and 3 Queens (3), a total of 28. He is very near a Repique, but there is no discard which would have given him one.

THE PLAY

Elder Hand leads out ♠ J. Younger Hand wins with the ♠ Q, returning the ◇ K; Elder Hand wins with the ◇ A, plays out his four winning Hearts and concedes the rest of the tricks.

Younger Hand scores 19 points to 7, making him 47 points to 7 on the deal.

VII

It is the *last* deal of a partie. The score is: Elder Hand, 77; Younger Hand, 154. The cards have been dealt as follows:

Elder Hand: ♠ A Q 8 ♡ K J 10 9 ♢ K Q J ♣ K 10.
Younger Hand: ♠ J 9 ♡ A 8 7 ♢ A 10 ♣ A Q 9 8 7.

First Question: What cards should Elder Hand and Younger Hand respectively discard?

1. *Elder Hand.* Elder Hand may take five cards, and from his scrappy hand should certainly discard the maximum. The ♠ Q 8 and ♣ 10 will at once be chosen for discard; the three Kings and the ♠ A must clearly be retained; the problem is, then, to choose between the Heart and Diamond possibilities.

The ♡ Q will give Elder Hand a Quint; if the ♠ K is also drawn there will probably be a Repique. To obtain a Quint, if Hearts are thrown, it will be necessary to draw ♢ A and ♢ 10. And since ♢ Q J do not matter much, since this suit is not likely to be dangerous, I prefer to keep the Hearts. Elder Hand then throws ♠ Q 8 ♢ Q J ♣ 10, and keeps ♠ A ♡ K J 10 9 ♢ K ♣ K.

2. *Younger Hand.* Here the discard (three cards) is fairly easy. The good Club suit should be kept; also the two other Aces; then the ♠ J 9 select themselves for retention, as a contribution towards a guard in the Spade suit. Hence Younger Hand throws ♡ 8 7 ♢ 10 and his hand, before drawing cards, is: ♠ J 9 ♡ A ♢ A ♣ A Q 9 8 7.

Second Question: The cards drawn being as stated below, what should be the outcome of the deal?

1. Elder Hand draws ♠ 10 ♢ 9 ♢ 8 ♣ J ♠ K. His hand then is: ♠ A K 10 ♡ K J 10 9 ♢ K 9 8 ♣ K J.

2. Younger Hand draws ♠ 7 ♡ Q ♢ 7. His hand is: ♠ J 9 7 ♡ A Q ♢ A 7 ♣ A Q 9 8 7.

DECLARATION OF HANDS

[In the declaration of hands I give the conversation which would occur in actual play.]

Elder Hand: 'Point of Four.'
Younger Hand: 'Not good.'
Elder Hand: 'Tierce to the Knave.'
Younger Hand: 'Good.'
Elder Hand: 'In Hearts (Three), Fourteen Kings (Seventeen).'

[Leads to first trick]

Younger Hand: 'Point of Five (Five).'

PLAY OF THE HAND

Trick	Elder Hand	Younger Hand
1	♡ K	♡ A
2	♣ J	♣ A
3	♣ K	♣ Q
4	♡ J	♡ Q
5	◇ 9	♣ 9
6	♠ 10	♣ 8
7	◇ 8	♣ 7
8	◇ K	◇ A
9	♡ 9	◇ 7
10	♠ A	♠ 7
11	♠ K	♠ 9
12	♡ 10	♠ J

NOTE. At Trick 7 Elder Hand takes a chance on Younger Hand's holding the ◇ A single.

Score				E.H.	Y.H.
In hand	..	..	..	17	5
In play	..	..	..	7	10
Cards	..	..	..	—	10
				24	25

Test Paper for Piquet Players

What would be your discards on the following hands (1) as Elder Hand, (2) as Younger Hand?

HAND I: ♠ K J ♡ A Q 10 9 8 7 ◇ K J ♣ K J
HAND II: ♠ K J ♡ A ◇ J 10 9 8 7 ♣ A K Q J
HAND III: ♠ A Q J 9 ♡ A J ◇ A J ♣ Q J 10 9

Here are my answers:

HAND I: ♠ K J ♡ A Q 10 9 8 7 ◇ K J ♣ K J

From the point of view of Elder Hand, about as awkward a collection as one can hold. The Hearts must all be kept, since the ♡ K gives Elder Hand the cards, and the ♡ J gives him not only the cards but a Sixième. If, however, the three Kings are kept, Elder Hand can only exchange three cards; and, apart from the fact that he needs one (or both) of the missing

Hearts, there are three Aces against him. I think, therefore, that Elder Hand must keep one King with his Hearts—it does not matter which—and resolutely sacrifice the rest of his hand.

Younger Hand has a much easier problem. He must keep his guarded Kings and will throw ♡ 9 8 7, with a good chance of the cards and two reasonable chances of a Quatorze.

HAND II: ♠ K J ♡ A ◇ J 10 9 8 7 ♣ A K Q J

This is another 'snorter' for the unfortunate player who, as Elder Hand, holds this collection. He has a Quint which is *not* good against the cards, and which is very little use from a trick-taking point of view; a Quart Major; three Knaves, but otherwise no great hopes of a Quatorze. What should he sacrifice?

The choices are:

(*a*) To throw the Diamonds and hope for the ♣ 10, which makes the cards fairly certain.

(*b*) To keep the Diamonds and the two Aces.

(*c*) To keep the Diamonds with the ♡ A and two Knaves, taking only four cards. This gives, on the whole, the best chance of a Repique.

(*d*) To throw ◇ 10 9 8 7, again taking only four cards.

On the whole, I prefer (*b*), *ie* the discard of ♠ K J ♣ K Q J. In five cards one can reasonably hope for two of the missing Diamonds.

Younger Hand might throw three Diamonds—which gives him a fair chance of the cards—but I think he will do better if he throws ♣ K Q J, keeping his Quint intact. 'A bird in hand,' etc.

HAND III: ♠ A Q J 9 ♡ A J ◇ A J ♣ Q J 10 9

Yet another exasperating deal from Elder Hand's point of view. Here is a Quatorze of Knaves (not good against the cards, since Younger Hand may hold four Kings), three Aces, and two chances of a Quint which *might* mean a Repique. But if Elder Hand keeps his Clubs and Knaves, and draws the ♣ 8, there is still the chance of four Kings against him, and even if he draws the ♣ K there are two suits in which Younger Hand may hold six cards.

I think the better plan, therefore, is to keep the Knaves and Aces, hoping to draw ♡ K Q 10 or ◇ K Q 10; this renders it unlikely that Younger Hand will score (provided one of the

four Kings is drawn) and also gives Elder Hand a reasonably
good chance of the cards.

Younger Hand has a puzzling discard, too. I think he should
throw ♠ Q 9 only, leaving one card; he cannot afford to part
with an Ace or Knave and there is no point in breaking up the
Club suit on the off-chance of getting something better.

CRIBBAGE

CRIBBAGE—ONE of the oldest of card games—is primarily a game for two, though it can also be played by three or four. Here, however, I shall deal with the game for two.

There are three distinct forms of the game, known respectively as Five-Card, Six-Card and Seven-Card Cribbage. They differ in the number of cards dealt to each player.

The scoring, which at Five-Card Cribbage is comparatively simple, becomes more complicated in the Six-Card game, and quite difficult in the Seven-Card game; indeed, one is well advised not to play Seven-Card Cribbage unless one has a good head for figures.

We will begin, then, with Five-Card Cribbage, which, from the point of view of tactical interest, is considered by many the best game of the three, in spite of its simplicity.

The objective of all forms of Cribbage is to reach a stated number of points before one's opponent does; at Five-Card Cribbage the game is 61 up. For scoring purposes a special board with holes and pegs is ordinarily used. This makes it possible to see at a glance that one's opponent has scored correctly, and shows throughout the game the relative positions of the two players. But one can, if one prefers, simply use pencil and paper.

To begin with, the players cut for deal, the full pack of fifty-two cards being used. The dealer is the player who cuts the lowest card (Aces ranking low). The dealer having shuffled the pack, the non-dealer cuts it to him, and he now deals (face downwards) five cards, one at a time, to each player. At this stage the scoring begins, the non-dealer pegging three points, which are known as 'three for last'. They are supposed to compensate the non-dealer for the slight disadvantage which would otherwise accrue.

The cards having been dealt, each player looks at his hand and discards two of his five cards. These discards are set aside (face downwards). They form what is called the crib, and their score will presently be taken into account.

The score in 'crib' accrues to the dealer, and therefore the principle of discarding (of which more will be said later) is different for the two players. The non-dealer will throw cards which, so far as he can judge, are of no advantage to his opponent, while, at the same time, he must try to retain cards which are of advantage to himself. The dealer, on the other hand, while also considering the scoring possibilities of his own hand, will try to secure a useful crib.

The cards for crib having been set aside, the non-dealer cuts the remainder of the pack to the dealer. (This should have been placed face downwards between the two players.) The non-dealer, that is, removes the top half of the pack, and the dealer turns up the top card of the bottom half.

This card is known as the 'start'. It plays, as we shall see, a very important part in the game. If the 'start' happens to be a Knave, the dealer at once pegs two points, known as 'two for his heels'.

Now begins the play of the cards. Each player will have three cards in his hand, and, beginning with the non-dealer, each in turn lays a card face uppermost on the table, so playing the three cards as to endeavour to score the maximum number of points.

POINTS SCORED IN PLAY

In play, points can be scored in respect of the following 'features':

1. Pairs

A player scores a Pair (pegging two) when he plays a card of the same denomination as that last played by his adversary. For example, suppose non-dealer leads off with a Queen, dealer puts down a second Queen, and at once pegs two for a Pair.

2. Pairs Royal

If a third card of the same denomination is played in succession, whoever has played it scores a Pair Royal, counting six. The reason why a Pair Royal carries six points is that, from three cards of the same denomination, three pairs can be formed.

3. Double Pairs Royal

A Double Pairs Royal—four cards of the same denomination played in succession—counts no less than twelve to the player of the fourth of these cards. For, from four cards, one can form six different pairs; hence the twelve points. As we shall see, however, it is not possible for, say, four Kings in succession to be played because, for scoring purposes, all court cards rank as ten, and the total pip count of the cards played may not exceed 31. Suppose, however, that the first card played is a 7, dealer may now play a second 7 (saying as he does so, 'Fourteen'), and scoring two for a Pair; non-dealer a third 7 (twenty-one), scoring six for a Pair Royal, and dealer a fourth 7 (twenty-eight), scoring twelve for his Double Pair Royal.

4. Runs or Sequences

If three cards played in succession can be so arranged as to form a sequence of three, the player of the third of these cards pegs three for his run. Thus, if the first card played is a 3, the second a 4, and the third a 5, three points are scored when the last-named card is played. But equally these points are scored if the three cards are played in any other order, *ie* 5, 4, 3; 5, 3, 4; 4, 5, 3; and so on. *This point is the cause of so much confusion and uncertainty that it is important that it should be grasped at the outset.*

Runs are not only scored for a sequence of three cards, but for a sequence of four, five or six. Thus, if the first card played is a 2, the second a 3, and the third a 4, a run of three is scorable; if, now, a 5 is played, whoever plays it scores four points for a run of four; now a 6 can be played, carrying five points for a run of five; and a 7, carrying six for a run of six.

As before, points are scorable at the conclusion of the play of any number of cards which can be arranged in sequence. Hence, it is not necessary for a run of four to have been preceded by a run of three. Suppose, for example, that 2, 3 and 5 are played, nothing is scorable, but a player now producing the 4 has made a sequence (*ie* the four cards last played *can* be arranged in the order 2, 3, 4, 5), and scores four points accordingly. Suppose, again, that the first three cards played are 7, 5, 6, non-dealer, on playing the 6, scores three for his run. Now let dealer play a 2; he scores nothing for this, and non-dealer, playing the 4, also scores nothing; but if, after these five cards, dealer produces a 3, a run of six has been completed and dealer pegs six points.

Court cards in sequences. For scoring purposes, court cards count as 10, but for purposes of runs, they rank in their natural order; *eg* 10, J, Q, played in any order, constitutes a sequence, so do K, Q, J, or J, 10, 9; but 8, 9, J is not a sequence.

5. Fifteen

If two or more cards are so played that their pip count equals Fifteen, the player who plays the last of them scores two. Thus, if non-dealer leads off with an 8, dealer can play a 7, making Fifteen, and scoring two. If non-dealer first plays a 6, and dealer a 5, non-dealer can now play a 4, making both Fifteen and a run of three, and scoring five points altogether.

It is for this reason that the 5s' are the most useful cards in Cribbage. There are no fewer than sixteen cards, counting ten for scoring purposes, with which they can be combined to form Fifteens.

6. Thirty-one

As already mentioned, the pip total of the cards played may not exceed Thirty-one. A player playing a card which makes this exact total scores two. Thus, if the first three cards are 10, 9, 6, a 6 may now be played for the dealer, for which he scores four: two for Thirty-one and two for a Pair. Once Thirty-one has been reached, no further cards are played. (This rule, by the way, applies only to Five-Card Cribbage; in Six- and Seven-Card Cribbage the cards are played out.)

7. 'One for Last'

A player who cannot play another card without exceeding the permitted total of thirty-one says, 'Go', if his opponent also can play no further cards, he also says 'Go'. If, however, his opponent can play his last card, he does so, scoring 'one for last', unless the play of that card makes the total exactly thirty-one, when he scores two as explained above.

The play of the hand is now over, and the players proceed to what is called 'the Show.'

THE SHOW

The non-dealer 'shows' his hand first; then the dealer. Lastly, the dealer turns up the four cards which have been thrown into crib, and that, too, is 'shown', its score accruing to the dealer.

Scoring in the show is on much the same lines as scoring in play.

For the purposes of the show, the *turned-up card or 'start'* *plays its part in all three scores*. It becomes, that is, an element in both hands and in the crib.

Suppose, for example, that non-dealer holds K 5 5, that

dealer holds 7 6 6, that there is Q 4 3 3 in crib, and that the turned-up card is another 5.

For scoring purposes, the hands now are: non-dealer's hand K 5 5 5, dealer's hand 7 6 6 5, Crib Q 5 4 3 3. As will be seen from what follows, the start can make an enormous difference.

Thus, in the case we have just given, non-dealer's three cards, worth only six in themselves, are now worth 14; dealer's cards, worth only two, are now worth eight, and the crib, worth only two, is now worth 12. Had the start been a worthless card, *eg* (in this case) an Ace, non-dealer would have scored eight points and dealer 16 points fewer than they actually got with a 5.

Scoring features in the show are as follows:

1. Fifteens

As in play, any combination, whether of two or more cards, which totals Fifteen counts two points. Thus, 10 5 counts two, so equally do 10 3 2, 8 7, 8 4 3, 9 3 2 A, and so on. One can, in crib, have all five cards combining to make 'Fifteen Two', *eg* A 2 3 4 5, A A 4 4 5, A 2 3 3 6, and so on.

The same card can be counted in more than one Fifteen provided that the other components of the Fifteen are different. Thus, for 10 5 5, 9 6 6, 8 7 7, 'Fifteen Four' is scored. In each of these combinations, one card scores twice. Similarly, 9 6 6 6 is 'Fifteen Six'—a very good hand, as the three 6's are independently worth another six points. 10 5 5 5 is worth even more, because there are not only three Fifteens each composed of 10 and 5, but a fourth Fifteen, made up of the three 5's.

Finally, perhaps, we should mention 5 5 5 5. How many Fifteens are there here? The beginner may be surprised to learn that there are no fewer than four, for included in the four 5's are four different groups each of three 5's, and each therefore ranking as Fifteen.

It follows that where, in crib, one has a 10 card and four 5's there are no fewer than eight Fifteens to be scored.

2. Pairs

As in play, any two cards of the same denomination rank as a Pair and score two. Thus, a hand consisting of 9 9 6 6 scores 12, for there is 'Fifteen Eight' here (each 9 combined with each 6) and also two Pairs.

3. Pairs Royal

Here again, as in play, three cards of the same denomination score six. This is an application of the logical principle to which I have already referred—a Pair Royal scores six because each of the three cards forms a Pair with each of the others. A hand containing a 9 and three 3's scores 12. There are three Fifteens here (the 9 combined with each pair of 3's) and also three pairs of 3's.

Novices will soon learn to recognize these 12-point hands. Others in the same category with 9 3 3 3 are 8 8 8 7, 8 7 7 7, 7 4 4 4, 7 7 7 A, 6 6 6 3. In each of these cases there are 'Fifteen Six' and a Pair Royal. 10 5 5 5 (also K 5 5 5, etc) are in a different category; these are hands that count 14 because the three 5's taken together make one Fifteen more.

4. Double Pairs Royal

A Double Pair Royal—four cards of the same denomination— scores 12 by a logical extension of the principle already enunciated. Where one has a Double Pair Royal in hand (as distinct from crib) there is, of course, no question of Fifteens unless the four cards concerned are 5's. Four 5's, for reasons already explained, score 20 in all.

Where, however, there is a Double Pair Royal in crib, one can get some complicated scores. A 10 with four 5's gives eight Fifteens, and the total score is 28. Four 6's and a 9 are worth 20. Four 8's and a 7 are similarly worth 20. Other 20 combinations can be deduced by analogy from the examples that I gave under Pairs Royal.

Runs

The principle which obtains in play equally applies here. Any three or more cards which can be arranged in sequence count as a run of three, four or five. Moreover, as with Fifteens and Pairs, the same card can be included in two or three runs. Thus, if in hand one has 3 3 4 5, one scores six for two runs of three (and also, of course, two for Fifteen and two more for a Pair). If in crib one has 3 3 3 4 5, the show is worth a good deal more. There are three runs of three and a Pair Royal, and also there are no fewer than three Fifteens, as each pair of 3's combines with the 4 and 5. Thus the hand is worth 21 in all.

A very nice assortment to hold in crib is 4 5 5 5 6. What is this worth? There are three runs of three and a Pair Royal, that is 15 to begin with. There are also three Fifteens, each made up of 4 5 6, and a fourth Fifteen made up of the three 5's. Thus the hand is worth 23 in all.

Flushes

Here is a scoring feature which does not count in the play. If the three cards in hand are all of the same suit, three is scored for a Flush. If the start is of the same suit as these three cards, four is scored for a Flush of Four. In crib, however, there is no score for four cards of a suit; the Flush is only scorable where five of a suit appear.

His Nob

'One for his Nob' is scored where hand or crib contains a Knave of the same suit as the start. Suppose, for example, that one has thrown into crib the ♡ 5 and ♣ 5, and that one's opponent (in an access of generosity or because of the state of the score) has thrown the ◇ J and ♠ 5. Now suppose that the start is ◇ 5, one has a total score, including his Nob, of 29, which is the largest single score possible at Five-Card Cribbage.

Some Notes on the Technique of Play

Cribbage is, quite definitely, a game of skill. How is skill exercised? In two ways: first, in selecting the right discards; secondly, in the play of the cards.

As one gains experience at Cribbage, one's capacity to discard quickly and effectively will rapidly develop. But, to begin with, one should not be afraid of taking plenty of time. The old hand will have seen the same combinations come up over and over again, and in most cases will decide automatically what is the right thing to do with them. He will have learned by a process of trial and error, if not actually by calculation, that from such-and-such a hand the most favourable discard is so-and-so.

But the beginner's case is quite different. Very often he is not even certain of his arithmetic; he will have to make mental calculations as to the value of his hand before he even begins to consider what its tactical possibilities are.

My advice, then, is: go slowly, and (unless you have a very impatient opponent) do not make your discard for crib until you have satisfied yourself that you have given reasonable thought to alternatives.

The following are the factors which should enter into this business of discarding:

1. You are going to throw two of your five cards. What are the relative scoring values of the various three-card combinations that you can keep?

2. How is the situation likely to be affected by the addition of the turned-up card? This should always enter into your calculations.

3. Are you keeping the most useful cards from the point of view of play?

More points are lost through neglecting to consider the 'play' element in the game, and to plan one's discard accordingly, than in any other way.

4. If it is your own crib, bear in mind that you want to give yourself a good 'show' in crib, as well as in your own hand. The largest scores, as we know, are obtainable in crib, and therefore it is often worth while sacrificing points scorable in hand in order to make a crib worth while.

5. *Per contra*, if it is your opponent's crib, give as little as possible away. Here again it may be desirable to sacrifice to some extent your own chances in order to cramp the adversary's.

6. Finally, whether it is your own crib or your opponent's, *keep an eye on the score*. As soon as one is on the homeward stretch, the score becomes an important factor. It is the player who pegs out first who wins, not the player who would have the better score if the hand were fully played out. Hence, when you are within sight of home (or, equally, when your opponent is within sight of home), some of the principles which you would normally apply need to be considerably modified.

Let us take one or two examples:

(i) Suppose you hold 10 7 5 4 4; if it is your own crib there could be no easier hand to discard from. You throw 10 5, giving yourself 'Fifteen Two' in crib (with the chance, of course, of considerably more), and you keep 7 4 4, which gives you 'Fifteen Two' and a Pair in hand.

But suppose it is your adversary's crib; now, in normal circumstances, you cannot possibly throw 10 5, for your adversary will almost certainly be doing his best to give himself a good crib, and if he has an odd 5 or so will be throwing them. Even if he is not throwing 5's, he may be throwing 10-cards, or a 10-card may turn up. Indeed you should make it a principle never to throw a 5 for your opponent except in most unusual circumstances.

Reluctantly, therefore, you will abandon the idea of keeping your 7 4 4; instead you will keep either 10 5 4 or (what seems to me preferable) 5 4 4. I prefer the latter combination for two reasons:

(*a*) You have here three cards towards a double run—if either a 3 or 6 turns up the hand becomes a very good one.

(*b*) It is a useful combination from the point of view of play— you lead off with a 4, and if by any chance your opponent has a 4 and Pairs yours, you play your second 4 and score a Pair Royal.

But now suppose that you are all but home—that you want, say, only six to get out. Once again you will revise your decision, and in these exceptional circumstances will risk throwing the 10 5, for you 'show' before your opponent does, and it would be hard luck indeed if you could not pick up a couple of points in play, or as a result of a favourable turn-up, to enable you to go out. You already have four, and these two points are all you need.

(ii) Suppose your hand is 10 9 9 8 6. Here is a puzzling affair. If it is your opponent's crib, your discard is, I think, quite simple. You throw 10 8, which is not likely to be worth much to him, and you keep 9 9 6—worth six as it stands and with fair possibilities of improvement. But suppose it is your own crib, do you make the same decision?

There is something to be said for doing so, but I think, on the whole, you stand to gain if you keep 10 9 8 and throw 9 6.

This gives you only five points for certain, as against six if you make the alternative discard. But your contribution to crib is a more useful one than if you throw 10 8, and also 10 9 8 has slight advantages from the point of view of potential improvement.

These two hands well illustrate the kind of difficulties with which you must teach yourself to grapple if you are to become a good player.

TRICKY SCORING COMBINATIONS AT 5-CARD CRIBBAGE

These, so far as 5-card Cribbage is concerned, are all of them *Crib* combinations.

Hand combinations, involving only four cards, are, by comparison, so easily calculated that it is not necessary for me to say any more about them; but some 5-card combinations involve difficulty for the beginner. The most important are:

1. 10-Card and 5-Card Combinations

Take, as an example, K and 5.

							15's	Pairs	Total
(a)	K	K	K	K	5	..	8	12	20
(b)	K	K	K	5	5	..	12	6 + 2	20
(c)	K	K	5	5	5	..	14	6 + 2	22
(d)	K	5	5	5	5	..	16	12	28

NOTES

(a) 12 for a Double Pair Royal.

(b) Fifteen 12; each K is matched with each 5.

(c) Fifteen 14. The extra 15 is composed of the three 5's.

(d) Fifteen 16. Each K is matched with each 5 (fifteen 8) and there are also four groups of three 5's each.

The only higher-scoring combination is J 5 5 5 5 where one 5 is the start and the Knave is of the same suit. Here there is one for 'his nob', making 29 in all.

2. 9, 6, 3 in Combination

This is a very interesting group.

								15's	Pairs	Total
	9	9	9	9	6	..	..	8	12	20
	9	9	9	6	6	..	..	12	6 + 2	20
	9	9	6	6	6	..	..	12	6 + 2	20
	9	6	6	6	6	..	..	8	12	20
	9	9	9	9	3	..	..	—	12	12
	9	9	9	3	3	..	..	6	6 + 2	14
	9	9	3	3	3	..	..	12	6 + 2	20
	9	3	3	3	3	..	..	12	12	24
	6	6	6	6	3	..	..	12	12	24
	6	6	6	3	3	..	..	12	6 + 2	20
(a)	6	6	3	3	3	..	..	10	6 + 2	18
	6	3	3	3	3	..	..	8	12	20
	9	9	9	6	3	..	..	6	6	12
(b)	9	9	6	6	3	..	..	10	2 + 2	14
	9	9	6	3	3	..	..	8	2 + 2	12
(c)	9	6	6	6	3	..	..	12	6	18
(d)	9	6	6	3	3	..	..	10	2 + 2	14
(e)	9	6	3	3	3	..	..	10	6	16

NOTES

(a) Fifteen 10	{	6 6 3 (3 combinations)
		6 3 3 3 (2 combinations)
(b) Fifteen 10	{	9 6 (4 combinations)
		6 6 3 (1 combination)
(c) Fifteen 12	{	9 6 (3 combinations)
		6 6 3 (3 combinations)
(d) Fifteen 10	{	9 6 (2 combinations)
		9 3 3 (1 combination)
		6 6 3 (2 combinations)
(e) Fifteen 10	{	9 6 (1 combination)
		9 3 3 (3 combinations)
		6 3 3 3 (1 combination)

3. 8, 4, 3 IN COMBINATION

	15's	Pairs	Total
8 8 8 4 3	6	6	12
8 8 4 4 3	8	2 + 2	12
8 8 4 3 3	8	2 + 2	12
8 4 4 4 3	8	6	14
8 4 4 3 3	8	2 + 2	12
8 4 3 3 3	6	6	12

Note that five of the six produce the same score (12). The exception—8 4 4 4 3—is worth 2 more because 4 4 4 3 = 15.

4. 7 AND 4 IN COMBINATION

	15's	Pairs	Total
7 7 7 7 4	—	12	12
7 7 7 4 4	6	6 + 2	14
7 7 4 4 4	12	6 + 2	20
7 4 4 4 4	12	12	24

That 7 4 4 4 4 should be worth as much as 24 is, at first blush, surprising. The reason is that the Double Pair Royal (4 4 4 4) produces *six* pairs of 4's, each combining with the 7 to produce 15.

A combination identical in structure is 6 6 6 6 3, also scoring 24 (see above).

5. FIFTEENS, PAIRS AND RUNS

Now let us look at some combinations including fifteens, pairs and runs. The most important of these belong to the 3–4–5–6 series.

		15's	Pairs	Rns.	Total
(a)	6 6 5 4 3 ..	6	2	8	16
	6 5 5 4 3 ..	4	2	8	14
	6 5 4 4 3 ..	4	2	8	14
	6 5 4 3 3 ..	4	2	8	14

(a) The extra fifteen consists of 6 6 3

	15's	Pairs	Rns.	Total
6 6 6 5 4 ..	6	6	9	21
6 6 5 5 4 ..	8	4	12	24
6 6 5 4 4 ..	8	4	12	24
6 5 5 5 4 ..	8	6	9	23
6 5 5 4 4 ..	8	4	12	24
6 5 4 4 4 ..	6	6	9	21
5 5 5 4 3 ..	2	6	9	17
5 5 4 4 3 ..	—	4	12	16
5 5 4 3 3 ..	4	4	12	20
5 4 4 4 3 ..	2	6	9	17
5 4 4 3 3 ..	4	4	12	20
5 4 3 3 3 ..	6	6	9	21

6. Two Combinations Similar in Structure to 6 3 3 3 3

Finally, note two combinations similar in structure to 6 3 3 3 3. This consists of a Double Pair Royal (12) and 6 3 3 3 in quadruplicate. The similar combinations are: 9 2 2 2 2 and 3 4 4 4 4.

6- and 7-Card Cribbage

The differences between the six- and seven-card games and the five-card game are very easily set out. They are three:

1. At Five-Card Cribbage game is 61 up; at Six-Card Cribbage it is 121 up; at Seven-Card Cribbage it is 181 up (in other words, a Six-Card Cribbage game is 'twice round the board' and a Seven-Card game is 'three times round the board').

2. At Five-Card Cribbage the non-dealer or elder hand pegs three before the game begins. This is done to counterbalance his opponent's advantage of first Crib. At the Six- and Seven-Card games these extra points are not scored.

3. At Five-Card Cribbage play ceases as soon as 31 (or the highest score below 31) has been reached. At Six- or Seven-Card Cribbage, however, all cards are played out, ie when a player scores for 31 or for 'go', the other player leads off again with

one of his remaining cards. Thus, at Seven-Card Cribbage (where each player has five cards in his hand) it is possible for 'go' to be scored three times and for one player still to have a card in hand and to score 'one for last' with that.

Scoring Combinations at 7-Card Cribbage

Six-Card Cribbage calls for no further comment, I think, since the possible scoring combinations in hand are exactly the same as the possible scoring combinations in Crib, and both are the same as the possible combinations in Crib when the five-card game is played. But at the Seven-Card game, where two cards are thrown out for Crib, hands have an extra card in them, *ie* including the turn-up there are six cards to be taken into account. I therefore set out below particulars of some of the most important Seven-Card Cribbage scoring combinations.

1. 10-Card and 5-Card Combinations
Suppose, as before, that Kings and 5's are held.

		15's	Pairs	Total
(a)	K K K K 5 5	16	12 + 2	30
(b)	K K K 5 5 5	20	6 + 6	32
(c)	K K 5 5 5 5	24	12 + 2	38

NOTES

(a) 12 for a Double Pair Royal.
(b) K + 5 nine times and 5 5 5 = 20.
(c) K + 5 eight times and 5 5 5 four times = 24.

2. 10, 3, 2 in Combination

	15's	Pairs	Total
Q Q Q Q 3 2	8	12	20
Q Q Q 3 3 2	12	6 + 2	20
Q Q 3 3 3 2	12	6 + 2	20
Q Q 3 3 2 2	16	2 + 2 + 2	22
Q 3 3 3 3 2	8	12	20
Q 3 3 3 2 2	12	6 + 2	20

Combinations of 10, 4, 1 are identical in structure.

3. 9, 6, 3 in Combination

		15's	Pairs	Total
	9 9 9 9 6 6	16	12 + 2	30
(a)	9 9 9 9 6 3	8	12	20
	9 9 9 9 3 3	8	12 + 2	22
	9 9 9 6 6 6	18	6 + 6	30
(b)	9 9 9 6 6 3	14	6 + 2	22

			15's	Pairs	Total
(c)	9 9 9 6 3 3	..	12	6 + 2	20
(d)	9 9 9 3 3 3	..	18	6 + 6	30
	9 9 6 6 6 6	..	16	12 + 2	30
(e)	9 9 6 6 6 3	..	18	6 + 2	26
(f)	9 9 6 6 3 3	..	16	2 + 2 + 2	22
(g)	9 9 6 3 3 3	..	18	6 + 2	26
(h)	9 9 3 3 3 3	..	24	12 + 2	38
(i)	9 6 6 6 6 3	..	20	12	32
	9 6 6 6 3 3	..	20	6 + 2	28
	9 6 6 3 3 3	..	20	6 + 2	28
	9 6 3 3 3 3	..	22	12	34
	6 6 6 6 3 3	..	24	12 + 2	38
	6 6 6 3 3 3	..	24	6 + 6	36
	6 6 3 3 3 3	..	24	12 + 2	38

NOTES

(a) The 3 has no scoring value.

(b) 9 + 6 six times, and 6 6 3 = fifteen 14.

(c) Scores 2 less than the above. Why? Because 6 3 3 has no value.

(d) Difficult. The 3's can be grouped to form three sixes; each six is paired with one of the 9's.

(e) Still more difficult! Fifteen 18 is made up as follows:

$$9 + 6 \text{ six times} = 12$$
$$6 + 6 + 3 \text{ three times} = 6$$

(f) Here we have:

$$\left.\begin{array}{ll} 9 + 6 \text{ four times} & = 8 \\ 9 + 3 + 3 \text{ twice} & = 4 \\ 6 + 6 + 3 \text{ twice} & = 4 \end{array}\right\} \text{fifteen 16}$$

(g)

$$\left.\begin{array}{ll} 9 + 6 \text{ twice} & = 4 \\ 9 + 3 + 3 \text{ six times} & = 12 \\ 6 + 3 + 3 + 3 & = 2 \end{array}\right\} \text{fifteen 18}$$

(h) Two 3's can be selected in *six* different ways to combine with a 9 for fifteen.

(i)

$$\left.\begin{array}{ll} 9 + 6 \text{ four times} & = 8 \\ 6 + 6 + 3 \text{ six times} & = 12 \end{array}\right\} \text{fifteen 20}$$

4. 8's, 4's AND 3's

			15's	Pairs	Total
	8 8 8 8 4 3	..	8	12	20
	8 8 8 4 4 3	..	12	6 + 2	20
	8 8 8 4 3 3	..	12	6 + 2	20
(a)	8 8 4 4 4 3	..	14	6 + 2	22

			15's	Pairs	Total
	8 8 4 4 3 3	..	16	2 + 2 + 2	22
	8 8 4 3 3 3	..	12	6 + 2	20
(b)	8 4 4 4 4 3	..	16	12	28
(c)	8 4 4 4 3 3	..	16	6 + 2	24
	8 4 4 3 3 3	..	12	6 + 2	20
	8 4 3 3 3 3	..	8	12	20
(d)	4 4 4 4 3 3	..	16	12 + 2	30
	4 4 4 3 3 3	..	6	6 + 6	18

NOTES

(a) 8, 4, 3 six times and 4, 4, 4, 3 once equals 15 fourteen.
(b) 8, 4, 3 four times and 4, 4, 4, 3 four times equals 15 sixteen.
(c) 8, 4, 3 six times and 4, 4, 4, 3 twice equals 15 sixteen.
(d) 4, 4, 4, 3 eight times equals 15 sixteen.

5. 5's, 4's AND 3's

			15's	Pairs	Runs	Total
	5 5 5 5 4 3	..	8	12	12	32
	5 5 5 4 4 3	..	2	6 + 2	18	28
(a)	5 5 5 4 3 3	..	8	6 + 2	18	34
(b)	5 5 4 4 4 3	..	2	6 + 2	18	28
(c)	5 5 4 4 3 3	..	8	2 + 2 + 2	24	38
(d)	5 5 4 3 3 3	..	12	6 + 2	18	38
(e)	5 4 4 4 4 3	..	8	12	12	32
(f)	5 4 4 4 3 3	..	10	6 + 2	18	36
	5 4 4 3 3 3	..	12	6 + 2	18	38
	5 4 3 3 3 3	..	12	12	12	36

NOTES

(a) 5, 4, 3, 3 three times and 5, 5, 5 once equals 15 eight.
(b) The only 15 is 4, 4, 4, 3.
(c) 5, 4, 3, 3 four times equals 15 eight.
(d) 5, 4, 3, 3 six times equals 15 twelve.
(e) 5, 4, 3, 3 four times equals 15 eight.
(f) This one is difficult. The five 15's (15 ten) are 5, 4, 3, 3 three times and 4, 4, 4, 3 twice.

6. 6's, 5's AND 4's

In this group are to be found the highest scores.

			15's	Pairs	Runs	Total
	6 6 6 6 5 4	..	8	12	12	32
	6 6 6 5 5 4	..	12	6 + 2	18	38
	6 6 6 5 4 4	..	12	6 + 2	18	38
(a)	6 6 5 5 5 4	..	14	6 + 2	18	40

	6 6 5 5 4 4	..	16 2 + 2 + 2	24	46
	6 6 5 4 4 4	..	12 6 + 2	18	38
	6 5 5 5 5 4	..	16 12	12	40
(a)	6 5 5 5 4 4	..	14 6 + 2	18	40
	6 5 5 4 4 4	..	12 6 + 2	18	38
	6 5 4 4 4 4	..	8 12	12	32

(a) These are the only two that present much difficulty. 15 fourteen equals 6, 5, 4 six times and 5, 5, 5 once.

Cribbage for Four Players

Cribbage makes an excellent game for four. The players play as partners, seated as in Whist, *ie* the North-South players are partners against East-West.

The only substantial difference between the two-handed and the four-handed games is that, in the latter, each player throws one card only into crib. Hence, to secure the same playing situations as in the two-handed game, one card less must be dealt to each player originally—*ie* four cards only for what is ordinarily five-card Cribbage; five cards for six-card Cribbage; and six cards for seven-card Cribbage.

AN ILLUSTRATIVE DEAL

Here is an illustrative deal at four-handed Cribbage with each player receiving five cards. North-South are partners against opponents sitting East-West.

South deals. The hands dealt are:

> To West: Q J 6 6 5.
> To North: K 9 9 6 5.
> To East: 7 5 3 2 A.
> To South: 10 8 7 7 5.

Players discard for crib: West throws 6; North, 5; East, 7; South, 5.

The pack is cut for the 'start', which is a Queen.

PLAY NOW BEGINS

					N-S	E-W
West plays Q	..	..	..	..	—	—
North plays K	..	..	..	..	—	—
East plays 5	..	..	..	..	—	—
South 'Go' ..	..	..	..	..	—	—
West plays 6	..	..	..	..	—	2
North plays 9	..	..	..	..	—	—

East plays 3 ..	..	..	..	..	—	—
South plays 10	..	..	..	..	—	—
West plays 5	..	..	..	..	—	—
North 'Go' ..	...	..	..	..	—	—
East plays 2 ..	..	..	..	..	—	—
S, W, N all 'Go'	..	..	..	..	—	—
East plays A	..	..	..	..	—	1
South plays 8	..	..	..	..	—	—
West plays J	..	..	..	..	—	—
North plays 9	..	..	..	..	—	—
All 'Go' ..	..	..	..	..	1	—
South plays 7	..	..	..	..	—	—
North plays 6	..	..	..	..	—	—
South plays 7	..	..	..	..	1	—
					2	3

THE SHOW

	15's	Pairs	Runs	Total
West: Q Q J 6 5 ..	6	2	—	8
North: K Q 9 6 6 ..	4	2	—	6
East: Q 5 3 2 A ..	4	—	3	7
South: Q 10 8 7 7 ..	4	2	—	6
South's Crib: Q 7 6 5 5 ..	4	2	6	12

Hence on this deal North-South peg 26 in all and East-West peg 18.

There is one point in connection with four-handed Cribbage that seems to occasion endless difficulty. This is the scoring of runs during play. The situation which has repeatedly been submitted to me is, in effect, the following:

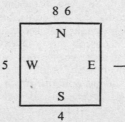

West leads a 5; North plays an 8; East cannot go. South plays a 4; West cannot go. North now plays a 6 (on top of his 8) and, seeing 4 5 6 on the table, claims a run of 3. Is this a valid claim?

Answer: No, it is not. The eligibility of a run depends not on what cards are visible, but on what cards have been last played, and the three cards last played are 8 4 6.

Had West played the 8, and North followed with a 5, a run would be scorable, because, though now it is 4 8 6 that are the visible cards, 5 4 6 are the three cards last played, and there are three cards in sequence. And again if, in the example given above, South plays a 7 after North's 6, he can score for a run of 5, because now five cards have been played—5 8 4 6 7—which constitute a sequence.

I must have answered fifty questions on this point during the last three years, so that evidently it is a source of much misunderstanding.

Four-handed Cribbage with seven cards dealt to each player

This is an 'unofficial' game, which gives pleasure to those who like large scores. Each player throws one card into crib: that leaves him with six cards, so that, with the 'start', he has seven cards that score.

Some nice problems in calculation result. Thus 4 4 5 5 6 6 scores 72, and 6 6 6 3 3 3 3 scores (appropriately) 66.

The game should be 241 up. Keen Cribbage players will (perhaps with justice) criticize it as being too much of a gamble.

Auction Cribbage

Auction Cribbage is a new offshoot of Cribbage.

At ordinary Cribbage there is one factor that spoils many a good hand, and that is the discarding when it is the opponent's turn to hold the crib. Suppose, for example, you hold 7 8 9 7 5 5. You have to discard two cards, and if you discard the two 5's it is highly probable that the crib will score as much as your own hand. Consequently you have to ruin your own hand to avoid making a present to your adversary. Again, when nearing game, the advantage of holding the crib, or, alternatively, of playing first, is, in my opinion, much too great. This new form of Cribbage has been devised with a view to counterbalancing this advantage. It is a Six-Card Cribbage and game is 121 up.

The cards are cut for deal in the ordinary way, but at Auction Cribbage there is little advantage to be gained by dealing first.

The dealer then says how many points he is prepared to bid for the right of holding the crib. His opponent can then overbid.

The dealer can again increase the bid, and then the opponent, each bidding in turn until one of the players declines to bid any higher. The points so bid are deducted from the score of the player immediately. If a player has bid for and won the crib at the beginning of the game it will be found convenient to back-mark on the board the number of points so bid; that is to say, if a player bids six points he places his peg six points from the start on the inner line of holes.

Let us take the above hand as an example. I am the dealer and bid four points. My opponent bids five. I bid six and he passes, and I take the crib.

Another difference between Auction and ordinary Cribbage is that in the former game the winner of the crib plays first and has the first show, whereas in ordinary Cribbage the opponent has the show. It follows that when the game is nearing its end the advantage of holding the crib is such that it is worth bidding high for it, but the advantage is counteracted by having to deduct from the score the number of points bid for the crib. The rest of the game is played in exactly the same way as ordinary Cribbage.

It will frequently be found that it is worth while to bid for the crib, even though you have nothing in your hand that will help the crib to any extent, but merely for the purpose of making it more expensive for your opponent. Care, however, must be taken not to overdo it, or you will be left in. If neither player makes a bid for the crib the hands are thrown in. The dealer may pass if he pleases and overbid the opponent in the next call.

When either player is 105 to 110 the advantage of holding the crib is worth two or three points more than during the earlier stages.

Cribbage for One

The solitary card player who is tired of patience games might like to try a one-handed Crib. It is quite simple (for those who know the rules of Crib), but affords plenty of amusement and a useful exercise in discarding.

Take an ordinary pack and shuffle it thoroughly. Then deal two cards to yourself, one card for crib, two more cards for yourself, one for crib, and two more for yourself, *ie* eight cards in all. Now you have a Six-Card Cribbage hand and an imaginary opponent's discard for your crib.

Look at your hand and throw out your own cribbage discard. Next, turn up the top card of the stock just as you would in an actual game and score, first what you have in hand, and then what you have in crib.

Put aside the eight used cards and continue as before: the turned-up card you will deal into your own hand, as, of course, your having seen it will not affect your discard.

The pack will admit of six deals along these lines, and there will be four cards left over, which you can turn up and score as a single crib.

Now add up your total score. If it exceeds 90, you may consider you have beaten Bogey.

The game could, of course, be played by two people, each with a separate pack. Before you begin, get a friend to arrange the cards so that their sequence in the two packs is identical.

BLACK MARIA

WHAT IS the best card game for three players? There are a number of possibilities. Booby is an excellent game; there is much also to be said for Knaves.

But, in my opinion, the best of them all is Black Maria. This, unlike all the games of the Whist family, is actually better as a game for three than when a larger number are playing. The reason is that, though any number of players can take part, the larger the number of players the greater is the element of chance.

The technique of the game lends itself peculiarly well to the requirements of three players. Superior skill will then show itself almost at once, and those who are really interested in card play will find endless fascination in the intricacies of this game. With seventeen cards to manipulate in each hand, there is always something new to think about.

This is how Black Maria, for three, is played. One card, the Two of Clubs, is taken from a full pack (this gives each player an equal number of cards. If there are four players, no card is removed; if five players, two cards; if six players, four cards, and so on). The players then cut for deal, the highest cut winning, and the dealer distributes seventeen cards face downwards to each player.

Next, the players look at their hands and each passes three cards face downwards to his right-hand neighbour. No one may look at the cards he is receiving until he has selected his own discards. The principle upon which cards are discarded will be clear enough from what follows.

When the cards have been exchanged, play begins, the player to the left of the dealer leading to the first trick. Tricks are won in the ordinary way, the Ace beating the King and so on, and there are no trumps. A player winning a trick leads to the next one.

The object of the game, however, is not to win tricks, but *not to win certain of the tricks*, ie those containing what are called Penalty Cards There are sixteen penalty cards in the pack. These are all the Hearts, each of which counts one point against the player taking the trick, and the Ace, King and Queen of

Spades. To collect any of these cards involves a player in much more serious penalties, as the Queen of Spades (Black Maria) counts thirteen points against whoever collects it, the King of Spades ten points, and the Ace seven points. Thus, the aggregate of penalty points is always forty-three.

The lines along which discarding and play should be planned will become evident after a very little practice. In discarding, one does not necessarily pass on the high Spades (as beginners are naturally inclined to do) since, if these are adequately guarded, it may be much better to keep them and so try and control their ultimate destination. Spades below the Queen should *never* be passed on (this is the one irrefragable rule).

Roughly what one tries to do in discarding is to set up in one's own hand either voids, which will give opportunities of discarding penalty cards, or long suits, *provided one has the low cards of them*. The manipulation of such long suits creates very similar problems to those which occur at Solo Whist, when one is trying to play a Misère hand.

As to the play, the first essential for success is an ability to count the cards. Towards the end of a deal, three good players will all know what cards are still in and will generally have also a shrewd idea of their distribution. Then, as play proceeds, tactical schemes need to be devised (and, if necessary, readjusted) which will enable those concerned to score the minimum of penalties.

End play at this game is very exciting. Here is an example from a recent game. The cards remaining in the three players' hands were:

In A's hand: ♠ A 7 ♣ 8.
In B's hand: ♠ Q 3 ♡ 5.
In C's hand: ♠ K ♡ 4 ♣ 4.

It was A's lead and, while he knew what other cards were out, he was not certain of their distribution. He led the ♠ 7; C, of course, took the trick, and led the ♣ 4. This meant that, in the course of these three tricks, 22 points were scored against A and 10 against C. But note that four other results were possible.

Had A led the ♠ 7 and C subsequently the ♡ 4, C would still have scored 10 points, but 22 would have been scored against B, as A discards the ♠ A on B's ♡ 5. Had A led the ♠ 7 and B, guessing that C's ♠ K was unguarded, played the ♠ Q, 23 points would have been scored against C. But even here there are two variations. If C leads the ♡ 4, B loses 9 points; if C leads the ♣ 4, A loses 9 points.

Finally, had A led the ♣ 8, on which, of course, B promptly discards the ♠ Q, each of the players are penalized: 13 points against A, 10 against C, and 9 against B.

When the play of nine cards can lead to so many variations, it will readily be perceived what complications are inherent in the play of fifty-one!

Black Maria for Three

A Deal with 'Unspoken Comments'

The players are Smith, Jones, and Brown. The ♣ 2 having been removed from the pack (so as to leave a number of cards divisible by three), Smith deals the cards as follows:

To Jones: ♠ J 8 3 ♡ K J 9 6 5 ♢ K J 10 7 5 2 ♣ 9 6 5.
To Brown: ♠ K Q 9 5 2 ♡ Q 10 7 ♢ A Q 9 6 4 ♣ K 10 4 3.
To Smith: ♠ A 10 7 6 4 ♡ A 8 4 3 2 ♢ 8 3 ♣ A Q J 8 7.

One should remember that the object of the game is to avoid taking tricks containing certain Penalty Cards.

The players inspect their cards. Each now passes *three cards* to the player on his *right*. Let us remind beginners that, in passing cards, there is no need to throw high ones if they are adequately guarded and if one holds the bottom cards of the suit.

Jones passes to Smith: ♣ 9 6 5.

'Don't like the look of this hand. Quite likely high Spades will be passed, and then where shall I be? Best plan is to void the Club suit.'

Smith passes to Brown: ♣ A Q J.

'I don't much mind about my ♠ A. But the Club position is horrid—a long suit with no low cards in it. That must be remedied at all costs!'

Brown passes to Jones: ♠ K Q ♢ A.

'I should think mine is the worst hand of the three. I'm bound to take a lot of tricks, but this seems about the best I can do.'

After passing cards, the hands are:

Jones: ♠ K Q J 8 3 ♡ K J 9 6 5 ♢ A K J 10 7 5 2 ♣ None.
Brown: ♠ 9 5 2 ♡ Q 10 7 ♢ Q 9 6 4 ♣ A K Q J 10 4 3.
Smith: ♠ A 10 7 6 4 ♡ A 8 4 3 2 ♢ 8 3 ♣ 9 8 7 6 5.

THE PLAY

Trick	Jones	Brown	Smith
1.	♡ 6	♡ Q	♡ 8

Jones: 'My hand is still a bad one. This seems about the best chance of getting rid of the lead.'

Brown: 'May as well play the highest, when my lowest is the 7.'

2.	♠ 8	♠ 9	♠ 10

Brown: 'With any luck, Smith is interested in this suit.'

3.	♠ J	♠ 5	♠ 7

Smith: 'A good idea! To continue the suit may be disagreeable for Jones!'

Jones: 'All wrong this. I must take the trick. But how can I best contrive to get rid of the lead again?'

4.	◇ A	◇ Q	◇ 8
5.	◇ K	◇ 9	◇ 3

Jones: 'Can't continue suit. Brown probably has the 6 and 4. If I lead the 5 he plays the 4, and I get a present from Smith. If I lead the 2 I lose control of the suit. I must try Hearts again.'

6.	♡ 5	♡ 10	♡ 4

Brown: 'Confound the fellow! Let's try him with another dose of Spades!'

7.	♠ 3	♠ 2	♠ 6

Smith: 'Now the only Spades I can't see are the King and Queen. What fun! Neither Jones nor I can afford to lead the suit.'

8.	♡ K	♡ 7	♡ 3

Jones: 'Seems there's nothing now but to lead a Diamond and hope they're divided after all. Surely someone will play a Club before long.'

9.	◇ 5	◇ 4	♠ A

Jones: 'The worst has happened. Brown, however, must take the next trick, and I don't think he has the Spade.'

10.	◇ 2	◇ 6	♣ 9

Brown: 'Now how are these Clubs divided? I think there's something fishy about the suit! I'd better begin with one of my low ones, keeping the other in reserve.'

11.	♠ Q	♣ 4	♣ 5

Brown: 'Ah, I was right! I suspected Jones was void!'

Smith: 'A bad show. But, at any rate, I can now fetch out Jones's ♠ K.'

12.   ♠ <u>K</u>   ♣ A   ♠ 4

Jones: 'Nothing left now but the Ace and 2 of Hearts. A Heart lead is therefore indicated.'

13.   ♡ 9   ♣ K   ♡ 2

14.   ♡ <u>J</u>   ♣ Q   ♡ <u>A</u>

All penalty cards have now been played. The scores against the three players are:

Against Jones:	♠ A ♠ K and 5 Hearts ..	22
„	Brown: 6 Hearts..	6
„	Smith: ♠ Q and 2 Hearts	15
		—
		43

Problems in Passing Cards and in Play

I

C has dealt the cards as under:

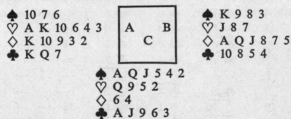

♠ 10 7 6
♡ A K 10 6 4 3
◇ K 10 9 3 2
♣ K Q 7

♠ K 9 8 3
♡ J 8 7
◇ A Q J 8 7 5
♣ 10 8 5 4

♠ A Q J 5 4 2
♡ Q 9 5 2
◇ 6 4
♣ A J 9 6 3

The ♣ 2 has been removed from the pack, so that there are only 12 cards in that suit.

A will lead to the first trick, after cards have been passed from player to player.

PASSING CARDS

A passes to C: ♣ K Q 7
B passes to A: ♠ K ♣ 10 8
C passes to B: ♡ Q ◇ 6 4

NOTES

A's hand is dangerous in that he has only three Spades. His obvious plan is to endeavour to void one suit by passing all three Clubs.

B's is a really bad hand. He is not safe in any suit. He *must* get rid of his inadequately guarded ♠ K and (unfortunately for A) the best cards to go with it are his two high Clubs.

C has a good hand. He has enough Spades to be able to retain the ♠ A Q.

After cards have been passed the hands are:

A: ♠ K 10 7 6 ♡ A K 10 6 4 3 ◇ K 10 9 3 2 ♣ 10 8.
B: ♠ 9 8 3 ♡ Q J 8 7 ◇ A Q J 8 7 6 5 4 ♣ 5 4.
C: ♠ A Q J 5 4 2 ♡ 9 5 2 ◇ None ♣ A K Q J 9 7 6 3.

As the hands now are, one predicts disaster for B.

THE PLAY

Trick	A	B	C	A	B	C
				Points Against		
1	♡ 3	♡ Q	♡ 9	—	3	—
2	♠ 10	♠ 9	♠ J	—	—	—
3	♡ 4	♡ J	♡ 5	—	3	—
4	♠ 7	♠ 8	♠ 5	—	—	—
5	♠ K	♠ 3	♠ 4	10	—	—
6	♠ 6	♡ 8	♠ 2	1	—	—
7	♣ 10	♣ 5	♣ J	—	—	—
8	♡ 6	♡ 7	♡ 2	—	3	—
9	♣ 8	♣ 4	♣ 3	—	—	—
10	◇ 10	◇ 8	♠ Q	13	—	—
11	◇ 2	◇ A	♠ A	—	7	—
12	◇ K	◇ J	♣ A	—	—	—
13	◇ 9	◇ 7	♣ K	—	—	—
14	◇ 3	◇ Q	♣ Q	—	—	—
15	♡ A	◇ 6	♣ 9	—	1	—
16	♡ K	◇ 5	♣ 7	—	1	—
17	♡ 10	◇ 4	♣ 6	—	1	—
Total ..				24	19	—

NOTES ON THE PLAY

Actually B, considering how bad his hand is, does remarkably well; both the major penalties fall to A. In the upshot, penalties

against A total 24, and against B only 19, so that on balance
A is −29 points, and B−14, C being +43.

A's opening lead is a Heart, and B, with only three small
Spades, naturally switches to that suit. B's third lead of Spades
(trick 5) compels A to play the ♠ K. (Otherwise, if A plays ♠ 6,
the lead of the ♠ Q will land him with a 23-point penalty.)

Now Clubs are played, followed by Diamonds.

The critical lead is at trick 10. A thinks it wisest to retain
his two low Diamonds—he has no inkling of the fact that C
has voided the suit—and, leading the ◇ 10, he secures the
♠ Q. The rest is obvious.

B is lucky, but makes the most of his poor material. C, with
the best hand, is on velvet throughout.

These three-handed deals are always of interest from the
point of view of in-and-out card play.

II

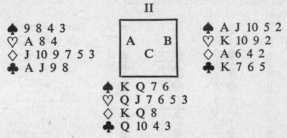

The ♣ 2 has been removed from the pack. C has dealt the
cards as above.

What cards should each player pass to his right-hand neighbour (A to C, B to A, C to B)?

What should be the upshot of the deal?

These are my answers:

PASSING CARDS

    A passes to C: ♡ A ♣ A J.

A's is an awkward hand. The long Diamond suit, with the 2
missing, is likely to be a nuisance, but A cannot well do anything
about that. His best plan is to throw three high cards and hope
for the best.

    B passes to A: ♡ K 10 9.

Here, again, it is difficult to dogmatize. On the whole, I prefer
to get rid of the high Hearts; the ♠ A is fairly well guarded and

the other suits, while not too good, are not outstandingly dangerous.

C passes to B: ♠ K Q ♡ Q.

This discard is obvious.

The hands as reconstructed (*ie* after cards have been passed) are:

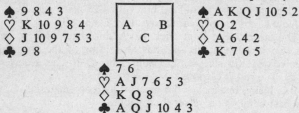

♠ 9 8 4 3
♡ K 10 9 8 4
◇ J 10 9 7 5 3
♣ 9 8

A   B
C

♠ A K Q J 10 5 2
♡ Q 2
◇ A 6 4 2
♣ K 7 6 5

♠ 7 6
♡ A J 7 6 5 3
◇ K Q 8
♣ A Q J 10 4 3

The 'hand-patterns' are now more irregular, and each of the three hands has a marked weakness. A's is the Diamond suit; B's is the Club suit; C's is Hearts.

THE PLAY

Trick	A	B	C	Points Against A	B	C
1	♠ 9	♠ 10	♠ 7	—	—	—
2	♣ 9	♣ K	♣ Q	—	—	—
3	♣ 8	♣ 7	♣ A	—	—	—
4	◇ J	◇ A	◇ K	—	—	—
5	♡ K	♣ 6	♣ 4	—	1	—
6	♠ 8	♠ J	♠ 6	—	—	—
7	♡ 10	♣ 5	♣ 3	—	1	—
8	◇ 10	◇ 6	◇ Q	—	—	—
9	♡ 4	♡ 2	♡ 6	—	—	3
10	♡ 9	♡ Q	♡ 7	—	3	—
11	♠ 4	♠ 5	♡ A	—	1	—
12	◇ 7	◇ 4	◇ 8	—	—	—
13	♡ 8	♠ Q	♡ 5	15	—	—
14	◇ 9	◇ 2	♡ J	1	—	—
15	◇ 5	♠ K	♡ 3	11	—	—
16	◇ 3	♠ A	♣ 7	7	—	—
17	♠ 3	♠ 2	♣ 10	—	—	—
Total ..				34	6	3

COMMENT

Trick 1. A's safest lead.

Trick 2. B, holding the ♠ A K Q, can make any lead with comparative impunity. He tackles his most dangerous suit first.

Trick 3. C takes a risk. But better take it now than later. And he knows ♠ K Q are both with B.

Trick 5. C counts the Clubs. He can now afford to play one of his low ones.

Trick 6. B now prudently tests the distribution of the Spades.

Trick 7. B gets rid of his last Club. Now he has only to dispose of the ♡ Q, and his hand will be foolproof.

Trick 9. C dare not lead the ◇ 8, lest B has no more of the suit.

Trick 11. The ◇ 4 would be just as good a lead.

III

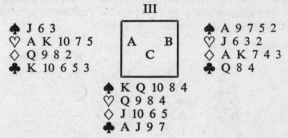

```
 ♠ J 6 3              ┌─────────┐       ♠ A 9 7 5 2
 ♡ A K 10 7 5        │  A    B │        ♡ J 6 3 2
 ◇ Q 9 8 2           │     C   │        ◇ A K 7 4 3
 ♣ K 10 6 5 3        └─────────┘        ♣ Q 8 4
                    ♠ K Q 10 8 4
                    ♡ Q 9 8 4
                    ◇ J 10 6 5
                    ♣ A J 9 7
```

C deals and distributes the cards as in the diagram.

What cards should each player pass to his right-hand neighbour (A to C, B to A, C to B)?

How should the hand be played?

My answers are as follows:

PASSING CARDS

A passes to C: ♡ A K 10.

A has 'too good' a hand, *ie* it is almost certain to be worsened by the exchange of cards. However, he gets rid of three penalty cards and must hope for the best as regards his being passed Spades.

C passes to B: ♠ K Q ♡ Q.

With a poor hand (and suits distributed 5 4 4 4) this is about the best that C can hope to do. His lack of 2's and 3's is almost sure to lead to trouble.

B passes to A: ♣ Q 8 4.

With four 'guards' to his ♠ A, B takes a chance on the Spades, and adopts the alternative plan of 'voiding' a suit.

The hands after cards have been passed are:

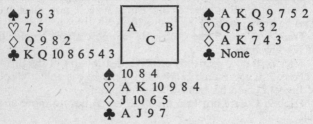

```
♠ J 6 3                         ♠ A K Q 9 7 5 2
♡ 7 5            A    B         ♡ Q J 6 3 2
◇ Q 9 8 2           C          ◇ A K 7 4 3
♣ K Q 10 8 6 5 4 3              ♣ None

                 ♠ 10 8 4
                 ♡ A K 10 9 8 4
                 ◇ J 10 6 5
                 ♣ A J 9 7
```

Looking at the hands before play begins, one can predict with confidence that there is likely to be trouble for C. A should emerge with a blank score, while B also has very nearly a 'misère' hand. Let us see how the situation develops.

THE PLAY

				Points Against		
Trick	A	B	C	A	B	C
1	♠ J	♠ 7	♠ 10	—	—	—
2	♠ 6	♠ 5	♠ 4	—	—	—
3	♠ 3	♠ 2	♠ 8	—	—	—
4	◇ Q	◇ K	◇ J	—	—	—
5	◇ 9	◇ A	◇ 10	—	—	—
6	◇ 8	◇ 7	◇ 6	—	—	—
7	♡ 5	♡ Q	♡ 10	—	3	—
8	◇ 2	◇ 4	◇ 5	—	—	—
9	♡ 7	♡ 6	♡ 4	3	—	—
10	♣ 3	♡ J	♣ A	—	—	1

COMMENTS

1. The safest lead from A's hand.

2. Neither B nor C wants the lead.

3. B has now four 'long' Spades.

5. It suits B to continue the suit—the principal source of danger to himself.

7. At trick 7, A leads ♡ 5 as an 'insurance premium'; otherwise he may find himself with the lead when he has nothing in his hand but established Clubs.

B wins trick 7, also as a matter of policy, to clear the Diamonds at trick 8.

9. A 'pays his premium' (3 points) when he wins this trick. He is now absolutely safe.

10. So is B. Note his discard here.

C inevitably takes the remaining seven tricks, losing in all 37 points, while A and B forfeit 3 each. For the hands when C leads to trick 11 are:

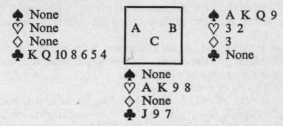

♠ None		♠ A K Q 9	
♡ None	A B	♡ 3 2	
◇ None	C	◇ 3	
♣ K Q 10 8 6 5 4		♣ None	

♠ None
♡ A K 9 8
◇ None
♣ J 9 7

C cannot blame himself. With both his adversaries discarding and playing intelligently, there was nothing to be done with his hand.

The feature of the play is A's lead of the ♡ 5 at trick 7. This apparently involves a gratuitous sacrifice of points. But let us see what *might* happen if A does not adopt this precaution:

Trick	A	B	C
7	♣ 3	♡ Q	♣ A
8	◇ 2	◇ 4	◇ 5
9	♣ 10	♡ J	♣ J
10	♣ 8	♡ 6	♣ 9
11	♣ 6	♠ Q	♣ 7
12	♡ 7	♡ 3	♡ 8
13	♡ 5	♡ 2	♡ 4

and A, with four established Clubs, must take all the rest of the tricks.

At this three-handed game one must watch every card played, conserving with the utmost care both one's entries and one's exits.

POKER

POKER is believed by many who do not play it, or who have only played it 'for fun', to be one of the easiest of card games; 'it's just a matter of bluff, isn't it?' they ask. Actually, Poker is not only one of the most difficult of all games to play well, but it has a higher skill factor than any other game played with playing cards.

By that I mean that, of all the games with which the card world is familiar, it is the one at which good players can be most certain of winning against bad players.

Here are its basic rules:

1. The number of players should be five, six or seven. Poker can be played with fewer players than five—sometimes, indeed, it is made into a game for two—but in these circumstances it quite loses its character. I shall describe the game as played in card clubs with five, six or seven participating.

2. Poker is played with one complete pack of fifty-two cards. The players cut for deal, high dealing first. The dealer—the cards having been cut to him—deals five cards face downwards, one at a time, to each player. The players then look at their hands, and those who are playing in that particular deal (I shall explain later how participation in the deal is determined) can exchange as many of their cards as they like for cards dealt to them, face downwards, from the top of the remainder of the pack.

Normally, players either stand 'pat' (*ie* exchange no cards), or exchange one, two or three. Only a lunatic stays in to exchange four. In giving these cards, the dealer begins with the player who is next to his left.

3. The object of these exchanges is to improve one's original hand (assuming it to be susceptible of improvement) with a view to securing one of the following scoring combinations. These are given in descending order of rank, *ie* a Royal Straight Flush is the best combination to hold; after that, a Straight Flush other than a Royal; after that, Fours, and so on.

SCORING COMBINATIONS IN DESCENDING ORDER OF RANK:

(i) *Royal Straight Flush*, *ie* A K Q J 10 of a suit.
(ii) *Straight Flush*, *eg* 9 8 7 6 5 of a suit. A Straight Flush

headed by a King beats a Straight Flush headed by a Queen. This, in turn, beats a Straight Flush headed by a Knave, and so on.

(iii) *Fours*, *ie* four cards of the same denomination. Four Kings, four 9's, four 3's, and so on. Four Aces beat four Kings, four Kings beat four Queens (this general principle following throughout). It is a matter of indifference what the fifth card of the hand is.

(iv) *Full House*, *ie* three cards of one denomination and two of another. Thus, three Queens and two 5's constitute a Full House, and so do three 5's and two Queens. The comparative value of Full Houses depends upon the denomination of the three similar cards contained in it. Thus, three Aces accompanied by two 2's are better than three Kings accompanied by two Queens.

(v) *Flush*, *ie* five cards of the same suit. Flushes, if in competition with one another, rank according to the highest card. Thus, A 9 6 3 2 is better than K Q J 10 8. If both Flushes are headed, say, by Aces, they rank according to their next card, and so on.

(vi) *Straight*, *ie* five cards in sequence regardless of their suit. Thus, a top Straight consists of such cards as ♠ A ♡ K ◇ Q ♠ J ♣ 10. Straights, in competition with one another, rank according to the top card. Straights headed by the same top card are equal, and if both have qualified for the 'pool' (to be explained later), the 'pool' is divided.

(vii) *Threes*, *ie* three cards of the same denomination accompanied by two others not of the same denomination. For example, three Kings, a 6 and a 4; or three 6's, a King and a 4.

(viii) *Two Pairs*, *ie* two Kings, two 4's and one other card, or two 6's two 4's and one other card. Where two pairs are in competition with one another, the player holding the higher pair wins. Where the higher pair is the same, the player with the better lower pair wins. Where both pairs are the same, the player whose fifth card is the higher wins.

(ix) *Pair*, *ie* two Kings, two 9's, etc, accompanied in each case by three 'worthless' cards. Where equal pairs are in competition, the highest outstanding card decides.

(x) Occasionally, the 'pool' may be won by a hand which has not even a pair in it. Such hands rank according to their top card and are described as 'Ace High', 'Queen High', etc.

4. We have now seen what, in exchanging cards, players are

endeavouring to do. But the winner at Poker is not necessarily the player who, by drawing cards that he wants, obtains the best hand. It is that player who, when it comes to a showdown, produces the best hand—or, if there is no showdown, that player who, by betting more money than others, has expressed the greatest confidence in the value of his own holding.

THE BETTING

Poker is always played for money, since a game which admits of 'bluffing' (ie betting in such a way as to give the impression that a worthless hand is of value) would clearly be impossible if there were nothing tangible at stake.

Moreover—and this, perhaps, is Poker's principal drawback—there is not really much point in it as a game unless you stand to risk just about as much as you can reasonably afford to lose. Naturally, I would not advise any reader to risk *more* than he can afford to lose; where a card game is played for money, you should never risk losing more than you would be prepared to spend on some other form of pleasure. But you do not get the full flavour of the game if you are playing it for stakes which are quite trivial in relation to your available resources.

Let us suppose that there are seven players in the game. Before a hand is dealt the player to the dealer's left puts up one chip; this is called the 'ante'. The next player puts up two chips; this is called the 'straddle'. (Play should be at a round table and each player places his chips in front of him.)

The hand is then dealt and the next player (ie the one who is number three from the dealer) looks at his hand and decides whether or not he wants to play; he is the 'first to speak'.

If he wishes to play, he puts up four chips, ie twice the amount of the 'straddle'.

Whether the player who is 'first to speak' plays or not depends upon what he has in his hand. If he is a good player he will not play unless he has a pair of Aces or better. He will just throw his hand in, and, so far as that deal is concerned, he takes no further part in the game.

Each of the other players in succession now decides whether or not he wants to play. Three courses are open to each of them: (1) he can come in for four chips, like the player who is 'first to speak'; (2) he can double the stake, ie he puts up eight chips; (3) he can throw his hand in.

When it comes to the player who has put up the 'ante', he can play, just like anyone else, by increasing his stake to the appropriate amount; if he does not want to play, he merely abandons his chip, and ultimately it goes to the winner of the 'pot'. Similarly, with the player who has 'straddled'.

This first part of the game—deciding whether to play or not—may take quite a long time, as, if one player has opened and another has doubled, it is open to the first player—or any one else who is in—to increase the stakes yet again, and this progressive increasing of the stakes will continue until no one wants to raise the stake any more.

The rules which govern the increase of the stakes vary from 'school' to 'school'. At private parties there is often no limit set. As the game is played in clubs, however, the following is the usual rule:

The opener must put up four chips; this can be raised to eight, and eight can be raised to sixteen. After sixteen, however, the next raise is only to twenty-four (not to thirty-two, as it would be if one went on doubling indefinitely), and, after twenty-four, to thirty-two, to forty, and so on. There is thus an automatic brake on the tendency to raise the stakes.

Now let me give an example showing how these rules operate.

Suppose the seven players are A, B, C, D, E, F, G—G being the dealer. A, on the dealer's left, puts up one chip; B puts up two chips; C is the 'first to speak'.

C's hand is: ♠ 8 5 ♡ 8 2 ◇ 8. This is a very good hand—three 8's—and C puts up four chips to play.

D now looks at his hand. He has ♠ 4 ♡ 4 ♣ J 9 7. This hand, with only a small pair in it, is worthless, and D throws it in.

E has ♠ A 10 ♡ A ◇ 10 3. This is 'Aces Up'—a good hand—and E says 'double' and puts up eight chips.

F has ♠ Q ◇ 6 5 ♣ Q 2. Only an idiot would play in a doubled pot on a pair of Queens, and F correctly throws his hand in.

G has five Clubs, the A 10 8 6 4. This is a Flush—a very good hand indeed—and G doubles the stakes again, putting up sixteen chips.

A and B have worthless hands and both throw them in, abandoning their respective chips.

C decides to stay and puts up twelve more chips, making sixteen altogether, and E, who is not prepared to put up eight more chips when he only holds Aces Up, abandons his eight chips and throws in his hand. Thus there are only two players to draw cards: C with his Threes and G with his Flush.

Now we come to the second part of the deal. Players who have stayed in (as we have seen C and G do in the example above) draw what cards they require from the dealer, and betting then begins all over again, beginning with the player who first came in.

In the above example it is C. He has already sixteen chips up and he cannot bet more than eight. He need not, however, bet as many as this; thus he can, if he likes, make no bid at all, merely saying 'check'.

Suppose that C, in our example, has drawn two cards, keeping, of course, the three 8's, and does not improve his hand. G, naturally, will have drawn no cards.

C says 'check', but G will probably raise the pot to the limit allowed him by putting up eight more chips, so that he has twenty-four in front of him.

C has now to decide whether to 'see' G, in which case he has to put up another eight chips, or to throw his hand in, in which case G takes all the money staked without exposing his hand.

If C and G are both good players, C will quite probably throw his hand in and G will collect twenty-seven chips apart from those he has put up himself.

This deal illustrates the element of *bluffing*, which is a feature of the game of Poker. If C is a weak player it is quite likely that G will have redoubled E's stake and will then have 'stood' on his five cards when he really holds nothing at all.

As Maurice Ellinger and others have pointed out, the two features of Poker—the original staking and the betting after the cards have been drawn—are quite different in character.

The first part of the game is based on mathematics, and no one can play Poker well who has not at least an intuitive knowledge of the mathematical chances governing the game. But the second part of the game (after the cards have been drawn) is not mathematical, but psychological: a player's bets are determined by his reading of the way in which other players are behaving, and by his judgment as to how they, in their turn, will read him.

Illustrative Deals

I

Here is a deal at Poker from actual play. A is the dealer, and the hands dealt are as follows:

D, 'first to speak': ♠ A ♡ 3 ♣ A 6 3.

E: ♠ 6 ♣ 9 8 5 2.

F: ♠ J ♡ A J ◇ A ♣ 10.

G: ♠ 7 ♡ 10 9 8 7.

A, dealer: ♠ 9 ♡ 4 ◇ 6 5 3.

B, ante: ♠ K Q ♡ K ◇ K Q.

C, straddle: ♡ Q ◇ J 10 8 7.

B puts up one chip and C two.

D, 'first to speak', has Aces Up and puts up four chips.

E, although he has four cards to a flush, will, if he is sensible, throw his hand in.

F, like D, has Aces Up, and this is a good enough hand to double on. F, therefore, puts up eight chips.

G has a very tempting hand; four cards to a Straight Flush. If he can draw either the ♡ J or the ♡ 6 he is virtually certain of winning the pool, and if he draws any Heart, any Knave or any 6, his chances of winning the pool will be very good. He therefore plays, putting up eight chips.

A has 'an open-ended Straight', *ie* if he throws his 9, he will make a Straight if he can draw either a 7 or a 2. Nevertheless, if he is wise, he will throw his hand in.

B has an enormous hand: a pat Full House, Kings High. He will therefore double, putting up fifteen more chips, making sixteen in all in front of him.

C, with four Diamonds in his hand, will reluctantly throw his hand in.

Now D has to decide whether to put up twelve more chips or to abandon four. There is so much money in the pool that he is tempted to take a chance; he puts up twelve more chips, hoping to make a Full House.

F and G each put up eight more chips, and the staking is now over. Four players are still in the game, each with sixteen chips in front of him.

The dealer now gives cards. B, with his Full House, stands pat. D takes one card, throwing the ♣ 6, but, alas, he does not improve his hand—he draws the ♣ 7. F, however, seems to be more fortunate; he draws the ♣ J, and has now a Full House,

Knaves Up. G throws the ♠ 7 and draws the ♡ 6; he has thus achieved his Straight Flush and is prepared to go on betting almost indefinitely.

The betting now opens, D 'speaking first'.

D, with only Aces Up, checks; F increases the stake to twenty-four, the maximum permissible, and G makes it twenty-eight.

B now has to think hard. Two players have already raised the Pot; nevertheless B's hand is so good that he ventures on one more raise. He puts up sixteen chips, the maximum permissible, and has now thirty-two in front of him.

F says 'See you', and puts up eight more chips, but G raises again to thirty-six.

It is now evident to B and F that G has Fours at least. B, however, 'sees' him, putting up four more chips, while F, very sensibly, throws his hand in. G's Straight Flush is better than B's Full House and G takes the Pool: 122 chips.

In this exampe there were three exceptionally good hands in conflict. This is unusual, though by no means impossible. I have given the hand in order to illustrate fully the principles on which the betting is conducted.

II

There are again seven players: A, B, C, D, E, F and G.

A, on the dealer's left, puts up one chip, as 'ante', B, putting up two chips, 'straddles'. C will be 'first to speak'. G now deals the seven hands as follows:

A: ♠ 7 3 ♡ K ◇ 7 ♣ 3.
B: ◇ 5 ♣ A Q 9 4.
C: ♠ K ♡ 8 ◇ K 9 ♣ 2.
D: ♠ Q 5 ♡ Q ◇ 8 ♣ 5.
E: ♡ 7 6 3 2 ◇ 10.
F: ♠ J ♡ J ♣ J 10 8.
G: ♠ A 6 ♡ A ◇ A ♣ 7.

C is first to speak. He looks at his hand; he has a pair of Kings. Most players will open on a pair of Kings; but actually, with seven players, it does not pay to do so. C throws his hand in.

D has 'Queens Up', ie a pair of Queens and a smaller pair. This is good enough to play on and D puts up four chips and plays.

E has four Hearts—a 'bobtail'. This, again, is the kind of hand on which a beginner is apt to play. But the odds against his drawing another Heart are approximately 4–1, and with only one player so far in the pool and the possibility that others will increase the stakes, it would be wrong for E to come in. Like C, he throws his hand in.

F has three Knaves—a very good hand—and doubles, putting up eight chips.

G has an even better hand—three Aces. This is, indeed, so good a hand that it is a very nice question whether G should not redouble. On a balance of considerations, however, he decides not to do so and contents himself with putting up his eight chips.

A has two small pairs and it would be very unwise of him to come into a doubled pot. He throws his hand in, abandoning his ante.

B's is a very difficult decision: he has four cards to a Flush—headed, moreover, by the Ace—and, as he is last to speak, there is no danger, if he comes in, of the pot being raised again before the draw. If he can take in another Club, he is more likely than not to win the pot. As, therefore, he has two chips up already, he decides to play and puts up six more, making him eight in all.

The dealer now gives cards to B, D, F and G.

B draws the ♣ K, making an 'Ace High' Flush. D, throwing the ◇ 8, takes in the ♠ 4, and ends as he began with 'Queens Up'. F throws the ♣ 10 8, and takes in the ◇ 6 and ♣ 6, which gives him a Full House, 'Knaves Up'. G throws his two worthless cards and takes in the ♡ 9 and ◇ 4. He has not improved on his three Aces.

Betting now begins. D, who knows, of course, that he is out of things, contents himself with saying 'check'.

F naturally doubles, putting up eight more chips.

This is a nasty blow for G. Let us suppose that G knows F to be a good player. The latter has doubled his stake in spite of the fact that two players have come into an already doubled pot after him and that one of these (B) has only drawn one card. G decides that, in these circumstances, F almost certainly has a Full House, and, with admirable morale, throws his three Aces in.

B also reads F with a Full House, but, at the same time, his hand and the size of the pot justify his making sure. He therefore 'sees' F, putting up another eight chips.

D, obviously, throws in his hand.

F's Full House, of course, wins and he collects the pool—forty-nine chips in all.

The above deal illustrates several points in respect of which the beginner would have gone wrong, and which deserve to be carefully studied.

'Pots' at Poker

'Straight' Poker is the basic form of a game which has many interesting varieties.

In some West End clubs it is the practice to have a round of 'pots' every quarter of an hour. The maximum number at the table is seven, and, if candidates are waiting to come in, they take the place of those who are due to come out before the round of pots begins. The pots played are usually a 'Jackpot', a 'Freakpot' and one or more 'Misère' pots, in that order. Sometimes 'Acepots' are played also.

The difference between an ordinary deal at Poker and a 'Pot' is that in the latter case everyone must contribute. Thus in a Jackpot, before the cards are dealt, each player puts up, say, two chips. Now cards are dealt to each player in the ordinary way.

The player to the dealer's left has the right to 'open' first. A Jackpot cannot be opened on a hand worse than a pair of Knaves. If the player to the dealer's left cannot, or does not, open (there is no obligation to open even if one is able to do so), the right to open passes to the next player, and so on round the table.

If no one opens the pot, the hands are thrown in and the deal passes; at the same time each player must 'sweeten' or 'refresh' the pot by putting up, say, one chip more.

The cards are now dealt again, and this process of re-dealing and 'sweetening' the pot continues until someone is able to open. It is not often that a Jackpot has to be 'sweetened' twice.

The opener can open for as many chips as he likes up to an agreed maximum—say, four. Now other players in turn can elect to play in the pot, raising the opener's stakes if they like to do so. Once a pot has been opened one does not need to have 'openers' to play.

Those who do not wish to play throw their hands in, merely forfeiting their entry money and refreshers, if any. Those who are in the pot receive cards and bet exactly as in 'straight' Poker.

ILLUSTRATIVE DEALS

A Jackpot

Here is an example of an actual Jackpot. We will suppose that it has been sweetened once (no player having opened it on the first deal) so that there are already twenty-one chips in the pot. Now, it is G's turn to deal, and the following are the players' hands:

(First to speak) A: ♠ 10 8 7 2   ◇ 9.

B: ♠ 6   ♡ K 5   ♣ 7 4.

C: ♠ 3   ♡ 3   ♣ Q 10 3.

D: ♠ A 5   ♡ A   ◇ 5 2.

E: ♠ 9   ♡ 9   ◇ Q 4   ♣ J.

F: ♠ K Q   ♡ 2   ◇ K 6.

G: ♠ J   ♡ 8 4   ♣ K 9.

A cannot open and says 'no'. B says 'no'. C, with three 3's (a good hand) says 'open' and puts up four chips. D has 'Aces Up' (a hand normally good enough to win the pot) and doubles, putting up eight chips. E, with a pair of 9's, should play in an undoubled pot, but not in a doubled one; E, therefore, throws his hand in. F also throws in, though he would play on a pair of Kings if the pot had not been doubled. G throws in, of course.

A has four cards to a Flush; there are, so far, thirty-three chips in the pot, and if C merely plays without redoubling, there will be thirty-seven. That means that by staking eight chips A has a reasonable chance of winning something like fifty. He therefore runs the risk of being redoubled and plays, putting up eight chips.

B has four cards to a Straight and is also tempted to play, though the odds against his making a Straight are longer than the odds against A's making a Flush. C, in the face of so much competition, is content with putting up another four chips.

Thus, before the 'buy', there are fifty-three chips in the pot. The players are now given cards.

A receives the ♠ 4 and makes his Flush. B fails to make his Straight, but C, throwing the ♣ Q 10, draws the ♠ A and ◇ 3, making him four 3's. D throws the ◇ 2 and draws the ♣ 5, which gives him a Full House. There are thus three exceptionally strong hands in competition.

Betting now begins. C, who has opened the pot, bets first. Holding four 3's, he not unnaturally doubles, putting up another eight chips. D reads C with at least a Full House (as the latter

has doubled in the teeth of two one-card buys) and has the sense
not to double again. He also puts up eight more chips. A, rather
reluctantly, also sees the opener. I do not think he is well advised
to do so since it is almost certain that either C or D holds a
Full House at least. But it requires considerable self-control to
throw in a Flush.

C, of course, wins the pot—seventy-seven chips in all—and
also receives a bonus of two chips from each player in respect
of his Fours.

A player who has opened a pot, and is subsequently driven
out in the betting, must retain his hand and exhibit his 'openers'
at the conclusion of the deal.

A Freakpot

In this pot all 2's are 'Freaks', ie Jokers; hence a 2 can represent any other card. Thus, a hand containing two Aces, two 2's,
and a 5, ranks as four Aces; a hand containing ♡ K 9 8 3 and
♣ 2 ranks as an Ace High Flush in Hearts.

It is obvious that with four Jokers in the pack, what seems
ordinarily a good hand is of little account in a Freakpot; thus
three natural 8's, which would ordinarily win a Jackpot or
Acepot, stand next to no chance of winning in a Freakpot.

The technique of the pot is the same as that of a Jackpot.
To begin with, each player puts up, say, two chips, and 'sweetens'
the pot with one chip if by any chance it is not opened. The
opener's requirements are the same as for a Jackpot, ie a Pair of
Knaves or better; this means, of course, that a player can open
on one Knave and a 'Freak'.

'FIVES'

There is one hand possible in a Freakpot which you cannot
obtain at 'straight' Poker, ie 'Fives'. If you hold, for example,
three Queens and two Freaks, this ranks as Five Queens. If it
comes to a showdown, Fives rank below a Royal Straight
Flush, but above any other Straight Flush.

Here is an example of a Freakpot from actual play:

G is the dealer, and the other players, as usual, are A, B,
C, D, E, F. A, on the dealer's left, is 'first to speak'.

Each player having put up his two chips, G deals the cards
as under:

   A: ♡ K ◇ K 9 ♣ 6 3.
   B: ♠ 2 ♡ A ◇ 8 ♣ J 4.

C: ♡ 5 3 2   ◇ 7   ♣ Q.
D: ♠ 10   ♡ 10   ♣ 10 8 5.
E: ♡ 7 6 4   ◇ A   ♣ A.
F: ♠ A K J 8   ◇ 3.
G: ♠ 9 4   ♡ 9   ◇ Q   ♣ 9.

A, with his Pair of Kings, can open, but he should not do so, as a Pair of natural Kings is a poor hand in a Freakpot. A, therefore, says 'no'.

B has a Pair of Aces and opens, putting up four chips.

C, with a Freak, elects to play. Unless the pot has been doubled, it is always worth while to draw four cards to a Freak.

D also plays, having three natural 10's. Although natural Threes stand but a moderate chance of winning, it is, I think, always worth while to play on them because of the chance of natural Fours, which carry a bonus with them.

E elects to play on his Pair of natural Aces, though this is doubtful policy with so many others in the pot.

F plays, as, of course, he should do, with four cards to an Ace High Flush.

G also plays, having three natural 9's. A throws his hand in.

NOTE: This is a somewhat unusual pot in that six of the seven players are competing, yet not one of them has a good enough hand to double.

THE DRAW

B keeps his Ace and Freak and draws ◇ 6 5   ♣ 7, leaving him slightly worse off than he was before.

C keeps his Freak and is rewarded by drawing ♠ 7 6 5 3, giving him a Straight Flush.

D, to three 10's, draws ◇ 2 and ♣ K, giving him four 10's.

E keeps his Aces and draws ◇ J 10 4.

F throws the ◇ 3 and draws the ♠ Q, which gives him an Ace High Flush.

G plays on his three 9's and draws ♡ Q and ♣ 2, making him four 9's.

THE BETTING

Before the betting begins, there are thirty-eight chips in the pot—two contributed by each of the seven players, and four by each of the six who have elected to play.

B checks.

C, with his Straight Flush, bets the maximum (say, four chips).

D says 'see you', putting up four chips in his turn.

E and F throw their hands in, but G also elects to 'see'.

C's Straight Flush, of course, wins against D's and G's Fours, and he takes the pool—fifty chips in all.

On the whole, C, holding a Straight Flush, has not done very well out of this pot. Quite often, he would meet a player with four Aces or Four Kings, and there would be some lively betting. Many players with C's hand, and with five others in the pot, would check in the hope that someone else would raise.

An Acepot

An Acepot is similar to a Jackpot, save that the minimum requirement for an opener is a pair of Aces.

There are seven players: A, B, C, D, E, F and G, of whom G, say, is the dealer. G distributes the cards as under:

A: ♡ J 10 9 8 ♣ 3.
B: ♠ 5 ♡ 3 ◇ 4 ♣ 9 2.
C: ♠ J 4 ◇ J 6 ♣ 6.
D: ♠ 9 2 ♡ Q ◇ 9 5.
E: ♠ 7 ♡ 7 ◇ 7 ♣ K 4.
F: ♠ K 6 ♡ K 6 ◇ 2.
G: ♠ A ♡ A ♣ A Q 10.

BETTING BEFORE THE DRAW

Each player has put up, say, four chips, so, when the pot opens, there are twenty-eight chips in all.

A has four cards to a Straight Flush and, naturally, much hopes that the pot will be opened. He, however, cannot open.

B also passes, though, like A, he will not be averse to seeing the pot opened.

C, with Knaves Up, opens, putting up eight chips.

D has a pair of 9's. The pot has just been opened to his left and therefore there are five more players to speak. If D is wise, he will throw his hand in.

E has three 7's and, as recommended above, doubles, putting up sixteen chips.

F has Kings Up. Should he play? In view of E's double, F can reasonably assume that he has at least Threes against him. That means he must make a Full House, a chance that is roughly 11–1 against. At present there are only fifty-two chips in the pot and therefore F is not justified in playing, which would mean putting up another sixteen chips. He throws his hand in.

G, with three Aces, doubles again, putting up twenty-four chips. (We are assuming that eight is the maximum raise permitted.) There are now seventy-six chips in the pot.

Now it is A's turn to reconsider his hand. He will stand a fair chance of winning if he can draw any Queen, any Seven, or any Heart, *ie* the odds against his drawing at least a Straight are only 30–17. Moreover, if he can draw the Queen or Seven of Hearts, filling the Straight Flush, he will be virtually certain of taking the pot, and will, in any case, secure a bonus. He is therefore justified in playing and puts up twenty-four chips.

B, on the other hand, should throw his hand in. The odds are roughly 5–1 against his making a very small Straight, and that may well be beaten if he does make it. It is not worth his while to put up twenty-four chips when there are only 100 in the pot.

C, the opener, should also throw his hand in. He is obviously up against three powerful hands: it is nearly 11–1 against his making a Full House and he would have to put up sixteen more chips. He therefore retires from the pot, keeping his cards, however, as he will have to show his openers at the conclusion of the deal.

E, who already has sixteen chips in, puts up eight more, and the betting before the draw is now finished.

There are 108 chips in the pot. C, the opener, has contributed eight; E, G and A have each put up twenty-four, and there were twenty-eight to begin with.

THE DRAW

In view of the evidently strong competition, each of the players goes 'all out'. E keeps his three 7's, to which he draws ◇ 8 and ♣ 8, making a Full House Sevens Up. G keeps his Aces and is lucky enough to draw ♠ 10 and ◇ 10, making a Full House Aces up. A throws the ♣ 3 and draws the ♡ 5, making a Knave-High Flush.

THE BETTING

C having retired, E bets first. With his Full House he has an odds-on chance of winning, and he therefore bets the maximum eight chips.

G, with an Ace-High Full House, has, of course, no hesitation in raising E, putting up sixteen chips.

A now reluctantly retires. His competitors, who both raised before the draw, cannot have been drawing to Straights or

Flushes; they must both have made Full Houses. Hence it is useless to continue with his Flush, though normally, of course, his hand would win the pot.

E 'sees' G, putting up eight more chips, and G takes the pot— 140 chips in all.

Had A filled his Straight Flush, he would, of course, have taken the pot, and, in addition, would have received from each player a bonus of, say, eight chips.

Misère Pots

Of recent years Misère pots have become very popular, and in many schools a 'round' consists of one Jackpot, one Freakpot and two Misères. Acepots have declined in favour, as, where there are fewer than seven players, several rounds may be dealt before the pot can be opened at all.

The winner of a Misère pot is the player who, at the finish, produces the worst hand. Their ranking is that of ordinary Poker hands but reckoning, so to speak, from the bottom upwards. Ace counts low, so the worst possible hand (which will win or divide any pot) is Ace, 2, 3, 4, 6—provided, of course, that the cards are not all of the same suit. (This hand is often called a 'Royal'.) The next worst hand is Ace, 2, 3, 5, 6; the next worst, Ace, 2, 4, 5, 6; and so on. Any hand in which 6 is the highest card stands a big odds-on chance of winning a Misère pot, and a hand in which 7 is the highest card is more likely than not to win. But quite often hands with a 9 or 10 will win, and it is by no means impossible to win a pot with a pair.

Any player in his turn can open a Misère pot. It does not matter what his holding is, but, when it comes to the draw, he may not draw more than three cards. Thus, even if one were foolish enough to want to draw four cards to an Ace, one is not allowed to do so.

A Misère pot affords exceptional opportunities for judgment and for the exercise of psychology. To begin with, playing in a Misère pot must be pure gamble unless one has a 'pat' hand. For, however good one's initial holding is, eg Ace, 2, 3, 6, and (say) another Ace, the draw may wreck it. One throws out the Ace with a good chance of making a 'Royal', and instead gets (say) a 6, which will almost certainly put one's hand out of court. Or a King or Queen, which reduces one's chances to a minimum. There is also more scope than in hands of other types for bluffing. For example, A opens a Misère pot; B—

known to have a penchant for doubling on four likely cards—doubles the stake; C now doubles again. This may well drive out the last four players, and perhaps will drive out A as well. Suppose A goes and that B was proposing to stand 'pat' on a hand in which a 9 is the highest card. B must now reconsider his tactics, for the redouble—unless a bluff—means that the third player, C, has certainly a better hand than B's. So B will throw his 9, and now C will stand pat and take a chance that B will not see him if he confidently doubles again. Sometimes a semi-bluff redouble of this kind is, so to speak, a 'two-way' affair. The redoubler has (say) 10, 6, 4, 3, Ace. If those who are competing against him draw, he stands pat and doubles again; if one of them stands pat, he throws his 10 and hopes that he may yet get the winning hand.

Tactical situations of this kind—which may, of course, be much more complicated, if there are three or four players involved—frequently occur in Misère pots.

Another situation which gives scope to the alert player arises when, first or second to speak, he holds an exceptionally good pat hand. If he passes, he takes a chance that the deal will be thrown in, but, with seven players, it is long odds that some-one else will open. Now, of course, one is perfectly placed for a double. Some players regard it as not 'playing the game' to pass on a Royal or near-Royal, but there is nothing unethical in doing so. The phrase 'playing the game' means nothing in this context: the one essential is that the game should be played in strict accordance with its rules.

It is very difficult to dogmatize as to when one should, or should not, participate in Misère pots. One certainly can't wait till one is dealt a good pat hand: one will lose much more in entries than one can hope to gain. One should normally play, therefore, on any hand which contains four cards of which only one is higher than a 7, eg K, 7, 5, 3, 2. From this collection, of course, one throws the King. There is one possible exception: where the four cards are in sequence, eg K, 6, 5, 4, 3. A 7 or 2 will ruin this hand, as well as a high card or a pair. Many players, however, regularly come in, drawing two cards. I believe that this policy must lose in the long run, though it is maddening to sit—as one may do—for perhaps an hour, and never have a four-card Misère to draw to. And the draw of two cards to (say) Ace, 2, 6 appears so often to produce a winning hand that one is sorely tempted to throw one's principle overboard.

The problem is complicated by the fact that mathematical odds, in connection with the Misère pots, are incalculable. One cannot assume, if one holds (say) Ace, 2, 6, that one has the normally calculable expectation of drawing a 3, a 4, or a 5. Everything depends on the number of other players and on the kind of game that they are playing. For example, if, when it comes to your turn to speak, there are five people in the pot already, it is sheer madness to draw two cards, since those five players have from fifteen to twenty low cards among them. If, on the other hand, you are last to speak, and there are only two players in the pot, a two-card buy affords a reasonably good chance.

Finally, the game varies very much in character according to whether the opening bet can be a 'check' (costing nothing) or a 'chip' (putting up the minimum stake). The player who has opened the pot, and is first to speak when the betting opens, will not waste even the minimum stake if he has a hopeless hand; he will just throw his hand in. And this may apply to the next two players as well. But if all these players can 'check'—and, of course, they will do so, since there is always the chance of a miracle—the first player with a good hand may well be deterred from betting, because there is always the possibility that some-one who has checked has, in fact, a winning hand and is lying low for a double. A player who 'chips' may also, of course, be lying low; the point is that the necessity to 'chip' eliminates the worthless hands as soon as the betting starts.

Stud Poker

Stud Poker is a most interesting variety of the game, in which each player exposes some of his cards, but keeps the others to himself. The most popular variety is Seven-Card Stud, which is played as follows.

First, there is a 'pot' to which each player contributes an initial stake, say, one chip. Next, the dealer deals, to each player, two cards face downwards and one card face upwards. These cards are placed in front of the player, so that there is no doubt as to which his exposed cards are. Each player looks at his own concealed cards, but—as in all forms of Poker—takes care that no one else sees them.

Betting on the hands now begins. There may be as many as five rounds of betting, so it is usual to limit the stakes in every round but the last. For example, if each player has put one chip in the pot, it would be quite usual for the rule to be that no player could bet or raise by more than one chip on any round and that the pot cannot, in the course of the round, be raised by more than four chips in all.

Let us assume, first of all, that we are playing an ordinary high-card Stud. The object here is to get the best Poker hand (*eg* a straight flush if possible, and so on downwards). When the first three cards have been dealt, the first player to speak is the one with the highest exposed card: *eg* if a player has an Ace, he speaks first; if there are two Aces, the player who first received cards speaks first. Whether a player bets, accepts a bet, or throws his hand in, depends, of course (*a*) on what cards he has concealed, (*b*) on what cards he can see in other hands, and (*c*), as in all Poker games, on the assumptions to be drawn from the bets which other players are making. The first player to speak, then, may either bet, check, or throw his hand in if he doesn't wish to go on. In the last case, he turns his exposed card, or cards, face downwards and abandons any money he may have put up. The first bet (or check) having been made by the player first to speak, each of the others speaks in rotation in the ordinary way. If one chip is the maximum bet allowed to any player, a second player can add another chip, a third one another, and a fourth another. After that, there can be no more betting till another card has been dealt. Or, of course, the hands may be so poor that no one wants to bet at all.

A second card is now dealt (face upwards) to each player—or, rather, to such of the players as have not thrown their hands in. Now, the same procedure is repeated, the player whose two exposed cards rank highest being the first to speak. Thus, a pair of 2's ranks higher than Ace King. Betting continues up to the prescribed limit, and then a third card is dealt, and a third round of betting follows. Each player left in the game has now two concealed cards and three exposed cards in front of him. There are two more rounds of cards to be dealt. Before each of these, every player left in the game will discard one of the cards in front of him. He can either discard an exposed card—in which case the next card is dealt face upwards—or one of his concealed cards—in which case it is dealt face downwards.

After the second exchange of cards the Stud is completed, and betting can now go on as long as any two players wish to compete. The final pot is likely to be a substantial one.

Here is an example of a high-card Stud. We will call the players

A, B, C, D, E, F, G, and let G be the dealer. Each player puts one chip into the pot, which thus starts with seven chips. G now deals cards as under:

	Concealed Cards:	Exposed cards:
A:	♡ 10, ◇ 8	♠ Ace
B:	♠ J, ♣ J	◇ 3
C:	◇ Ace, ◇ 10	♣ Ace
D:	◇ 5, ♣ 3	♡ 8
E:	♡ 7, ♣ 6	♠ 5
F:	♠ K, ♠ Q	♠ 4
G:	♡ 2, ◇ 4	♡ 6

Betting now begins. A (first player with an exposed Ace) is first to speak. A checks. B (with a concealed pair of Knaves) bets one chip. C (with a pair of Aces) makes it two chips. D throws his hand in. E (who has three cards towards a straight) puts up two chips, and F (with three cards towards a flush) also puts up two chips. G throws his hand in, and A (perhaps not very sensibly) decides to stay, and puts up two chips. B puts up a second chip.

Ten chips now have been staked (in addition to the seven in the pot), and G deals the second exposed card. These are: A: ♠ 10; B: ♣ 4; C: ♡ 9; E: ♠ 8; F: ♡ 3. And the hands are now as under:

	Concealed cards:	Exposed cards:
A:	♡ 10, ◇ 8	♠ Ace, ♠ 10
B:	♠ J, ♣ J	◇ 3, ♣ 4
C:	◇ Ace, ◇ 10	♣ Ace, ♡ 9
E:	♡ 7, ♣ 6	♠ 5, ♠ 8
F:	♠ K, ♠ Q	♠ 4, ♡ 3

The first player to speak is A, whose Ace 10 is better than anything else exposed. A checks, ie leaves his stake at two chips. So does B. C bets another chip, making three. E puts up another chip; so does F; and so do A and B. There are now fifteen chips plus seven in the pot, and the third round of exposed cards is dealt: A: ♣ 7; B: ♡ J; C: ♡ 4; E: ◇ 2; F: ♠ 7. The hands are:

	Concealed cards:	Exposed cards:
A:	♡ 10, ◇ 8	♠ Ace, ♠ 10, ♣ 7
B:	♠ J, ♣ J	◇ 3, ♣ 4, ♡ J
C:	◇ Ace, ◇ 10	♣ Ace, ♡ 9, ♡ 4
E:	♡ 7, ♣ 6	♠ 5, ♠ 8, ◇ 2
F:	♠ K, ♠ Q	♠ 4, ♡ 3, ♠ 7

The game is now 'warming up'. B has three Knaves; E has four cards to an open-ended straight; F has four cards to a flush. And there are two more rounds to be dealt. A (with Ace, 10, 7 exposed) is still the first player to speak.

A, who has only a pair of 10's, checks; B bets another chip, making four; C puts up one more chip; E puts up one more chip; F puts up two more chips (raising B by one). A now decides to throw his hand in, but B, C and D all put up another chip. There are now twenty-three chips staked, plus seven in the pot.

The four players left in the game now each discard one card. All four throw exposed cards: B, the ◇ 3; C, the ♡ 4; E the ◇ 2; F, the ♡ 3. So G deals another card, face upwards, to each player. B gets ◇ 6; C, ♡ Ace; E, ♠ 9; F, ♠ 2. The hands are now:

	Concealed cards:	Exposed cards:
B:	♠ J, ♣ J	♣ 4, ♡ J, ◇ 6
C:	◇ Ace, ◇ 10	♣ Ace, ♡ 9, ♡ Ace
E:	♡ 7, ♣ 6	♠ 5, ♠ 8, ♠ 9
F:	♠ K, ♠ Q	♠ 4, ♠ 7, ♠ 2

With one card still to be dealt, an unusually good lot of hands are in competition. B has three Knaves; C, three Aces; E has made a straight; and F has made his Spade flush. What makes it more amusing is the fact that all E's exposed cards are Spades, so it looks to some of the players as though E has a flush too.

The first to speak is now C, who has a pair of Aces on the table. He bets one chip, making six; E makes it seven; F makes it eight; and B—far from happy in the face of such strong betting—somewhat reluctantly puts up three more chips. C, however, raises again, making nine; E puts up two more chips (also making nine); F puts up another chip (making ten); and B, C, E make up to this total.

The dealer now announces that each player can discard one more card. B discards ♣ 4, and, to his delight, receives ♠ 6. C throws his concealed ◇ 10, and is dealt (face downwards) ♣ 5. E and F announce that they are satisfied with their hands. These are the full hands:

	Concealed cards:	Exposed cards:
B:	♠ J, ♣ J	♡ J, ◇ 6, ♠ 6
C:	◇ Ace, ♣ 5	♣ Ace, ♡ 9, ♡ Ace
E:	♡ 7, ♣ 6	♠ 5, ♠ 8, ♠ 9
F:	♠ K, ♠ Q	♠ 4, ♠ 7, ♠ 2

It is still C's turn to bet first. With two pat hands announced against him (though it is, of course, possible that E or F is bluffing), C does no more than check. E, suspecting that F has a flush, checks also. F bets four chips (which we will assume to be the maximum single bet allowed). B raises F by four chips, making his stake eighteen. C and E throw their hands in, and F sees B at eighteen chips. B's full house wins against F's flush, and B collects the pool: sixty-six chips in all.

Misère Studs

With many players, Misère Studs are more popular than high-card Studs (such as the one just illustrated), because there is more scope for sudden improvement or dramatic failure.

The play is on exactly the same lines as that of the high-card Stud, except, of course, that the object is to get the worst hand, and that, in each round of betting, the worst card, or combination of cards, bets first. Thus, where there are three exposed cards, a player holding 3, 4, 6 will have priority over a player holding A, 2, 7. Novices should play in Misère Studs with extreme caution. Unless you have two really good concealed cards, *ie* two cards not a pair and not higher than six, you should retire from any pot where there are ostensibly good hands against you and betting threatens to be heavy. In nearly every school there will be one or more gamblers who will boost up a Misère Stud from the outset, in the hope of eliminating competition, and it is a mistake to play their game in preference to one's own.

There is, of course, a good deal of scope for bluffing in this particular type of pot, *eg* a player with Ace, 2, 6 on the table, who announces that he is 'standing' before the final round is dealt, stands a good chance of getting away with the pot whatever his concealed cards may be.

QUINTET

CARD-PLAYERS who are looking for a new game for two may like to try 'Quintent'. This is a game invented by the writer Tom Brown, in the dialogue which follows, introduces Quintet to Joe Smith.

'The game is based,' Tom explained, 'on Poker. But Poker for two is pointless, while this game offers, I think, considerable scope for skill. It is played with two Piquet packs; *ie* from two ordinary packs we take out all the cards from the 2 to the 6 inclusive. That leaves us with thirty-two cards in each pack.

'Next, suppose I'm dealer—it makes no difference whatever who deals—I shuffle my pack—you cut—now I turn up the seven top cards.' Tom did so. They were: ♠ K; ♡ Q 10 8; ◊ J 10; ♣ Q.

'I put these cards aside,' said Tom. 'Now you, Joe, take your pack and throw out the same seven cards. That leaves us with twenty-five cards each. Now, what we have to do is to arrange our twenty-five cards in five Poker hands. When we've done that— we'll allow, say, ten minutes—the fun begins. We expose the first of our hands, and whoever has the better hand (scoring as in Poker) wins. Then we similarly expose each of our remaining hands.

'But the point is that they don't all score equally. The winner of the first hand scores 3 points. The winner of the second hand scores 4 points. The third, fourth and fifth hands score respectively 5, 6 and 7 points.

'The game is won on aggregate points. So you see, Joe, you can win if you take the last two hands. The fun comes in trying to frame hands which are most likely to win points, having regard to the variety of tactics which are open to your opponent, just as they are to you. The skill factor is obviously very large.'

'For which reason,' grinned Joe, 'you're pretty sure to beat me.'

The twenty-five cards with which each player had started were: ♠ A Q J 10 9 8 7; ♡ A K J 9 7; ◊ A K Q 9 8 7; ♣ A K J 10 9 8 7.

'Before we begin, I should add this,' said Tom. 'If we have equality on any pair of hands, the points for that hand are divided.'

In selecting his five hands, Joe, not unnaturally, was out-manœuvred. Remembering that a player winning the last two hands would, *ipso facto*, win the game, Joe put aside the ♠ Q J 10 9 8 (the strongest possible hand) for his No 5, and the ♣ J 10 9 8 7 for his No 4. 'At the worst,' he said to himself, 'I shall divide on these two hands.' But Tom, foreseeing precisely these machinations on Joe's part, had taken effective steps to meet them.

For the first hand Joe produced ♡ K J 9 7; ♠ 7.

'No good, I'm afraid,' said Tom. His hand was a Full House: ♠ 7; ♡ 9 7; ◇ 9 7.

For the second hand, Joe had a Flush: ◇ K Q 9 8 7.

Tom countered with Four Aces: ♠ A; ♡ A J; ◇ A; ♣ A.

'I begin to see what's happened,' said Joe. 'My four Aces appear next, and I suppose they meet a Straight Flush.'

'Quite right,' said Tom. The hands were:

Joe: ♠ A; ♡ A; ◇ A; ♣ A K.
Tom: ♣ J 10 9 8 7.

Similarly on the fourth show Joe's Straight Flush met a better one:

Joe: ♣ J 10 9 8 7.
Tom: ♠ Q J 10 9 8.

Of course, Joe won the last show hands down. He had the Queen high Straight Flush against Three Kings; but he had lost the game by 18 points to 7.

'Talk about a wagonload of monkeys!' said Joe. 'I knew you'd have it in for me. Come on, Tom; let me try again.'

CANASTA

CANASTA, A game of the Rummy family, originated in South America. In 1949 it spread like wildfire across America, and it has since become popular all over the world. The game is easy to learn and extremely exciting, but at the same time its strategy is sufficiently complex to interest serious card players. Many famous Bridge experts are among the keenest devotees of Canasta.

Canasta can be played two handed, three handed, or as a four handed partnership game. The four handed game is the best and most popular, and we will consider this first.

Before describing the procedure of the game, it will help to define some of the terms used.

THE PACK

Canasta is played with two ordinary fifty-two card packs with four Jokers added—108 cards in all. In addition to the four Jokers, the eight 2's are wild; that is, they can be used as cards of any denomination. The cards have the following values:

Joker	..	50 points each	Ace	..	20 points each
Two	..	20 ,, ,,	K Q J 10 9 8	10 ,, ,,
		7 6 5 4 & black 3	..	.. 5 points each

Red 3's have a special function. They count 100 each, but if a side has four red 3's, the score is 800.

As in all Rummy games, there is a stock pile and a discard pile. After the deal, one card is turned face upwards, and the rest of the pack (the stock) is face downwards. The players in turn draw from the stock and discard on the discard pile.

THE MELD

A meld is three or more cards of a kind. A player melds by withdrawing three or more cards from his hand and laying them on the table. A meld must contain at least two natural cards. Thus Q Q 2 is a valid meld, but Q 2 2 is not.

There are no sequences in Canasta.

No meld may contain more than three wild cards.

Partners may add to one another's melds, but never to those of opponents.

Red 3's are never melded. Black 3's (which, as we shall see

later, play a special part in the game) can be melded only when a player goes out at the finish of the game; and then they may not be melded in conjunction with a wild card.

Wild cards themselves cannot be melded with one another.

MAKING A CANASTA

The main object of the game is to meld seven of a kind. This is called a canasta and carries with it a bonus far exceeding all other scores that can be made (except for four red 3's—and this is an automatic score, like honours at Bridge). A canasta may be *natural* or *mixed*. A natural canasta contains no wild cards; for this the bonus is 500. A canasta containing wild cards scores 300.

To be valid a canasta must contain a base of four natural cards. When a canasta has been completed, it is folded up. If it is a natural canasta, a red card is left face upwards on top: if a mixed canasta, a black card. Cards of the same denomination (or wild cards) can be added to a completed canasta.

HOW THE GAME IS PLAYED

Now that you understand the terms 'meld' and 'canasta', you can follow a description of the game.

In the cut for deal and partners the cards have the same rank as at Bridge, except that a player who cuts a Joker, or two players who cut identical cards, must cut again. The players with the highest cards are partners, and the first deal is made by the player in front of the player who has the highest card. Imagine the four players sitting in the following positions:

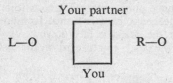

Your partner

L—O   R—O

You

L—O stands for left-hand opponent, R—O for right-hand opponent. Say that you have cut the highest card. R—O deals eleven cards to each player, then spreads out the remainder of the stock, running into the centre of the table, so that all players can easily reach to draw a card. He turns the top card face upwards.

You have to make the first draw and discard. Your first action is to remove from your hand any red 3 and lay it face upwards on the table. This is compulsory. Whenever you put a red 3 on the table you draw a card from the stock to replace it, so that the cards in your hand are not reduced in number.

Your first action, then, is to place a red 3 on the table and to draw from stock. Then you have eleven cards in your hand, which you will sort into pairs, keeping the Jokers and 2's distinct. So your hand may look like this:

Joker 2 K K 5 5 5 7 6 4 3

The 3, of course, is a black 3.

Now, if the up-card were a 5, you might take it, but if it were any other card (a wild card would be covered by a natural card—see below) you would draw from stock. Suppose that you draw a 9. Now you would discard one of your loose cards. You would probably choose one of the low cards; but not, for the moment, the black 3.

Making the First Meld

You may have noted that your hand contained cards with which you could have made a legitimate meld, for example, the two Kings with the Joker or the three 5's with or without the Joker. Moreover, you have the necessary count for the first meld.

It is a rule that the cards in a side's first meld should total at least 50 points. This requirement you can easily meet, for the Joker by itself counts 50. You could not, at this point of the game, put down simply 5 5 5, or K K 2.

As the game progresses the requirements for the initial meld become higher. Game is 5000 up and the minimum count for the initial melds is as follows:

When the partnership's score is:

0 to 1495	..	..	50	1500 to 2995	.. 90
		3000 to 4995	..	120	

When a side has a minus score (you will see later how this can happen) there is no minimum requirement for the first meld.

With the hand we are considering at present, you could, in theory, go down for 70, by melding Joker K K plus 2 5 5 5, totalling 105. Nevertheless, for reasons that will become clearer as we go on, it would be a tactical error to meld so soon, especially if the count required were only 50.

'Capturing the Pack'

On the great majority of hands the player's object in the early part of the game is to 'capture the pack', that is, to pick up the discard pile, containing all the cards that have so far been discarded.

Before a side has made its first meld, a player can pick up the discard pile when he has a natural pair matching the last discard by his R—O, together with the count required for the initial meld. Suppose that, in our present example, the pack were not picked up by any of the next three players, and that on the next round R—O were to discard a King or a 5. Then, having a natural pair to match the discard, together with the required count for the initial meld (you can include for this purpose the value of the card you are picking up from the top of the pack), you can make your first meld and pick up the pack. The proper way to do this, supposing that a 5 were discarded, would be to show first of all your natural pair of 5's, and then to add the Joker. Then you take the 5 from the top of the pack and add this to your meld. Only then do you take the rest of the cards into your hand; before taking up the pack you had to show all the players that you had both the pair of 5's and the necessary count.

To acquire extra cards in this way is a decided advantage. To build up a good score, you require a large number of cards with which to make several canastas.

Black Threes and Stop Cards

Black 3's have a special rôle in the game. They are 'stop cards'. When a black 3 is the last discard, in no circumstances may the next player take the pack.

Black 3's also cannot be used for any meld, except that three or four of them can be melded at the final turn by a player who is going out. Since they have no constructive value in building up the hand, inexperienced players tend to discard them at the first opportunity. When more cards are urgently needed to build up a big count, this may be sound play, but when that is not so it is better to retain the black 3's until you are under pressure to find a safe discard; for example, when you or R—O has made the first meld.

A card matching a completed canasta is also a stop card to this extent, that an opponent can take the pack only if he has a natural pair—possible but unlikely. It must be mentioned, however, that this is a rule on which all Canasta players are not in agreement; some permit the pack to be taken just as though the card matched an ordinary meld, not a completed canasta.

AFTER THE FIRST MELD

Once a side has made its first meld, it is, for the time being, in a stronger position to take the next pack. From then on, unless the pack is frozen (see next section), either player of the partnership can pick up the pack not only with a natural pair, but with one card matching the last discard plus a wild card. A minimum count is no longer required; and the pack can also be taken if an opponent makes a discard matching any meld on the table.

To return to our game, on the second round you pick up a pack containing five cards or so. You meld three 5's and a Joker. You could at the same time meld K K 2, but this would be very poor play for three reasons:

1. It would leave you with too few cards at this stage of the game.

2. Kings might not suit your partner, and then you would be wasting your 2 on them; and

3. You would have no wild card left to help you take the pack.

Having melded Joker 5 5 5 you would discard another loose card. L—O draws and discards. Partner draws and perhaps adds a 5 to your meld. He might make other melds, but in most cases it would not be good play; for it is generally a mistake to reduce one's hand early in the game. Partner discards, R—O draws and discards a 9. You have a 9 and a 2 in your hand, and although the pack is quite small, you should take it, for at any rate you increase the cards in your hand by two. You meld 9 9 2 and again discard.

FREEZING THE PACK

Making the first meld will appear to you so far to be a big advantage. When both sides have to go down for 120, then it is indeed an advantage to go down early if you are lucky enough to be able to do so without using too many cards. At 50 up, however, it is not such a big advantage as it may seem up to now.

The reason is that opponents have a valuable and important counter. They can discard a wild card, thus freezing the pack.

The effect of this is that, until the pack has been won, a

player can pick it up only if he has a natural pair in his hand matching the last discard. In other words, two of the three advantages gained by making the first meld are cancelled: you can no longer take the pack with a wild card and one matching card; and you can no longer take the pack because the discard matches one of your melds. The only advantage you have is that, having made your first meld, you do not have to worry about the count.

You can see now why it would have been a mistake for you to meld Joker 5 5 on the first round of play, and a still worse mistake to meld Joker 5 5 and K K 2. As soon as the pack began to grow beyond four or five cards, one opponent would certainly freeze. Then your side would be at a big disadvantage. R—O would have no trouble in discarding to you; and you, with only five cards, would have great difficulty in discarding safely to L—O. Almost surely, the first sizeable pack would go to your opponents.

Opponents might play the same game, it is true, after you had taken the small pack on the second round; but, since you picked up as many cards as you put down, you would not be at the same disadvantage as if you had melded from hand. Your side would be in a bad position, however, if you melded other cards, leaving yourself with fewer cards than L—O.

It is not only at this early stage, after the first meld, that this manœuvre of freezing the pack is valuable. It often happens later in the game that a side which has taken the pack on several occasions has various melds on the table. Then, if the opponents have cards matching these melds, it may pay them to freeze; for the time being at least they will be able to discard the danger cards without conceding the pack; they may well be able to play for 'out' before anyone has taken the pack.

The struggle for a big pack is the great thrill of Canasta. Sometimes it happens that a pack is frozen early and that it mounts until almost the whole stock—sometimes the whole stock—is exhausted. Players will often throw further wild cards into the pack with the double object of building up their own hands with pairs and making what for the time being is a dead safe discard; for an opponent can never pick up the pack when a wild card has been thrown.

HOW THE GAME ENDS

A hand of Canasta ends when a player melds all his cards.

At his turn, he must draw; he may discard or not, as he chooses. Thus, suppose your last five cards are 2 K K 9 4, and that your side has a meld of 9's, and at least one canasta. You can meld K K 2, add the 9 to your meld, and discard the 4.

Note that, to go out, you must have a canasta. Since a hand cannot end until this requirement is met, the player is never allowed to reduce himself to less than one card (it is, by the way, obligatory when you meld to the point at which you have only one card, to announce it by saying 'One card'). There is a bonus of 100 points for going out. There is a special bonus of 200 points for 'going out concealed'. A player is said to meld out concealed when he melds his complete hand at one turn, including a canasta, and not adding to partner's meld. This happens rarely. To go out at Canasta is not, as it is in most Rummy games, an objective in itself. In fact, it is generally a defensive measure adopted by the side that is having the worse of the hand. The side that has the majority of cards and melds should not consider going out.

When a player is in a position to go out he has the right to say to his partner, after drawing from stock, but before making any play, 'May I go out, partner?' Partner can answer Yes or No, and the answer is binding. Either player may repeat the same question at a later turn. A player should ask only if he is genuinely in doubt whether or not it is wise to finish the hand.

ADDING UP THE SCORE

When a hand ends, one player on each side should be responsible for adding up the score. This is generally calculated in two parts—base and cards. The base consists of bonuses as follows:

BONUSES

Natural canasta (no wild cards) ..	500 points
Mixed canasta (1 to 3 wild cards) ..	300 "
Red 3's	100 "
Four red 3's for one partnership ..	800 "
Melding out	100 "
Melding out 'concealed'	200 "

CARDS

All cards that have been melded count their normal value— Joker, 50; Ace and 2, 20; King to 8, 10; 7 to 3, 5.

Cards left in a player's hand, and not melded, count the same values against the partnership. Also, when neither player has melded at all, red 3's count against the partnership. It is possible, therefore, for a side to score a minus on a hand. However, this is not a tragedy. Most players jump at the opportunity to go out before opponents have melded, thus setting them back 300 to 400 points. In many cases, however, it is better to continue the hand, even though sooner or later opponents will go down.

Although it is not part of the official rules, many players add a bonus of 500 for winning the game.

SOME SPECIAL SITUATIONS

Initially Frozen Pack. If the card turned up by the dealer is a black 3, another card is turned up, but the pack is not thereafter frozen.

If the up-card is a Joker or a red 3, it is covered, and, the pack remains frozen until captured. When a player acquires a red 3 in this way, he does not draw an extra card from the stock.

The Last Card. When a game continues to the end of the stock the last card is drawn and the player discards in the usual way. The next player may take the last discard if he is able to do so. He must take this last card if it is a 'player', that is, a card matching one of his side's melds. If the next player takes the pack and discards, the same rules apply to the player after him. The hand ends when the discard is not taken.

If the last card of the stock is a red 3, the player exposes it and can meld, but does not discard.

One Card. A player who has only one card in his hand cannot go out by taking up a discard pile consisting of one card. He must draw from stock.

Wild Cards and Canastas. Wild cards can be added to completed canastas, but if added to a natural canasta they make it a mixed canasta.

SOME HINTS ON PLAY

In this outline of the rules and procedure in Canasta it has not been possible to describe the varied tactics of this fascinating game. Here are a few hints that will help a beginner:

1. In the early discarding, concentrate on winning the first pack. If you can afford to do so without sacrificing the count to go down, discard from threes; by so doing you increase your chance of obtaining pairs and you make it difficult for R—O to read your hand. Be very careful not to miss the early discards of L—O, so that you will know how to discard to him later.

2. If your side won the first pack, don't reduce your hand unnecessarily. Don't hesitate to discard from your longest holdings. At all costs keep a grip on the pack. If your side wins a fair-sized pack, you should keep opponents out throughout the game.

3. Distinguish between attack and defence. If opponents win the first pack, your only defence, if opponents are good players, is to play for out. If you need a high count, and it looks as though you will have to rely on your partner, match his discards, so that when partner does at length go down, you will be able to add to his melds. Don't worry about giving successive packs to the opponents.

4. Don't freeze simply because you have inconvenient discards. You should freeze only when (i) your side has the majority of cards, so that you can expect ultimately to win the pack, or (ii) you expect to be able to hold on until either the stock has been exhausted or your side is able to go out.

Two-Handed Canasta

In this game each player has fifteen cards, and a player must have two canastas to go out.

This is a game of big swings. All depends on who wins the first pack, provided it is not taken too soon. The player who wins the first pack should have no difficulty in discarding so that his opponent never wins the pack. As a defence against freezing, the player who holds the majority of the cards should hold them up and, for the most part, should meld only when he has a natural canasta.

The player who is on the defensive should run for home and not break up his hand to fight for the pack.

Three-Handed Canasta

Each player has thirteen cards, and two canastas are needed to go out. This is a cut-throat game. A player should build up his own hand, and not try to keep the pack from his left-hand opponent. There is scarcely ever any advantage in freezing.

GIN RUMMY

THERE IS an infinitude of games of the Rummy family, of which Canasta is today more widely played than any other. But, before Canasta became fashionable, Gin Rummy had a considerable vogue. This differs from many other Rummy games only in the complications of its scoring—designed to make it not so much a family game as a gamble.

Gin Rummy is primarily a game for two players. It is played with an ordinary fifty-two card pack, the cards ranking in order from King down to the Ace.

For scoring purposes, the King, Queen and Knave each count 10 points; the Ace, 1 point; each of the other cards, its pip value. Game is 100 points up.

The initial deal is determined by cutting, the player with the lower card dealing. If both players cut, say, a 4, they cut again. The dealer deals one card to his opponent, then one to himself, and so on until each player has ten cards. The twenty-first card is turned face up on the table. The remainder of the pack is placed face downwards beside it, and forms the stock.

The winner of the first hand will deal the next one, and so on throughout the game.

The object of the game is to arrange the cards in one's hand in 'sets' of three or four of the same denomination (eg three Kings, four eights, and so on) or in 'sequences' of three or more cards of the same suit (eg Spades: Ace, 2, 3; Diamonds: 6, 7, 8, 9, 10). Queen, King, Ace, or King, Ace, 2, do *not* constitute a sequence.

The same card may not figure in both a sequence and a set, *ie* each scoring arrangement is a separate entity.

A player may 'go down' when the pip value of the cards remaining in his hand is ten or under. When he goes down he places his sets and sequences face upwards on the table. Either player may, of course, be able to go down with the cards that he has in his hand. This, however, is unusual, and normally play will proceed.

The mechanics of the play are very simple. The non-dealer, having looked at his hand, has the option of taking either the upturned card (the first card of the 'discard pile'), or the top card from the stock. If he does not want the upturned card, the dealer in his turn may take it, throwing face upwards a card from his own hand. If neither player wants the upturned card, the non-dealer must take the top card from the stock. Having done so, he discards one of his own cards. If he has taken a card from stock, he places his discard on top of the faced card already on the table, in such a manner as to conceal it. Dealer, in his turn, follows the same procedure, and play continues until one player or the other goes down.

As has been mentioned, a player can go down—although he is not obliged to do so—as soon as the pip value of the unmatched cards in his hand is not higher than ten. He may only go down after drawing a card and making the consequent discard. It is the decision when to go down which gives the game its tactical interest. For as soon as a player has gone down, his opponent will also lay his 'melded' cards on the table (*ie* his sets and sequences), and may also contribute to any of the melds of the player who has gone down first. Thus, if the melds of the player who has gone down first include three Kings, the other player can, if he has it, contribute the fourth; or, if the player first going down has laid ♠ 6, 7, 8, 9 on the table, his opponent could contribute ♠ 5 or ♠ 10 J.

Hence, if the player who elects to go down does so having a comparatively high score, *ie* with, say, five or more points left in his hand, he stands the risk of losing on that deal through giving his opponent facilities to get rid of too many cards.

When both players have put their cards down in accordance with the above rules, the pip values of their unmatched cards are totalled. If the player who has first gone down has the lower total, he scores the difference in points between the totals announced. But if the player who has not gone down has the same or a lower pip total in unmatched cards, he scores the difference in points plus a bonus of 10, known as an 'undercut' bonus. *Eg* if the player who first goes 'down for 6', and the pip total of his opponent's unmatched cards is 19, he scores 13. But if he has gone down for 6 and the pip total of his opponent's unmatched cards is only 3, the latter scores not 3 (6 minus 3), but 3 plus a bonus of 10, *ie* 13.

If a player does not go down until he can meld the whole of the ten cards in his hand, he scores a 'gin'. This carries a 20-point bonus in addition to the value of the unmatched cards in the other player's hand. If the other player, after matching his cards against those of the player who has gone down, is able to dispose of all of them, this does not affect the 20-point bonus, which the player who went down first still scores.

The scores are cumulative. The player who has first reached 100 wins the game. The scores are then totalled as follows:

(*a*) Each player scores 20 points for every deal won.

(*b*) The winner adds to his score the difference in the total scores after he has reached 100.

(*c*) The winner also receives a bonus of 100 points for game. If his opponent has scored nothing at all during the game, this bonus becomes 200 points.

Example:

After 9 deals A has scored 104 points to B's 83. A has won 5 of these deals. He scores:

(*a*) Difference in bonuses (100–80)			..	..	20
(*b*) Difference in points (104–83)			..	..	21
(*c*) Game bonus	..	..	..	..	100
			A's net score	..	141

If the game is played for stakes, B will pay so much a point, or so much for every 10 points, or whatever has been agreed.

Illustrative Deals at Gin Rummy

I

We will call the players A and B. B deals as follows:

To A: ♠ 4 3 ♡ 8 A ◇ K 7 5 4 A ♣ Q
To B: ♠ J 7 4 2 A ♡ Q 7 2 ◇ None ♣ K 9 5 ♣ A turned up.

  A takes ♣ A, throws ♣ Q; B draws ◇ 3, throws ♡ Q.
  A draws ♣ 8, throws ◇ K; B draws ♠ K, throws ♠ K.
  A draws ♠ 6, throws ◇ 7; B takes ◇ 7, throws ♣ K.
  A draws ♡ 3, throws ♠ 6; B draws ♣ 4, throws ♠ J.

The hands are now:

  A: ♠ 4 3 ♡ 8 3 A ◇ 5 4 A ♣ 8 A (at this stage he can meld three Aces).

  B: ♠ 7 2 A ♡ 7 2 ◇ 7 3 ♣ 9 5 4 (B can meld three 7's).

The game proceeds:

A draws ◇ 10, throws ◇ 10; B draws ♣ 7, throws ♣ 9.
A draws ◇ 8, throws ◇ 5; B draws ◇ 9, throws ◇ 9.
A draws ♣ 3, throws ◇ 4.

(A can now go down for 4. He has three 8's, three 3's, three Aces and the ♠ 4. Suspecting, however, that B must also be nearly out, he decides to try for a 'gin'.)

Now B draws ♡ 6, throws ♡ 6.

A draws ◇ J, throws ◇ J; B draws ◇ 2, throws ♣ 5.
A draws ♠ 10, throws ♠ 10; B draws ♣ 2, throws ♣ 4.

B decides to go down for 4, laying on the table four 7's and four 2's, and retaining ◇ 3 and ♠ A. A still has the hand shown above. He can meld nothing on B's cards, but, as he has only the ♠ 4 left in his hand, there is equality of pips, and A scores the 'undercut' bonus of 10 points.

II

A is the dealer. The cards dealt are:

To B: ♠ None ♡ K J 10 A ◇ 10 5 3 ♣ 7 5 3
To A: ♠ Q 10 ♡ 9 4 2 ◇ 9 6 ♣ 10 9 A

♠ K is turned up. Both B and A decline the ♠ K. So B draws the top card from the stock. It is the ♠ 8, and he throws the ♡ K.

A draws ♡ 8, throws ♠ Q; B draws ♠ 4, throws ♠ 8.
A draws ♡ 5, throws ◇ 6; B draws ♠ 9, throws ♠ 9.
A takes ♠ 9, throws ♠ 10; B takes ♠ 10, throws ♡ J.
A draws ♣ 4, throws ♣ 4; B takes ♣ 4, throws ♣ 7.
A draws ♠ J, throws ♠ J.

The hands are now:

B has two melds: three 10's and the ♣ 3 4 5. He has also ◇ 5 3, ♠ 4 and ♡ A.

A has only one meld: four 9's. He has also ♡ 8 5 4 2 and ♣ 10 A. His ♣ 10 is at this point a source of embarrassment, because he has seen B take up one 10 already. The game proceeds: B draws ◇ A, throws ♠ 4.

A draws ♡ 3, throws ♡ 8; B draws ♣ 6, throws ◇ 5. (This draw adds a card to B's sequence, and he could now go down for 5. He decides, however, to carry on.)

A draws ◇ Q, throws ◇ Q; B draws ♠ 3, throws ◇ A. (He

can now go down for one. He decides, however, to go for a gin, since he is quite safe if A is hanging on to the ♣ 10, and, if not, that card may appear.)

A now draws ♠ 2 and throws ♣ 10, deciding that he cannot afford to hang on to it any longer. B takes up ♣ 10, throws ♡ A, and announces a gin. He has four 10's, three 3's, and ♣ 6 5 4. A melds his four 9's and sequence ♡ 5 4 3 2. His remaining cards are ♣ 2 A. B scores 3 points plus 20 for his gin.

III

B is the dealer. The cards dealt are:

To A: ♠ K 5 A ♡ K 9 4 ◇ K 4 3 ♣ 3
To B: ♠ 3 2 ♡ Q 5 ◇ Q 5 ♣ J 8 5 2

♣ Q turned up. A declines the ♣ Q, B takes it, and throws ♣ J.

A draws ♠ 8, throws ♡ 9; B draws ◇ A, throws ♣ 8.

B now decides to go down for 8. He melds three Queens, three 5's. His remaining cards are ♠ 3 2, ◇ A, ♣ 2. A melds his three Kings, and throws ♠ 5 on the three 5's which B has already put down. A's remaining count is 22. B wins by 22 minus 8, equal 14 points.

IV

A deals. The hands are:

B: ♠ 7 6 ♡ Q J 10 A ◇ 6 3 2 ♣ 7
A: ♠ K ♡ K ◇ K Q J 10 8 ♣ 8 6 5

♣ K turned up. B declines ♣ K. A takes ♣ K, throws ♣ 8. B draws ♠ J, throws ♠ J.

A draws ◇ 9, throws ♣ 6; B takes ♣ 6, throws ♣ 7.

A draws ◇ 7, throws ♣ 5, and announces a gin. He has four Kings in his hand and the sequence ◇ Q J 10 9 8 7. B melds three 6's and sequence ♡ Q J 10. His remaining cards total 11. A wins by 11 plus 20 points for his gin.

OTHER GAMES OF THE RUMMY FAMILY

SEVEN-CARD RUMMY

ANY REASONABLE number, from two upwards, can play this game. Two packs, well shuffled together, are required. Each player begins with so many counters, and, before the first deal, an agreed number of counters—say two from each player—are put into the 'kitty'. Now the players cut for deal, lowest card (Ace low) dealing.

The dealer deals seven cards, one at a time and face downwards, to each player, beginning with the player to his left. Having dealt the cards, he places the remainder of the pack, face downwards, on the table, but turns the top card (*ie* the card next to the card last dealt) face upwards and places it beside the stock.

Play now begins. Each player in turn (beginning with the player to the dealer's left) takes in one card, which can be either the exposed card that has been placed beside the stock or the unseen top card of the stock itself. He then discards one card from his hand, placing it face upwards on top of any other card or cards exposed. This card, in lieu of the one underneath it, is now available for the next player. Each player throughout has the same option: to take the top exposed card or the top unseen card from the stock.

The object of the game is to assemble in one's own hand certain scoring combinations. These are: (*a*) sequences of three or more cards in the same suit, *eg* ♠ J 10 9 8 ♡ 8 7 6, etc; and (*b*) sets of three or more cards having the same denomination, *eg* three King's, four 7's, etc.

All 2's are Jokers and can represent any other card.

As soon as a player has seven cards in his hand composed entirely of sequences and/or sets, *or* has six cards so composed and one card left which is not higher than a 7, he can put his hand down. It sometimes happens, for example, that the player to the dealer's left is dealt some such hand as ♠ A K Q ♡ 9 8 7 ◇ 4, in which case he can put his hand down right away, stating as he does so: 'Down for four.'

As soon as a player 'goes down', the other players must lay their cards face upwards on the table. Points are now scored against each of them in respect of any cards in their hands which do not belong to sequences or sets. Thus, suppose, when one player 'goes down', another one holds ♣ 7 6 5 ♠ 2 ♡ Q 9 ◇ 8, there is no score against him in respect of his Clubs, or, of course, his Joker, but the pip value of his other cards is added up (all Court cards counting ten), and the score against him is 27. Aces count as one.

There is, however, this further point: that when a player 'goes down', say, for four, any 4's held by other players which are not included in a sequence or a set can be thrown on to his 4. Note that a player cannot 'go down' immediately after he has exchanged a card; he must wait until his turn comes round again. As soon as a player has 'gone down', the various scores are recorded, and each player refreshes the 'kitty' with, say, one counter. Now the cards are reshuffled and dealt again, the deal passing to the left, and the game proceeds as before.

After three or four rounds, it will be found that the scores against some one or more of the players are beginning to approach 100. The game now becomes more intriguing. As soon as a player's score reaches 100 he is eliminated from the game, and, of course, contributes nothing further to the 'kitty'. The process of elimination goes on until there are only two players left; it is then customary for these two to divide the 'kitty', generally in the proportion of 3–1, the player who is in the better position, *ie* who has the lower score, taking the lion's share of the counters.

A little experiment will show that, while there is a high element of luck in this game, there is plenty of scope for good play.

An Illustrative Deal

Let us suppose that there are five players—Amy, Bernard, Claire, David and Esmé. It is the first deal of the game. The two packs are well shuffled together, and Amy, the first dealer, gives each player seven cards. These are dealt one at a time, face downwards.

CARDS DEALT

To Bernard: ◇ K ♡ 10 ♠ 9 ◇ 9 ◇ 6 ◇ 5 ♠ 4
To Claire: ◇ Q ♠ 10 ♠ 7 ♣ 7 ♡ 6 ◇ 3 ◇ A

To David: ♠ K ♠ J ♠ J ♡ J ◇ J ♡ 5 ♡ A
To Esmé: ♡ 10 ◇ 8 ♣ 8 ◇ 7 ♠ 6 ♣ 5 ◇ 2
To Amy: ♡ Q ♠ Q ◇ 10 ♡ 9 ♠ 8 ♡ 7 ◇ A

The ◇ 2 is underlined because any two is a Joker and can represent any other card.

The object of the game is to exchange cards, one at a time, until one has a hand that will 'go down'. One can lay down all seven cards, or six only, provided the seventh card is not higher than a 7. In that case the value of the odd card is scored against one.

To lay down a hand one must have six (or seven) cards consisting of sequences and sets. A sequence consists of three or more cards, in sequence, of the same suit. A set, of three (or more) of a kind.

David, for example, has four Knaves to begin with—a very promising start. Each player in turn exchanges a card against the last player's discard (to begin with, the top card of the stack, which is exposed) or against the (unexposed) top card of the pack.

To enable the game to be clearly followed, we give below each player's hand after he has made his draw.

The cards having been dealt, play begins. The ♡ 8 is exposed. Bernard, who draws first, can take either this card or the next (unseen) card from the pack. Before drawing, of course, each player looks at his hand.

Bernard takes top card (♠ 2) and discards (face upwards) ◇ K.

♡ 10 ♠ 9 ◇ 9 ◇ 6 ◇ 5 ♠ 4 ♠ 2

NOTE. This useful draw of a Joker means that Bernard has now three 9's, or ◇ 6 ◇ 5 ♠ 2—a sequence.

Claire takes top card (♣ J) and discards ◇ Q.
♣ J ♠ 10 ♠ 7 ♣ 7 ♡ 6 ◇ 3 ◇ A

David takes top card (♣ Q) and discards it.
♠ K ♠ J ♠ J ♡ J ◇ J ♡ 5 ♡ A

Esmé takes top card (♠ 5) and discards ♡ 10.
♣ 8 ◇ 8 ◇ 7 ♠ 6 ♠ 5 ♣ 5 ◇ 2

Amy takes top card (♡ 3) and discards ◇ 10.
♠ Q ♡ Q ♡ 9 ♠ 8 ♡ 7 ♡ 3 ◇ A

Note that the general tendency is to throw high cards. The

reason is that when one player goes down, the ungrouped cards in other players' hands count against them.

SECOND ROUND

Bernard takes top card (♣ 3) and throws ♡ 10.

♠ 9   ♢ 9   ♢ 6   ♢ 5   ♠ 4   ♣ 3   ♠ 2

Claire takes top card (♣ 4) and throws ♣ J.

♠ 10   ♠ 7   ♣ 7   ♡ 6   ♣ 4   ♢ 3   ♢ A

David takes the ♣ J just discarded and throws ♠ K.

♠ J   ♠ J   ♡ J   ♢ J   ♣ J   ♡ 5   ♡ A

Esmé takes top card (♣ 9) and throws it.

♣ 8   ♢ 8   ♢ 7   ♠ 6   ♠ 5   ♣ 5   ♢ 2

Amy takes top card (♣ 6) and throws ♠ 8.

♠ Q   ♡ Q   ♡ 9   ♡ 7   ♣ 6   ♡ 3   ♢ A

On the whole, an unprofitable round.

THIRD ROUND

Bernard takes top card (♣ 6) and throws ♠ 4. (He has one 6 already.)

♠ 9   ♢ 9   ♣ 6   ♢ 6   ♢ 5   ♣ 3   ♠ 2

Claire takes top card (♢ 5) and throws ♠ 10.

♠ 7   ♣ 7   ♡ 6   ♢ 5   ♣ 4   ♢ 3   ♢ A

David takes top card (♢ Q) and throws it.

♠ J   ♠ J   ♡ J   ♢ J   ♣ J   ♡ 5   ♡ A

Esmé takes top card (♣ 2) and throws ♣ 8.

Esmé has now a hand which will go down, but cannot lay it down immediately after drawing: ♢ 8   ♢ 7   ♣ 2—♠ 6   ♠ 5   ♢ 2—♣ 5. (Esmé can 'go down for 5' next time.)

Amy takes top card (♣ A) and discards ♡ 9.

♠ Q   ♡ Q   ♡ 7   ♣ 6   ♡ 3   ♢ A   ♣ A

Another poor round.

FOURTH ROUND

Bernard takes discard (♡ 9) and throws ♣ 6.

(Bernard has now a hand which can go down: ♠ 9   ♡ 9   ♢ 9—♢ 6   ♢ 5   ♠ 2—♣ 3.)

Claire takes top card (♣ 5) and discards ♡ 6.

♠ 7   ♣ 7   ♢ 5   ♣ 5   ♣ 4   ♢ 3   ♢ A

David takes top card (♣ K) and discards it. David has had bad luck in making no more progress with his hand.

Esmé now announces 'down for 5'.

She shows ◇ 8 ◇ 7 ♣ 2 (sequence) ♠ 6 ♠ 5 ◇ 2 (sequence) and the ♣ 5 over, on which other players can throw odd 5's, to that extent minimizing the score against them.

The other players now expose their hands, and announce scores against them:

Amy: ♠ Q ♡ Q ♡ 7 ♣ 6 ♡ 3 ◇ A ♣ A—38. (Court cards count 10, Aces 1.)

Amy, without a single sequence or set, has been quite exceptionally unlucky.

Bernard: (♠ 9 ♡ 9 ◇ 9) (◇ 6 ◇ 5 ♠ 2) ♣ 3—3.

Claire: (◇ 5 ♣ 5) ♠ 7 ♣ 7 ♣ 4 ◇ 3 ◇ A—22. The 5's do not count against Claire, because of Esmé's 5.

David: (♠ J ♠ J ♡ J ◇ J ♣ J) (♡ 5) ♡ A—1.

The scores are now 'clocked up' against the players thus:

Against Amy	..	..	..	38
Against Bernard ..	..	..	..	3
Against Claire	..	..	..	22
Against David	..	..	..	1
Against Esmé	..	..	..	5

Now the cards are shuffled for the next (Bernard's) deal.

The scores are cumulative, and a player reaching 100 is out of the game. The remaining players continue till only one is left. The winner takes the pool, or it may be divided: three-quarters to the winner, quarter to the next player.

RUMMY. In the rare event of a player obtaining a seven-card sequence, he has 'Rummy'. This wipes out any score against him.

THE POOL

To begin with each player puts in (say) two chips. At the end of each deal all the players, except the one who goes down first, refresh with one chip. This is the special advantage of going down early.

KINGS AND QUEENS

IN KINGS AND QUEENS, which is a variant of Seven-card Rummy, two full packs are used and any number of players can take part. Each player is dealt seven cards, face downwards; the remaining cards form the stock. The top card of the stock is turned face upwards. All 2's are Jokers, *ie* a 2 can represent any other card.

The object of the game is to 'go out' as quickly as possible. One can 'go out' as soon as one has six cards in one's hand which can be arranged in sequences or in sets, as long as the remaining card is not higher than 7. A sequence consists of three or more consecutive cards of the same suit, *eg* the 10 9 8 of Diamonds, while a set consists of three or more cards of the same denomination, *eg* three Queens or four 4's. If all seven cards are cards which can be arranged in sets or sequences, so much the better; one is then 'out for nothing'.

The following represent hands on which one can go out:

    ♠ 9 8 7   ♡ 5   ◇ 2   ♡ 3   ♣ A.

The ◇ 2 (a Joker) here represents the ♡ 4, and one is 'out for one'.

    ♠ Q   ♡ Q   ◇ Q   ♣ J   ♣ 10   ♠ 2   ♡ 4.

Here one is 'out for four'.

    ♡ J   ♣ 2   ♡ 10   ♡ 9   ♠ K   ◇ K   ◇ K.

Here one is 'out for nothing'.

So far the rules of the game are those of ordinary Seven-card Rummy. But in 'Kings and Queens' these two denominations have a special value. For every King in one's hand which is part of a scoring combination, one is entitled to deduct five from one's score; and for every Queen, three. These cards have thus a high *premium value*, provided they are part of a scoring combination.

Let us now return to the method of play.

The cards having been dealt and the top card of the stock exposed, the player to the left of the dealer has the first right of exchanging a card. He can either take the exposed card or the next (unexposed) card; having taken in a card, he discards, face upwards, one card from his hand.

The next player now has the option of taking the card last discarded, or the top unexposed card from stock. And so the game goes on, each player, in turn, drawing and discarding until someone can put down his hand. Of course, it is possible that the first or some other player can 'go out' right away. This is hard luck on the others, but it is just one of the possibilities that make the game exciting.

As soon as a player lays down his hand, the others must lay down theirs. If the player who went down first is out for, say, four, any surplus 4 can be discarded on his card. Otherwise each player is penalized to the extent of the total pip value of such cards in his hand as are not part of a scoring combination. For this purpose, Kings, Queens and Knaves each count ten.

It will now be seen how much added excitement is given by the special status of the Kings and Queens. Normally, one is in a hurry to get rid of these high-scoring cards. But in this game one is tempted to take the risk of keeping them, partly because of the premium which they may carry and partly because the next player may be waiting to snap them up. In other words, they give one the option of taking an extra risk.

THE SCORING

Rummy is usually played with counters. At the beginning of the deal each player puts two counters into the 'kitty' and at the end of the deal one additional counter is put in by each player except the one who has 'gone out'. In addition, the score is kept on paper. Against each player is 'chalked up' his adverse score on the deal. When he reaches the total of 100 he is 'out'. This goes on until only two players are left, when they divide the counters in the 'kitty' in the proportion of three to one.

In ordinary Seven-card Rummy one's score begins at nought and mounts slowly up to 100. But in Kings and Queens one may, of course, have a *minus* score. Let us suppose, for example, one 'goes out' on the first deal with this hand:

$$\diamondsuit K \quad \spadesuit K \quad \heartsuit K \quad \clubsuit K \quad \diamondsuit Q \quad \clubsuit Q \quad \heartsuit 2.$$

One has the very agreeable bonus of 29 points. Hence, it is desirable that the scorer should start each player at, say, 100, counting them out as they reach 200. Then, in the case just given, a player beginning at 100 would go back to 71. Theoretically the game could go on indefinitely, but it will be found this does not happen in practice.

I suggest that any players who have found ordinary Rummy a trifle monotonous should give 'Kings and Queens' a trial.

SEQUENCE RUMMY

THE GAME is played with two full packs, shuffled together and including Jokers. (If Jokers are not available, any other two cards can be nominated.) Any reasonable number can play—five, six or seven are the best numbers. *Eight* cards are dealt to each player, and, as in all forms of Rummy, the remaining cards form the stock. One card from the stock is exposed and placed beside it.

The rules of play are as follows:

1. Each player, in turn, draws a card or cards, discarding one, which is placed face upwards beside the stock, at the completion of his turn. Either he takes the top (unexposed) card of the stock, *or he can take all discards exposed beside the stock up to, and including, any card which he is able to play forthwith*.

Thus, suppose it is your turn to play and you hold

♠ K J 10   ♥ Q 10 8   ♣ 5 3

and suppose the last four exposed cards (in order of their availability) are ♣ 4   ♦ K   ♣ 7   ♠ Q.

You can either take the ♣ 4, provided you play ♣ 5 4 3 immediately to the table, or you can take all four cards, in which case you must play your Spade sequence, ♠ K Q J 10, and can also (and probably should) play ♣ 5 4 3 as well.

2. No player can score anything until he has put down a run or sequence (*eg* ♣ 5 4 3 above). After he has played a sequence, he can play:

(*a*) Other sequences;

(*b*) Sets of three or more cards of a kind, *eg*, three (or more) Kings, 8's, etc.;

(*c*) Cards which will continue other players' sequences or can be added to their sets.

3. The scoring is complicated. Someone who is good at addition must be appointed as scorer. Each player scores for all cards as he plays them—Aces, 15; Court cards (K Q J), 10 each; other cards, their pip values. Thus, a player putting down ♠ 9 8 7   ♥ K Q J, and adding a ♦ 3 to someone else's set of 3's, scores 24 plus 30 plus 3, equals 57 in all. Quite large

scores—perhaps 100 at one 'go'—can be attained by players who have taken a long sequence from the table.

4. At the end of a deal, which occurs as soon as a player has disposed of all his cards, the cards in his hand are counted and their aggregate deducted from his score. A Joker not played counts 25 against the holder; other scores are as above. Quite often a player will not have had a sequence at all, and his final score will be negative. An Ace in sequence (A 2 3) scores only 1.

5. The Joker may represent any card which has not been played to the table. Thus, if both Kings of Clubs are exposed, the Joker cannot be a King of Clubs. Any player holding the card which the Joker is supposed to represent may, when his turn comes, exchange it.

6. A player discarding a card which he is eligible to play— *eg* the ◇ A when the ◇ 4 3 2, or three Aces are on the table— can be 'rummied'. That is to say, someone calls 'Rummy' and the offender must accept a card from each player.

PROGRESSIVE RUMMY

IN THIS form of Rummy, a game consists of seven deals. Two packs are shuffled together, and each player is dealt ten cards. The top card of the stock is exposed in the usual way.

All 2's are Jokers. No player may get rid of any cards from his hand (except, of course, when he discards after drawing) until he has laid down the minimum requirements for the deal. This minimum requirement varies from deal to deal; that is why the game is called 'progressive'.

These are the minimum requirements:
1st round: Three of a set or sequence.
2nd round: Four of a set or sequence.
3rd round: Five of a set or sequence.
4th round: Two threes (sets or sequences).
5th round: A three and a four (sets or sequences).
6th round: A three and a five (sets or sequences).
7th round: Two fours (sets or sequences).

There is one difference between this and some other forms of Rummy. The three cards in a set of three must all be of different suits, and the four cards of a set of four must be of four different suits. In a set of five, also, all four suits must be represented.

Sequences are the same as in other forms of Rummy. That is, a sequence consists of three (or more) cards of the same suit; the Ace can be either high or low. Thus ♥ 9 8 7, ♠ A K Q, ◇ A 2 3 are all three card sequences.

In the first round (threes) a player could lay down ♠ 7 6 5 or ♠ Q ◇ Q ♣ Q, and after that would be free to contribute cards to other sets or sequences on the table, or, of course, to put down other sets or sequences of his own. Thus, if there were three 9's on the table, he could get rid of any 9's; if there was ♥ 6 5 4 on the table, he could throw ♥ 7 or ♥ 3.

In the second round, similarly, he could begin by laying down ◇ 8 7 6 ♣ 2, the ♣ 2 (a Joker) representing the ◇ 5. Or he could lay down ♠ A ♥ A ♣ A with any 2 to represent the ◇ A.

In subsequent rounds, the following could be laid down:
3rd round: ♠ J 10 9 ♣ 2 ♠ 7, or ♠ K ♠ K ♥ K ♣ 2 ♣ K. Here the Joker represents the ◇ K.

4th round: ♠ 7 6 5 and ♡ 4 ◇ 4 ♠ 2.

5th round: ♠ 7 6 5 4 and ◇ K ♠ 2 ♡ 2 ◇ 10. Here there are two sequences. But two sets, or a set and a sequence, are equally permissible.

6th round: ♠ 5 ♡ 5 ♡ 5 ◇ 5 ♠ 2 and ♣ K Q J. (The ♠ 2 represents ♣ 5.)

7th round: ♠ A ◇ 2 ◇ A ♣ A and ♠ 9 ♡ 9 ◇ 9 ♣ 9.

Two other rules should be mentioned. First, a Joker, once played, remains on the table. Players may not (as they can do at some Rummy games) take them in exchange for the cards which they represent.

Secondly, players may *buy* cards. That is to say, when a player discards after taking a card in, anyone else who wants the discard may say 'Buy'. If the next player does not want the card, the buyer may have it, taking in with it the unexposed card next to it. But no player may buy more cards than will bring the total in his hand up to sixteen.

Scoring. A player is out when he has got rid of all his cards. He must, however, throw his last card to the centre. He cannot, for example, go out by putting down a set or sequence if he has no card for the centre left over.

As soon as a player is out, the others expose their hands and the total pip-values are reckoned against them. In this reckoning, Aces count as 11; all picture cards as 10, and Jokers as 15.

Each player's total is carried forward and when he reaches 100 he is out. The winner is the player with the lowest score at the end of the seven rounds.

A DEAL AT PROGRESSIVE RUMMY

The Smith family are playing Progressive Rummy. We will not attempt to follow everyone's fortune, but will confine ourselves to watching Millie.

It was the third round of the game. For the first round, the minimum requirement is *three* (set or sequence); for the second it is *four*. For this third round it is *five*.

Millie sat on the left of Dorothy, the dealer. She looked at her hand and saw: ♠ K ◇ K ◇ Q ♣ Q ♠ 9 ♡ 9 ♡ 8 ♡ 6 ♡ 4 ◇ 2. A puzzling hand, but full of possibilities. With a Joker, Millie has already four cards towards the needed sequence of five.

The exposed card was the ♠ 7.

Millie rejected this card as useless and took in the top unexposed card from the stock. This was a second ♣ Q. 'Dear

me!' murmured Millie. She threw the ♠ 9 and her hand was
now ♠ K ♦ K ♦ Q ♣ Q ♣ Q ♥ 9 ♥ 8 ♥ 6 ♥ 4 ♦ 2.

Leonard, on Millie's left, played next. He took in an unexposed
card and ,threw the ♦ Q. 'Buy!' cried Millie. 'Very well,' said
Joan, the next player. 'I don't want it.' So Millie took up the
♦ Q and with it the next unexposed card. This proved to be the
♠ K. 'Oh dear!' she said to herself. 'I shall soon be getting
what they call an *embarras de choix*.' She now had three Kings
and four Queens (but, in each case, only two suits); four cards
which might fit into a sequence; and a Joker.

Nothing of interest happened, from Millie's point of view, till
it was again her turn to play. The card thrown by Dorothy was
the ♦ J. 'I'll take that,' said Millie. For this card gave her a
second chance of a sequence. So she took in the ♦ J and threw
her least useful card, the ♥ 4. Her hand was now: ♠ K ♠ K
♦ K ♦ Q ♦ Q ♣ Q ♣ Q ♦ J ♥ 9 ♥ 8 ♥ 6 ♦ 2.

So far no one had laid any cards down. When the ♥ K was
thrown, a moment later, things looked promising. Millie was
permitted to buy this card, and with it, to her delight, she drew
the ♥ 7! She now had two possible fives, and her next decision
was going to be interesting.

Her turn arrived with the table still void of cards. Dorothy's
next discard was the ♠ 3. Millie took the top unexposed card
and it proved to be the ♠ 2. A second Joker! Millie sat back
in her chair and scrutinized her cards: ♠ K ♠ K ♥ K ♦ K
♣ Q ♣ Q ♦ Q ♦ Q ♦ J ♥ 9 ♥ 8 ♥ 7 ♥ 6 ♠ 2 ♦ 2.

'It was doubtful policy,' she said to herself, 'to buy that
second ♦ Q. These Queens may be an embarrassment. I'll
unload one, and, as no one has gone down yet, I'll hold up the
rest of my cards.' She threw a ♣ Q.

'Buy!' shouted Joe Smith. 'No objection,' said Leonard.
Joe took the ♣ Q and another card, and, when it came to his
turn, he took an unexposed card and said, 'Off we go'. He laid
down ♠ Q ♠ Q ♥ Q ♣ Q ♥ 2 and ♣ 7 6 5. 'Going out?'
asked Millie. 'Not quite,' answered Joe. 'But I thought it time
to unload.'

No one else had laid down anything when Millie's turn came
round again. If she drew a favourable card she was out.

Alas! Dorothy threw the ♦ 5—quite useless to Millie. So
she drew the unexposed card. It was the second ♥ 4.

'Hooray!' said Millie. 'Going out.'

She laid down her hand. 'A Heart sequence of seven,' she said, 'including two Jokers. Three Kings, with an extra one. Three Queens for you, Dad. And the ◇ J for the table.'

Millie had scored heavily on the round. Only Joe Smith, of the other players, had got rid of any cards at all.

CHALLENGE

THIS IS the name which I have given to the Russian game of
SVOYI KOZIRI. It was shown to me about a year ago by Mr
J. A. Fotheringham, of Trinity College, Cambridge, and—so far
as I know—Cambridge is the only place where it is played. Its
sponsor in the University is Professor A. S. Besicovitch.

Challenge differs from all other card games—with a single
exception—in that the element of luck is eliminated. The exception is my game of Quintet (originally published under the name
of Pochette), of which an account will be found on page 193.

But Quintet is a game in which all one's thinking is done
at the outset: the better player is bound to win in the long run,
but it is by no means certain that he will win every time. His
calculations are in part based on assumptions as to what his
opponent will plan to do, and these assumptions may not always
be right: in short, there is a large psychological factor (as in
Poker, from which Quintet derives).

Challenge is a game of pure skill in quite a different sense.
For here the two players play alternately, as in Chess; and, as
in Chess, the player will win who can calculate accurately for
the larger number of moves ahead. The mental processes required
for Challenge are, indeed, very similar to the mental processes
required for Chess. This is not true of any other card game.

The standard form of the game of Challenge is played with
a Piquet pack of thirty-two cards. But it can also be played
with twenty-four, twenty-eight, thirty-six, or even more cards.
In every case, the pack used consists of four suits of equal length,
headed by the Ace. Thus, in the standard form of the game, each
suit consists of the Ace, King, Queen, Jack, 10, 9, 8, 7; but
the 7's may be omitted, or the 7's and the 8's, or—if one wants
a really difficult game—one can add 6's, 5's, and so on. So far
as I know, no one has attempted to play the game seriously with
a pack of more than thirty-two cards.

How Challenge Is Played

Preliminaries

To begin with, two suits—it doesn't matter which two—are
nominated by the dealer; moreover, he chooses one of them as

his trump suit. The non-dealer now chooses one of the two remaining suits as *his* trump suit. For example, the dealer may nominate Spades and Diamonds, Spades being his trumps, and the non-dealer may then choose Hearts as his trumps. Now the pack of thirty-two cards is well shuffled and cut, and the dealer deals sixteen cards *face upwards*. He throws out the Hearts and Clubs, which are of no importance, and sets aside the Spades and Diamonds, which will be part of his own hand. Thus, he may have dealt: ♠ A Q 10 8   ◇ A K J 9 7. These nine cards determine the pattern of the two hands. The dealer's hand will be ♠ A Q 10 8   ♡ K J 9 7   ◇ A K J 9 7   ♣ Q 10 8, and the non-dealer's hand (exactly corresponding) will be: ♠ K J 9 7 ♡ A Q 10 8   ◇ Q 10 8   ♣ A K J 9 7. It is thus theoretically possible (though, of course, most unlikely) for a player to hold no cards whatever in his own trump suit. But, should this be the case, his opponent also will hold no cards in *his* trump suit. I suggest (below) that hands as unbalanced as this should be rejected, and that the dealer should deal again.

The Play

The cards having been distributed in accordance with the above formula, and taken into the players' hands, play begins. The object of the game is to play on to the table the last card in one's hand: whoever does this first is the winner. Play begins with the non-dealer laying a card face upwards on the table. Dealer must now either play a better card, or pick up the card from the table. By a 'better card' is meant a higher card of the suit led or one of one's own trumps. There is no obligation to play a better card, or to follow suit.

For example, if, in the case set out above, the non-dealer begins by playing the ♣ 7, dealer can either play one of his three higher Clubs or one of his trumps, or he can take the ♣ 7 into his hand. In the last-mentioned case, the non-dealer will play another card.

A player who is unable, or unwilling to play a card better than that last played by his opponent, must take up, not only the last-played card, but all the cards on the table.

Let us consider how the game might have gone in the case of the deal set out above. We will call the players A (non-dealer) and B (dealer). A card underlined is a 'better card' than that which has just been played, and whoever played it has next led the card shown underneath it. And 't.u.' means that

the player concerned takes up all the cards on the table. For the
sake of clarity, let us set out the two hands again.

A: ♠ K J 9 7 ♡ <u>A Q 10 8</u> ◇ Q 10 8 ♣ A K J 9 7
B: ♠ <u>A Q 10 8</u> ♡ K J 9 7 ◇ A K J 9 7 ♣ Q 10 8

A	B
♣ 7	♣ 8
◇ 8	◇ 7
♣ 9	♣ 10
♡ 8	◇ K
♣ J	♣ Q
♡ 10	◇ A
♣ 10	♠ 8
◇ 10	◇ 9
◇ Q	♠ 10
t.u.	◇ J

(A now has in his hand 26 of the 32 cards, the holdings of the
two players being: A: ♠ K J 10 9 8 7 ♡ A Q 10 8 ◇ A K
Q J 10 9 8 7 ♣ A K Q J 10 9 8 7, B: ♠ <u>A Q</u> ♡ K J 9 7. Play
now continues.)

t.u.	♡ 7
t.u.	♡ 9
♡ Q	♡ J
◇ 7	♠ Q

And now, of course, B has won. His only remaining cards
are the ♡ K and the ♠ Ace, which will beat any card his
opponent plays. So he plays the ♡ K, and—whatever A does—
goes out next time.

This is *not* an example of good play; indeed, A's play is very
poor. He goes on collecting cards, with the idea of staging a
counter-attack when he has enough of them, but he waits far
too long before doing so. I give the game, however, as an example,
because games between two good players (like games of Chess)
can go on for a very long time. It is important, first of all, to
grasp the mechanics of the game.

It may be thought that, with only sixteen cards in each hand,
Challenge offers very little scope. In fact, however, there is
enough variety in it to last two skilled players a lifetime. With

the standard game (played with thirty-two cards) there are about 48,000 possible initial distributions, each of which presents a range of problems far too complex for *a priori* analysis. Here is another point of resemblance between Challenge and Chess. Indeed, it might not be unfair to say that the resemblance is really between Challenge and a Chess game in which the sixteen pieces on either side can be arranged before the game begins in thousands of different ways.

Of the 48,000-odd possible initial distributions of the cards, there is a very small number which should undoubtedly be rejected—and the cards dealt again—as these distributions give the non-dealer a win out of hand. If he holds the whole of his opponent's trump suit and either the whole of one of the plain suits or a sequence headed by the Ace in both of them (*eg* A K Q; A K Q J 10), he can force his opponent to take up the cards by playing out first the plain suits from the lowest card upwards, and then his opponent's trump suit in the same way. Other similarly 'unbalanced' distributions are in various ways equally unsatisfactory.

I suggest, therefore, as one of the rules of the game, that there should be a new deal if either of the two suits nominated by the dealer is distributed at the outset 8–0 or 7–1.

An Illustrative Game

A game at Challenge between two well-matched players may, as I have remarked, go on for a long time, and may, indeed, end in a draw by agreement. The illustrative game which follows is one which was played with a twenty-eight card pack (*ie* seven cards of each suit, instead of the eight required for what I call the 'standard' game).

A deals as follows:

To A: ♠ A Q J 9   ♡ K 10 8   ◇ K Q 10 9 8   ♣ A J
To B: ♠ K 10 8   ♡ A Q J 9   ◇ A J   ♣ K Q 10 9 8

A's trumps are Spades. B's are Hearts. A to lead.

	A	B		A	B
1.	◇ 8	◇ J	31.	t.u.	◇ 9
2.	♣ J	♣ 8	32.	t.u.	◇ 10
3.	♡ 10	t.u.	33.	t.u.	◇ J
4.	◇ 9	◇ J	34.	t.u.	◇ Q
5.	♠ 9	♣ 8	35.	t.u.	♣ K
6.	◇ 10	◇ A	36.	t.u.	♣ Q

7.	♠ J	♠ 8	37.	t.u.	♠ 8
8.	♦ Q	♥ 9	38.	t.u.	♠ 9
9.	t.u.	♠ 10	39.	♠ Q	♠ 10
10.	♠ 8	♣ 9	40.	♥ 8	♥ K
11.	♦ 9	♥ 10	41.	♠ K	♠ J
12.	♠ 9	♣ 10	42.	♥ 9	♥ A
13.	♦ 10	t.u.	43.	♠ 8	♣ A
14.	♦ J	♥ 10	44.	♣ 8	t.u.
15.	♠ 10	♣ 9	45.	♣ 9	♥ 8
16.	♦ Q	♥ J	46.	t.u.	♠ 10
17.	♣ A	♣ 10	47.	♣ 9	♣ 8
18.	♦ K	t.u.	48.	♣ 10	♣ A
19.	♥ 8	♥ 10	49.	t.u.	♠ J
20.	♠ J	♣ 9	50.	♠ 9	♠ 8
21.	♥ K	t.u.	51.	♥ 10	♥ K
22.	♥ 9	♥ 10	52.	♠ A	♠ Q
23.	t.u.	♠ K	53.	♥ J	t.u.
24.	♠ Q	♣ 9	54.	♣ 8	♥ 9
25.	♥ 9	♥ J	55.	♠ 10	♠ 8
26.	♠ K	♣ 10	56.	♥ Q	t.u.
27.	♥ 10	♥ Q	57.	♣ 9	♥ 9
28.	♣ A	♣ J	58.	t.u.	♠ Q
29.	♦ A	♥ 8	59.	t.u.	♠ K
30.	t.u.	♦ 8	60.	t.u.	♠ A

Now B must win. He has the five top cards of his trumps, the 10 9 8 of Spades, and two cards in the plain suits. He can, therefore, lead, trump A's lead and then lead a plain suit again, and so on, going straight out whatever A does.

OTHER GAMES FOR TWO PLAYERS

GERMAN WHIST

THE CARDS are cut for deal, the lower cut taking the deal and Ace counting low. Thirteen cards are dealt to each player and the top card of the remainder is turned face up, the suit it belongs to being declared trumps.

The elder hand, *ie* the dealer's opponent, leads a card, the dealer following suit if possible. The winner of the trick, namely, the player who plays the higher card, takes the exposed card, and the loser the top card from the pile. Before placing this card in his hand, the loser shows it to the other player.

The next card is then turned up and the winner of the preceding trick leads again. The winner of this trick takes the exposed card again, the loser the top card of the pile, and so on until the pile is exhausted.

The hands are then played out, and each player counts the tricks he has made. If each player makes thirteen tricks, no score is entered; but otherwise, the player with the greater number of tricks scores the difference between his tricks and his opponent's. For example, if a player makes sixteen tricks and his opponent ten, he scores 6 points. The game is 50 points.

As in Whist, a player having no card of the suit led by his opponent may trump if he please. It must be remembered, however, that it is not always desirable to take a trick, for a lot depends on the value of the exposed card.

If your opponent, for example, leads the ♠ 9 (Hearts being trumps), and you hold ♠ K 7 4, the exposed card being the ♠ 8, play the 4, reserving the King for a more important card later; but if the exposed card is the Queen, then, of course, you should take the trick with the King, as the Queen is then as good as the King.

If you hold a strong hand of trumps it generally pays to play them early, so as to command the game in its later stages. It is advisable to attempt to take the trick when the exposed card is a trump.

Another point in the game worth remembering is that it is a very big advantage to command as many certain tricks as possible, not merely for their trick value, but because they enable you to take the trick whenever the exposed card is a valuable one.

Suppose you hold:

♠ K Q 6 4
♡ A 10 8 3
◇ 10
♣ A Q 6 2

The exposed card is the ♡ K, Clubs being trumps. Instead of leading the ♡ A, lead the ♠ K, for although by taking the trick with the ♡ A the value of your hand will remain the same; by playing the ♠ K you make your ♠ Q the best Spade if your opponent takes the trick with the Ace, thus giving you the commanding cards in three suits. Of course, your opponent may not have the ♠ A, in which case you have improved your hand.

If, on the other hand, you hold:

♠ A K Q 4
♡ J 10 6
◇ 10 4
♣ A Q 6 2

Here the exposed card is the ♠ 10, and it is better to lead the ♠ A and maintain the three winning tricks in Spades.

German Whist is primarily a test of memory and is good practice for those who wish to improve their card-technique.

NULLOS

NULLOS is a form of Bridge for two which I have long recommended. I do so because, while the *mechanics* of the game are simple (much simpler, for example, than those of Bezique or Piquet), its *strategy* evolves unfailing interest. Let us look at an illustrative deal, explaining as we proceed how the game is played.

Suppose A and B are the players. They cut for deal, and A wins. He deals the cards as under (from a full pack):

To B: ♠ K Q 8 7 ♡ A K J 3 2 ◇ A 6 5 ♣ Q.
To A: ♠ A 9 ♡ 10 6 4 ◇ K 9 7 4 2 ♣ J 9 4.

The players look at their hands. Each has the right of exchanging as many cards as he wishes—if he likes, even the whole thirteen —for new ones.

B exchanges first. His hand has possibilities, both in Hearts and Nullos, and he might think of keeping the Spades, with a view to No Trump. At this game, however, No Trump is often a delusion. Let us suppose that B throws the Spades and Club. He takes in:

♠ J ♡ 7 ◇ 3 ♣ 10 3

and his hand is now:

♠ J ♡ A K J 7 3 2 ◇ A 6 5 3 ♣ 10 3.

A's hand is less promising. As it stands it is useless, and A therefore decides to sacrifice the ♠ 9, the Hearts and the Clubs. He throws out these seven cards, taking in:

♠ 6 5 2 ♡ Q ◇ J ♣ A 5.

His hand, after taking cards in, is:

♠ A 6 5 2 ♡ Q ◇ K J 9 7 4 2 ♣ A 5.

NOTE.—Both players keep their spare Aces for defensive purposes. Otherwise game may be made against them in their unprotected suits. At Nullos, the all-important cards are the Aces and the 2's!

THE DECLARATIONS

Bidding and scoring are as at Auction Bridge. Dealer bids first. Let me recapitulate the hands:

A: ♠ A 6 5 2 ♡ Q ◇ K J 9 7 4 2 ♣ A 5.
B: ♠ J ♡ A K J 7 3 2 ◇ A 6 5 3 ♣ 10 3.

A: One Nullo (*ie* a contract not to win more than six tricks).

B: One No Trump. (B had intended to bid Nullos. A's declaration, though it may be a bluff, takes the wind out of his sails. He bids a No Trump to conceal his Nullo strength, hoping that A will bid again.)

A: Two Nullos.

B: Two Hearts.

(NOTE that Hearts count the same as Nullos—8 per trick— but will overbid them.)

A: Three Nullos. (A contracts not to win more than four tricks.)

B: Double!

Now note the play. The card underlined takes the trick.

Trick	B	A
1	♠ J	♠ <u>A</u>
2	♡ J	<u>♡ Q</u>
3	♣ 10	<u>♣ A</u>
4	♣ 3	<u>♣ 5</u>
5	♢ A	<u>♠ 6</u>
6	♢ 6	<u>♢ 7</u>
7	♢ 3	<u>♢ 4</u>
8	♢ 5	<u>♢ 2</u>
9	<u>♡ 2</u>	♢ K
10	<u>♡ 3</u>	B
11	<u>♡ 7</u>	lays his
12	<u>♡ K</u>	hand
13	<u>♡ A</u>	down

A is defeated by three tricks, *ie* he makes seven tricks when he contracted to make not more than four.

B, having doubled, scores 300 points.

We will now review more closely the play of this Nullo hand, which is typical of the strategy of this game.

Trick 1.—B begins by getting rid of his single spade. A, as an 'insurance', takes this trick (he naturally cannot read the ♠ J as a singleton) and, similarly, leads out his single Heart.

Trick 2.—B, with ♡ A K J in his hand, sees no point in taking this trick.

Trick 3.—Now A must get rid of his dangerous doubleton in Clubs. His only hope is that after that he will be clear.

Trick 5.—A sad blow for A! B has no more Spades. The outlook at this stage is menacing.

Trick 6.—How to play the Diamond suit? B may be short. On the other hand, to play the ♢ 2 early may land A with the rest of the tricks. For example, if A plays this card at trick 7, B takes with the ♢ 5 and returns the ♢ 3. It is such situations as these that lend Nullos its fascination.

Suit and No Trump contracts are comparatively uninteresting

(though these can produce some difficult play situations, similar to those at Piquet) but a high proportion of the hands will be played at Nullos—normally the only contract at which there is a good chance of game. And these hands are never dull.

Contract Nullos

Nullos with Contract scoring is an improvement on the original game, where the scoring and conditions are based on Auction.

The change to a Contract basis has two advantages. First, it means that only contracts actually bid are scored 'below the line', and secondly, it adjusts what I have always thought was too severe a disparity between the reward for making tricks and the penalty for failure.

1. The game is played with a full pack of fifty-two cards. The players cut for deal and the pack is shuffled and cut in the ordinary way (the first deal goes to the player who draws the highest card).

2. The dealer deals thirteen cards face downwards to each player, putting to one side the remaining twenty-six cards (the stock).

3. Elder Hand, *ie* the non-dealer, now looks at his cards and discards as many of them as he likes. He can, if he wishes, discard none, or he can discard the whole thirteen, or any intermediate number. He places his discards face downwards and may not look at those cards again.

Now he draws from the stock cards equal in number to those he has discarded. When Elder Hand has discarded and drawn cards, the dealer does the same thing. He also can discard as many cards as he likes, so that it is possible in an extreme instance for the whole twenty-six cards of the stock to be utilized.

4. The auction now begins on the same lines as at Contract Bridge. Each player's object (which, of course, he has in mind in discarding and taking in cards) is to make as many tricks as he can at a suit or No Trump declaration, or to lose as many as he can at a Nullo declaration, and also, if possible, to score game.

The dealer has the right to the first bid. Whatever bid he makes may be overcalled by Elder Hand and the dealer can then bid again; the players can go on bidding against each other until the maximum bid (Seven No Trump redoubled) is reached. If, however, either player's bid is not overcalled, that is the final declaration. (This means that a player who thinks he has game in his hand will do well to open with a game call. Otherwise a wary opponent will pass.) There is no obligation for either player to bid; if both pass the hand is thrown in.

5. The sequence of bids, and the trick values of each, are as follows:

Clubs, 20 (the lowest bid is One Club: a contract to take seven tricks with Clubs as trumps).

Diamonds, 20.

Nullos, 30.

Hearts, 30.

Spades, 30.

No Trump—first trick, 40; subsequent tricks, 30.

Game is 100 up, *ie* a contract for game is a contract to take eleven tricks at Clubs or Diamonds, ten tricks at Hearts or Spades, nine tricks at No Trump, or to lose four odd tricks (*ie* to take not more than three tricks) at Nullos.

6. Any bid can be doubled by the adversary, which gives the player who has made it the right to bid again. He can either pass the double, redouble, or make a new bid of a higher denomination. Doubling doubles the trick value 'below the line', and redoubling redoubles it.

7. Scoring is throughout as at Contract Bridge. The trick values have been given above. A player who has won two games wins the rubber; he receives a bonus of 700 points if he wins a two-game rubber, and 500 points if he wins a three-game rubber. After winning one game he is 'vulnerable' and an increased scale of penalties applies should he fail to make a contract. Penalties for undertricks are:

(*a*) *When not vulnerable* (*ie* when a player has not won a game), 50 per trick.

If doubled, 100 for the first undertrick, and 200 for each subsequent undertrick.

Where the contract is redoubled, double the above penalties.

(*b*) *When a player is vulnerable:*

Undoubled, 100 points for each undertrick.

Doubled, 200 for the first undertrick, and 300 for each subsequent undertrick.

Redoubled, double the above penalties.

Where a player, not vulnerable, is doubled and makes his contract, he scores 100 for each overtrick. (NOTE that there is no bonus for making the contract: the doubled trick score suffices.) Where a vulnerable player is doubled and makes his contract, he scores 200 points for each overtrick. Where a contract is redoubled (vulnerable or not vulnerable) overtrick bonuses are double the above.

Slams: Again, slam bonuses are as at Contract. A *Small Slam* bid and made, where declarer is not vulnerable, scores 500 points; where vulnerable, 750 points.

Grand Slam bid and made, where not vulnerable, 1,000 points; where vulnerable, 1,500 points.

Where a Small Slam is bid and a Grand Slam is made, only the Small Slam bonus is scored.

BEZIQUE

BEZIQUE is one of the standard card games for two players, the others—so far as this country is concerned—being Cribbage and Piquet. By a standard game I mean one which has been established for some generations and which has universally accepted rules.

Bezique as ordinarily played (*ie* with two packs) has, perhaps, more of the element of luck in it than Piquet or Cribbage. Nevertheless, there is considerable scope for skill.

By two packs I mean that two Piquet packs are used, *ie* sixty-four cards in all. Special Bezique packs, including a 'marker', are sold, but it is not necessary to have a Bezique set. The game can be played with two ordinary packs, shuffled together, from which the 2's, 3's, 4's, 5's and 6's have been removed.

To begin with, the players cut for deal; the player getting the highest card deals, and Ace counts high. The dealer gives each player eight cards, face downwards, dealing first three to his adversary and then three to himself; then two and two; then three and three again.

Next, the top card is turned up from the remainder of the pack. The suit of this card is the trump suit. If it is a 7, the dealer scores 10 points.

The play proper now begins.

The play of each hand is in two parts: First, each player plays a card from his hand, taking in exchange a card from the pack, until the pack is exhausted; second, the eight cards which remain to each player are played out under different scoring conditions. I will explain these two stages separately.

THE PRELIMINARY PLAY

The top card of the pack, which indicates the trump suit, is laid face upwards by the side of the remainder of the pack or 'stock'. Now the non-dealer leads to the first trick, to which the dealer will then play a card. The winner of the trick draws the top card from the 'stock'; his adversary draws the next card. And so play goes on until the 'stock' is exhausted. The cards of the 'stock' are not exposed.

The lead to the first trick will normally be a worthless card, but a player who wishes to change the 7 of Trumps, or to make an immediate Declaration (see below) will play a small trump. In play, the 10 ranks next after the Ace (*ie* above K Q J). And note that *during this preliminary part of the play* Bezique differs fundamentally from games of the Whist family in that there is no need to follow suit.

During this preliminary stage of the game the only objects of taking tricks are (*a*) to cash in on Aces and 10's (Brisques)— any Ace or 10 included in a trick counts 10 points to the winner of it; and (*b*) to make a Declaration. The scores mainly depend upon the Declarations that are made.

A Declaration can only be made by a player immediately after taking a trick.

A Declaration consists in laying the appropriate cards face upwards on the table, at the same time mentioning the scoring combination claimed. Each Declaration, as claimed, is scored.

Declarations are as follows:

1. *A Common Marriage* (King and Queen of any suit other than trumps), 20 points.

2. *A Royal Marriage* (King and Queen of the trump suit), 40 points.

3. *Bezique* (Queen of Spades and Knave of Diamonds), 40 points.

As a variant, some people make the ♣ Q and ♡ J Bezique when either Spades or Diamonds are trumps.

4. *Four Knaves*, 40 points.

5. *Four Queens*, 60 points.

6. *Four Kings*, 80 points.

7. *Four Aces*, 100 points.

8. *Sequence* (A 10 K Q J of the trump suit), 250 points.

9. *Double Bezique* (both Queens of Spades and both Knaves of Diamonds), 500 points.

In addition, as noted above, a player scores 10 points for

any Ace or any 10 included in tricks won by him. Thus, if he leads the ♣ A, and his adversary plays the ◇ 10 (Diamonds not being trumps), 20 points are scored in respect of that trick.

Finally, a player holding the 7 of trumps in his hand may, immediately after taking a trick, exchange it for the turned-up trump card. This, of course, he should always do at the first opportunity if the turned-up card is one of trump honours. Exchanging the 7 ranks as a Declaration, and another Declaration cannot be made at the same time. Once the 7 has been exchanged, the player who has the second 7 cannot do anything special with it. He scores 10, however, when he plays it.

Only one Declaration can be made at a time in Bezique. Thus, you cannot put down a trump Sequence and score both for the Sequence and for a Royal Marriage.

On the other hand, the same cards may figure in more than one Declaration provided they are of different kinds. That is to say, if Spades are trumps, the same Queen of Spades may figure in Declarations of (a) Bezique, (b) a Royal Marriage, (c) Four Queens, (d) a Sequence and (e) Double Bezique, but she cannot figure in two Royal Marriages or in two sets of Four Queens.

A card that has been declared stays on the table until it is played. Thus, a player may have seven of his eight cards in front of him (in which case, of course, his opponent knows exactly what he has got and can plan to play accordingly). An exposed card can be led, or played to a trick on the table, in exactly the same way as a card in the hand.

A subsidiary Declaration must be made before a more important one if it is to be made at all; but sometimes it is advisable to 'sink' the subsidiary Declaration in case one will not have the opportunity for both. Thus, if one has all four Bezique cards, one can declare the two Simple Beziques separately and then the Double Bezique. But if the four cards have come into your possession towards the end of this first part of the game, and if your opponent is known to have sufficient good cards to lead to prevent one making many Declarations, it would be the height of stupidity to waste time declaring the Simple Beziques. You would put down your four Bezique cards, declare the Double Bezique, which is worth 500, and let the 40's go.

This first stage of the game, as I have called it, goes on until there are only two cards left which are not in the possession of the players, ie the bottom card of the pack, which is the last card to be played for, and the card turned up to indicate the trump suit (or, as is normally the case, the 7 which has been exchanged for it). The winner of the previous trick takes the former, and the loser takes the latter, and to the winner of this trick falls the last opportunity of making a Declaration.

Now comes the second part of the play. This is sometimes called the 'Play-Off'. Each player takes into his hand such exposed cards as he has on the table, and (the winner of the last trick playing first) the eight tricks are played out.

The Play-Off differs from the Preliminary Play in that a player must follow suit; if he cannot follow suit he may either trump or discard. No Declarations can be made in the Play-Off, but each player scores 10 points for every Ace or 10 contained in tricks won by him. The simplest plan is, thus, for each player to collect the tricks which have been taken by him and to count his Aces and 10's at the finish.

The game, as usually played, is 1,000 up.

I will give an illustrative deal at this interesting game, but the above account should be sufficient to show that the element of skill in it is considerable.

The following are what may be described as the 'skill factors' in the game:

1. Deciding at what stage to play out your winners, *ie* balancing the desirability of using them in order to make Declarations against their potential usefulness later on and the fact that they may develop a scoring value.

2. Deciding what scoring combinations it is best worth while to go for in the light of the cards that you hold and that you know your opponent to hold.

3. Noting and memorizing the cards played to each trick and the cards which your opponent takes in. (A player equipped with a perfect card memory will know at the end of the game exactly what cards his opponent holds, and, long before the end of the Preliminary Play, will be able to make a shrewd guess at his opponent's tactics and decide accordingly how far it is desirable to sacrifice valuable tricks in order to obtain the lead. The six-pack game played with 192 cards is, for that reason, a game in which the skill factor is very high.)

4. Judging what we may call the 'tempo' of the game, *ie* making sacrifices of winning cards where necessary in order to prevent your opponent from making Declarations. ·

AN ILLUSTRATIVE DEAL

The players are A and B. They cut for deal. A cuts ◇ Q, B cuts ♡ A. B deals as follows:

To A: ♠ J 9 7 ♡ 8 7 7 ◇ 8 ♣ K.
To B: ♠ K K ♡ A 10 ◇ J 8 ♣ 10 9.

Now the ♠ 10 is turned up and Spades are trumps. The ♠ 10 is laid beside the stock.

THE PRELIMINARY PLAY

Trick	A Plays	B Plays	Winner	Declarations A	Declarations B	Brisques A	Brisques B	Running Score A	Running Score B
1	♡ 8	♡ 10	B	—	—	—	10	—	10
2	♠ 9	◇ 8	A	Exchanges ♠ 7 (10)	—	—	—	10	10
3	♡ 7	♣ 9	A	—	—	—	—	10	10
4	♡ 7	♡ A	B	—	—	—	10	10	20
5	◇ 8	◇ 10	B	—	—	—	10	10	30
6	♠ 9	♣ 10	B	—	—	—	10	10	40
7	♡ Q	◇ 9	A	—	—	—	—	10	40
8	♣ K	♡ 10	A	—	—	10	—	20	40
9	◇ 7	◇ 9	B	—	4 Knaves (40)	—	—	20	80
10	♣ K	♣ J	A	—	—	—	—	20	80
11	◇ K	♣ J	A	4 Aces (100)	—	—	—	120	80
12	♣ A	♣ Q	A	—	—	10	—	130	80
13	♣ A	◇ 10	A	Marriage ◇ K Q (20)	—	20	—	170	80
14	◇ K	◇ A	B	—	—	—	10	170	90
15	♠ 8	♡ J	A	Bezique (40)	—	—	—	210	90
16	◇ J	◇ A	B	—	—	—	10	210	100
17	♣ 8	♣ 7	A	—	—	—	—	210	100
18	♣ 8	♠ 7	B	—	4 Kings (80) Exchanges ♠ 7 (10)	—	—	210	190
19	♡ J	♡ K	B	—	—	—	—	210	190
20	♡ 9	◇ 7	B	—	—	—	—	210	190
21	♡ 8	♡ K	B	—	—	—	—	210	190
22	♠ J	♠ 9	A	—	—	—	—	210	190
23	♠ 10	♣ Q	A	—	—	10	—	220	190
24	♠ A	◇ J	A	—	—	10	—	230	190

| Cards Drawn | | After the Draw Players Hold | |
A	B	In Hand	Exposed on the Table
♠ A	♣ J	A: ♠ A J 9 7 ♥ 7 7 ♦ 8 ♣ K	—
		B: ♠ K K ♥ A ♦ J 8 ♣ J 10 9	—
♣ A	♣ J	A: ♠ A J 10 ♥ 7 7 ♦ 8 ♣ A K	
		B: ♠ K K ♥ A ♦ J ♣ J J 10 9	
♣ 9	♦ 10	A: ♠ A J 10 ♥ 7 ♦ 8 ♣ A K 9	
		B: ♠ K K ♥ A ♦ J 10 ♣ J J 10	
♦ K	♥ 9	A: ♠ A J 10 ♦ K 8 ♣ A K 9	
		B: ♠ K K ♥ 9 ♦ J 10 ♣ J J 10	
♥ Q	♣ Q	A: ♠ A J 10 ♥ Q Q ♦ K ♣ A K 9	
		B: ♠ K K ♥ 9 ♦ J ♣ Q J J 10	
♣ A	♣ J	A: ♠ A J 10 ♥ Q Q ♦ K ♣ A A K	
		B: ♠ K K J ♥ 9 ♦ J ♣ Q J J	
♠ Q	♥ 10	A: ♠ A Q J 10 ♦ K ♣ A A K	
		B: ♠ K K J ♥ 10 ♦ J ♣ Q J J	
♦ 7	♦ 9	A: ♠ A Q J 10 ♦ K 7 ♣ A A	
		B: ♠ K K J ♦ J 9 ♣ Q J J	
♣ K	♦ A	A: ♠ A Q J 10 ♦ K ♣ A A K	
		B: ♠ K K ♦ A ♣ Q	♠ J ♦ J ♣ J J
♠ A	♦ A	A: ♠ A A Q J 10 ♦ K ♣ A A	♠ J ♦ A ♣ J
		B: ♠ K K ♦ A A ♣ Q	♠ J ♦ J
♦ Q	♦ 10	A: ♠ Q J 10 ♦ Q	♠ A A ♣ A A
		B: ♠ K K ♦ A A 10 ♣ Q	♠ J ♦ J
♦ K	♥ K	A: ♠ Q J 10 ♦ K Q	♠ A A ♣ A
		B: ♠ K K ♥ K ♦ A A 10	♠ J ♦ J
♦ J	♥ J	A: ♠ Q J 10 ♦ J	♠ A A ♦ K Q
		B: ♠ K K ♥ K J ♦ A A	♠ J ♦ J
♠ 8	♦ Q	A: ♠ Q J 10 8 ♦ J	♠ A A ♦ Q
		B: ♠ K K ♥ K J ♦ A Q	♠ J ♦ J
♥ J	♠ 7	A: ♠ J 10 ♥ J	♠ A A Q ♦ Q J
		B: ♠ K K 7 ♥ K ♦ A Q	♠ J ♦ J
♣ 8	♣ 7	A: ♠ J 10 ♥ J ♣ 8	♠ A A Q ♦ Q
		B: ♠ K K 7 ♥ K ♦ K Q ♣ 7	♠ J ♦ J
♣ 8	♥ K	A: ♠ J 10 ♥ J ♣ 8	♠ A A Q ♦ Q
		B: ♠ K K 7 ♥ K K ♦ Q	♠ J ♦ J
♥ Q	♠ 9	A: ♠ J 10 ♥ Q J	♠ A A Q ♦ Q
		B: ♠ 9 ♦ Q	♠ K K J ♥ K K ♦ J
♥ 9	♦ 7	A: ♠ J 10 ♥ Q 9	♠ A A Q ♦ Q
		B: ♠ 9 ♦ Q 7	♠ K K J ♥ K ♦ J
♥ 8	♣ Q	A: ♠ J 10 ♥ Q 8	♠ A A Q ♦ Q
		B: ♠ 9 ♦ Q ♣ Q	♠ K K J ♥ K ♦ J
♥ A	♠ 8	A: ♠ J 10 ♥ A Q	♠ A A Q ♦ Q
		B: ♠ 9 8 ♦ Q ♣ Q	♠ K K J ♦ J
♦ 9	♠ 10	A: ♠ 10 ♥ A Q ♦ 9	♠ A A Q ♦ Q
		B: ♠ 10 8 ♦ Q ♣ Q	♠ K K J ♦ J
♣ 7	♠ Q	A: ♥ A Q ♦ 9 ♣ 7	♠ A A Q ♦ Q
		B: ♠ Q 10 8 ♦ Q	♠ K K J ♦ J
♣ 10	♠ 7	A: ♥ A Q ♦ 9 ♣ 10 7	♠ A Q ♦ Q
		B: ♠ Q 10 8 7 ♦ Q	♠ K K J

The Play-Off

The players take up their exposed cards from the table. Their hands are:

A: ♠ A Q ♡ A Q ◇ Q 9 ♣ 10 7.
B: ♠ K K Q J 10 8 7 ◇ Q.

With B holding so many trumps, there is little in the play. It goes as follows:

Trick	1	2	3	4	5	6	7	8
A	♡ A	♠ Q	♣ 10	♠ A	♣ 7	◇ 9	◇ Q	♡ Q
B	♠ 7	♠ 8	♠ J	♠ K	♠ 10	♠ K	♠ Q	◇ Q

A scores 10 points (♠ A).
B scores 40 points (♡ A ♣ 10 ♠ 10, 10 for last trick).
Score at the end of the deal: A, 240; B, 230.

Comments

The scores (A 240, B 230) are below the average for a deal. Neither player secures a sequence; only three out of eight possible 'Fours' are declared, and only one out of eight possible marriages.

Notes on the Preliminary Play

Trick 7.—B is anxious to declare his four Knaves, but A (most annoyingly) takes the trick.

Trick 8.—B is reluctantly obliged to surrender a 'brisque' to A.

Trick 9.—B is lucky: he draws the ◇ 9 with which to win A's ◇ 7.

Trick 11.—When A exhibits four Aces, including two ♠ A's, B knows he has no hope of sequence, or of four Aces (for an Ace was played at trick 4).

Trick 14.—A hopes to declare Bezique, but is temporarily thwarted.

Trick 17.—B's patience is rewarded. He draws a fourth King.

Trick 18.—B declares four Kings and A, in his turn, sees all hope of a sequence disappear.

Tricks 22, 23, 24.—A makes sure that B shall declare nothing further. This is excellent play. B's accumulation of trumps, now almost useless, has come too late.

KALABRIASZ

THIS is primarily a game for two players: a good game, too: its
skill factor is very high. It is played, with slight variations, in
many parts of the world and under many different names. The
simplest of its alternative names is 'Clob', which is a contraction
of the variant 'Clobberyash'. The name Kalabriasz is perhaps
Hungarian, but the polyglot terminology of the game suggests
a cosmopolitan origin.

KALABRIASZ FOR TWO PLAYERS

A Piquet pack (thirty-two cards) is used. The ranking of the
cards (in play) is different in the trump suit and in plain suits. In a
trump suit the ranking is: Knave (highest), 9, Ace, 10, King,
Queen, 8, 7 (lowest). Special names are given to the Knave, 9
and 7 of trumps. The Knave is known as 'Jasz' (pronounced
'Yass'); the 9 of trumps as 'Menel'; the 7 of trumps as 'Dix'
(pronounced 'Deece').

In plain suits (*ie* suits which are not trumps) the ranking is:
Ace (highest), 10, King, Queen, Knave, 9, 8, 7 (lowest).

The game somewhat resembles Piquet. Points are scored
partly for taking tricks and partly for 'melding' winning combinations. A game (unless otherwise agreed) is 500 points up.

THE DEAL

Players cut for deal: whoever cuts the lower card deals first.
If both players cut (say) an eight, they cut again, as in Piquet.
The dealer (Younger Hand) shuffles the cards; his opponent
(Elder Hand) cuts to him; he then deals three cards (face downwards) to his opponent; three to himself; three more to his
opponent; and three more to himself. The thirteenth card is
turned up and placed beside the remainder of the pack, which
is deposited face downwards between the two players. This is
called the 'talon'.

MAKING THE TRUMP SUIT

The first objective is the 'making' of a trump suit. Elder Hand
(the non-dealer) has first say. He looks at his cards, and, if he is
satisfied with the suit of the card turned up, he says 'I accept',
otherwise he says 'Pass'. Now Younger Hand (dealer) has the
chance of accepting, but he also may pass.

If both players have passed, Elder Hand may name another trump suit. If he passes again, Younger Hand may name the trump suit. If he too passes, the hands are thrown in, and the deal passes to Elder Hand.

Either player, instead of accepting or passing when it is first his turn to speak, may say 'Schmeiss' (pronounced 'Schmice'). This is a proposal for a new deal. If the other player accepts, the cards are dealt again. If not, the other player names the trump suit.

COMPLETION OF DEAL

The trump suit having been established, Younger Hand deals three more cards to Elder Hand and three more to himself—face downwards, as before. Each player now has nine cards. When the deal is completed, the bottom card of the talon is placed faced upwards on top of the talon. This is to mark the conclusion of the deal, but the exposed card plays no further part in the game.

EXCHANGING THE DIX

Before play begins, whoever holds the Dix (7 of trumps) may exchange it for the trump card originally turned up, provided that that trump suit has been accepted.

COMPARISON AND SCORING OF MELDS

Now (as in Piquet) players disclose their scoring combinations, these are (a) sequences of three; (b) sequences of four or more; (c) the King and Queen of trumps. A sequence is three or more successive cards of the same suit.

Here—for the purpose of scoring sequences—the cards have yet another ranking order. This time it is that which one would normally expect: Ace, King, Queen, Knave, 10, 9, 8, 7.

The procedure is very much as in Piquet. Elder Hand begins by announcing the point value of any sequence he holds, or, if he has more than one, of his best sequence. The point value is 20 for a sequence of three, and 50 for a sequence of four or more. Other things being equal, a sequence in trumps is better than a non-trump sequence.

Examples:

1. Spades are trumps. Elder Hand holds:

♠ A K Q J; ♡ None; ◇ Q J 10 9; ♣ Ace.
Younger Hand holds:
♠ None; ♡ K Q J 10; ◇ 7; ♣ K Q J 10.

The dialogue would go:
    Elder Hand: 'Sequence of 50.'
    Younger Hand: 'How high?'
    Elder Hand: 'Ace high.'
    Younger Hand: 'Good.'

Elder Hand now scores 50 for his sequence in Spades and also 50 for his sequence in Diamonds. Younger Hand scores nothing, because points for sequences can only be scored by one player. (Here again this game resembles Piquet, where the player with the best sequence scores for all his other sequences, and the other player—though he may hold the second best sequence—scores nothing.)

2. If Elder Hand holds the same cards:

    ♠ A K Q J; ♡ None; ◇ Q J 10 9; ♣ Ace
and Younger Hand holds:
    ♠ None; ♡ A K Q J; ◇ 7; ♣ K Q J 10

Elder Hand still scores the points, because his best sequence is in the trump suit. And if Diamonds were trumps, Elder Hand would still score the points, because, where there is equality, priority of claim goes to the non-dealer.

3. Spades are trumps. Elder Hand holds:

    ♠ None; ♡ A K Q; ◇ A K Q; ♣ K Q J
Younger Hand holds:
    ♠ Q J 10 9 7; ♡ 9 8 7; ◇ None; ♣ Ace

Younger Hand's sequence of four cancels out Elder Hand's three high sequences. He scores 50 for his trump sequence and 20 for his sequence in Hearts, and Elder Hand scores nothing.

If Elder Hand has no sequences, he says so, and Younger Hand may then declare his.

A player is not obliged to declare any or all of his sequences. For example, Elder Hand may announce a sequence scoring 50, and Younger Hand may hold two such sequences, but—knowing that Elder Hand's is better—will say 'Good' without contesting the claim. Or again, a low sequence of 20 may be 'sunk' if the player holding it thinks this is tactically profitable. Note that a sequence of more than four cards has not, for that reason, priority over a sequence of four. If Elder Hand has declared the sequence K Q J 10, and Younger Hand has a sequence Q J 10 9 8 7, it is Elder Hand who scores.

'BELLA'

The meld of King and Queen of trumps (sometimes known as 'Bella') scores 20 points for the holder. It should be claimed by the player holding these cards when he produces the second one in play.

THE PLAY

Sequences having been duly claimed, Elder Hand leads to the first trick. A trick consists of one card contributed by each player. The winner of a trick leads to the next one.

In the play, the second player to the trick must follow suit if he is able to. If he has no card of the suit led, he must play a trump is he has one; if he has no trump, he can play any card he likes. If the lead is in the trump suit, the second player must, if possible, win the trick by playing a higher trump; if he can't do that, he must, if possible, follow suit.

A trick is won by the higher card of the suit led, the ranking value being as already stated: in trumps: J, 9, A, 10, K, Q, 8, 7; in plain suits: A, 10, K, Q, J, 9, 8, 7. If a plain card has been trumped, the trump, of course, wins. The winner of a trick places it face downwards in front of him, and then leads to the next one.

The object of winning tricks is not to win tricks as such—which, save for the last one, score nothing—but to win tricks containing certain scoring cards. These are:

Knave of trumps (Jasz)	20 points
9 of trumps ('Menel')	14 ,,
Any Ace	11 ,,
Any 10	10 ,,
Any King	4 ,,
Any Queen	3 ,,
Knave of any suit but trumps	2 ,,

The winner of the last trick scores 10 points.

SCORING

The scoring is complicated. At the end of the play, the deal is over. The players now add what they have scored in melds and play. There are three scoring situations: (a) If the 'Bidder' (ie trump-maker) has scored more (in melds and play combined) than his opponent, each scores his own total. (b) If the non-bidder has the higher score, he scores the whole of his points, plus those of his opponent. In this case, the bidder is said to have 'gone bate': the situation is somewhat similar to that of being rubiconed at Piquet. (c) If there is an equality of scores, the non-bidder reckons his own points, but the bidder scores nothing. This is said to be going 'half bate'.

These somewhat drastic scoring rules explain why experienced players throw so many hands in. A player nominating a trump suit not sufficiently powerful to ensure him a good score in the play runs the risk of losing everything.

There is no universal code of rules for this game. I have come across a number of variations. Players should agree beforehand on any doubtful points, or on any departures which they may wish to make from the rules as set out above.

BEZIQUE, POKER AND CRIBBAGE PATIENCE

THOSE who are familiar with the rules of Bezique may like to try a Two-Handed Bezique Patience. Though based upon Bezique, it is a competitive game of a different type, calling for a fair amount of skill. It needs preliminary organization.

Each player requires a specially prepared pack of forty cards, consisting of the honour cards only, ie Aces to 10's inclusive, taken from two packs. (It will thus be seen that four ordinary packs will be required to make up the two Patience packs.)

One of the packs of forty Honour Cards is now well shuffled and the other pack should be arranged in suits from the 10 to the Ace. The dealer, whose pack has been shuffled, now turns up his top card and calls it aloud, and the other player selects the card called and both place it face up on the table. I should mention that some partition should be placed between the two players so that neither sees what the other is doing. The dealer then calls a second card and this must be placed on the table in a position so that it touches the previous card. It can be placed immediately above, below, at either side, or in any of the four corners, so that there are eight places in which this card can be placed. The dealer then continues to play one card at a time, calling it out aloud as he draws it, and each player puts it in the position he considers best, remembering that he must always place his card so that it touches one already placed

on the table.[1] When twenty-five cards have been played and the
square is complete the scores are checked.[2]

	Points
Marriage (*ie* King and Queen of a suit)	2
Bezique (*ie* Knave of Diamonds and Queen of Spades or Knave of Hearts and Queen of Clubs)	4
4 Knaves	4
4 Queens	6
4 Kings	8
4 Aces	10
Sequence (*ie* Ace, King, Queen, Knave, Ten of a suit)	25
Double Bezique (*ie* two Knaves of Diamonds and two Queens of Spades or two Knaves of Clubs and Two Queens of Hearts)	50

Scores are reckoned in respect of each row and of each column.
Here is an example:

Trick	A	B	C	D	E
1	♦ K	♣ K	♣ Q	♡ K	♠ K
2	♦ A	♣ A	♣ A	♡ 10	♠ 10
3	♦ Q	♣ Q	♡ Q	♡ Q	♡ 10
4	♦ J	♣ J	♦ J	♦ 10	♠ J
5	♦ 10	♣ 10	♠ Q	♦ A	♠ A

This will produce a score of:

Row 1.	Four Kings	..	..	..	..	8
	Marriage ..	..	..	..	..	2
Row 2.	.. ..	..	..	..	..	0
Row 3.	Four Queens	..	..	..	..	6
Row 4.	Four Knaves	..	..	..	..	4
Row 5.	.. ..	..	..	..	..	0
Column A.	Sequence	..	..	..	..	25
Column B.	Sequence	..	..	..	..	25
Column C.	Bezique	..	..	..	..	4

[1] It must be understood that not more than five cards may be placed
in a line in either direction, so that when twenty-five cards have been
dealt there is a complete square of twenty-five cards. (Some players,
to make the game more amusing, permit of a maximum of five cards
being discarded by either player. In this case thirty cards are played
altogether, but only twenty-five used.)

[2] In order to simplify the scoring the table given is generally used
at Bezique Patience.

Column D.	Marriage	..	..	..	..	2
Column E.	..	..	..	..	..	0
						76

When each player has laid out his twenty-five cards—all of which, of course, will be identical, as the packs have been prepared beforehand—the scores are added up, and the player with the highest score wins. If desired, however, stakes may be played on the differences in points.

The same principle may equally be applied to Poker and to Cribbage. At one time Poker Patience was a very popular amusement. Although it is primarily a game for two, it can be played simultaneously by any number of players.

GAMES FOR TWO, THREE OR FOUR PLAYERS

TABLANETTE

'TABLANETTE,' LIKE several other card games, is said to have come originally from Russia. It is one of the best of the lesser-known games for two. It is a game of skill, but not at all difficult to learn.

The cards are cut for deal, the lower card taking the deal. Six cards are then dealt to each player, and four cards are turned face upwards on the table. (In the three-handed game only four cards are dealt to each player. We will assume that in this instance only two persons are playing the game.)

When the dealer has exposed the four cards, his opponent has to play. If he plays a card of the same denomination as any of the four cards on the table, then he takes such card. Or, if there are any two or three cards on the table whose pips added together make a total equal to that of any one card, then he takes such cards. He may be able to do both.

A King counts fourteen; a Queen, thirteen; an Ace either one or eleven. The Knave is treated differently, but we will deal with him in a moment.

Let us suppose the four cards exposed are the King, 9, 4 and 3. If the opponent plays a King he takes the King; if he plays a Queen he takes the 9 and 4 (thirteen); if a 7, the 3 and 4. These cards are put in a pile on one side, each player having his own pile. Should either player, now or at any time, be able to take with one card *all* the cards on the table (sometimes there is only one) then he calls 'Tablanette', and scores the total pip value of all such cards, including that of the card he himself plays.

Suppose, for example, that for the 9 in the above-mentioned cards we substitute a 7. If the opponent of the dealer holds a King he scores forty-two (fourteen for the King on the table, fourteen for the 7, 4, 3, and fourteen for his own King). If he is, however, unable to score a Tablanette, he will play a card, if possible, that will not allow his opponent to score Tablanette. In the instance first quoted, if he plays a King, then he leaves 9, 4, 3, which cannot be taken by one card.

The Knave plays a different rôle. He cannot in any circumstances score Tablanette, but a Knave can always take *all* the cards on the table, such cards being put on the pile at the side.

The Knave is an extremely useful card, because it forces the opponent to play a fresh card with which the other player may be able to make Tablanette. If a Knave is among the four dealt out, it is taken up and placed at the bottom of the pack (so that the dealer will ultimately receive it). Should there be two or more Knaves in the four exposed cards, then only one Knave is placed at the bottom of the pack, and the other, or others, placed in the middle of the pack, a fresh card, or cards, being dealt to replace the Knaves so taken. It should be noted that two cards on the table making twelve cannot make a Tablanette, as the Ace counts only eleven and the Queen thirteen.

The opponent having played, the dealer, in his turn, plays a card. This continues in turn until each player has played his six cards. If either player makes Tablanette, then the opponent must play a card (at choice) on to the table. In doing so he will play either a card of the lowest denomination possible (in order to give his opponent the minimum score in case he can again make Tablanette), or else a card which he thinks it improbable or impossible for his opponent to match.

For example, if you have two 4's in your hand and one 4 has previously been played, the chances are against your opponent holding the remaining 4. When each player has played his six cards, the dealer deals a further six to each player (any cards on the table remaining face upwards), and the game continues until these six cards are also played. Then a third six, and finally the last six.

When the last six cards have been played, any cards left on the table are taken by the player last taking a card from the board. That is to say, if neither player can take a card from the board for the last three times, then the player who before that matched a card or cards takes the remaining cards. Each player then counts from his pile one point for every Ace, King, Queen, Knave and 10, and one for the 2 of Clubs. The 10 of Diamonds counts two.

The player with the greater *number* of cards counts three extra. The cards are then shuffled and the deal passes, and the next hand is played as before. The player who first makes 251 wins.

CASSINO

THIS is an excellent game for two, three or four players: not difficult, but with scope for mental alertness. A knowledge of arithmetic is helpful.

Here I describe the game for two players. The game for three is similar, each player playing against each; the four-handed game is a partnership affair, partners sitting opposite to one another.

Let us call the players A and B. They cut for deal, the player who cuts the lowest card dealing.

A full pack of fifty-two cards is used, and in cutting and play the Ace ranks as the lowest card and has a pip value of one. Other cards carry their own pip values.

Court cards have no special pip value, because, as will be seen, they can only be 'paired' like with like.

The dealer (A) begins by dealing, two at a time, four cards to his opponent (B), to the table, and to himself. The cards dealt to the table are dealt face upwards and constitute the 'layout'. The remainder of the pack (forty cards) A places to his left; there will be ten more deals and A will deal them all.

The object of the game is to score points on the following basis:

	Points
For taking in Great Cassino (the ◇ 10)	2
For taking in Little Cassino (the ♠ 2)	1
For taking in a majority of the cards	3
For taking in a majority of Spades	1
For taking in any Ace	1
For a 'sweep' of the cards on the table	1

The cards having been dealt, play begins. B plays first, then A, and so on till each player has played his four cards, when A deals again. After the first deal, the cards are only dealt to the players; nothing to the table.

In play, a player produces a card from his hand and can do one of the following things:

1. He can *pair* a card from his hand with one or more like cards on the table. Thus, if he has a 6 and there are two 6's on the table, he plays his 6 face upwards and gathers in all three cards, placing them face downwards in front of him.

2. He can *combine* a card from his hand with one or more cards on the table. This does not apply to court cards, which can only be used for pairing. In *combining*, a player takes two or more cards which have an aggregate pip-value equal to his. Thus, suppose there are 8, 7, 3, 2 on the table. A player holding the ◇ 10 can bring off a very useful *coup*. He combines his 10 with 8 2, and with 7 3, collecting all four cards; thus, with his ◇ 10 he gathers in five cards and also scores for Great Cassino and for a sweep of the cards on the table.

3. He can *build* from his hand on the table. In building, a player plays a card from his hand to another card on the table to make a pip-aggregate equal to that of some other card in his hand. Thus, suppose there is a 7 on the table and a player holds a 9 and a 2. He lays his 2 on the 7, announcing 'nine'; then, next time, he can play his 9 and gather in all three cards. Of course, if his opponent happens to have a 9 the original builder can be forestalled.

A card built on cannot now be claimed separately: it has become part of a combination which can only be collected as a whole.

The 'building', however, can be continued to make a combination of three, four, or even five cards. Suppose there is an Ace on the table and B holds 9, 4, 3 and 2. He plays the 2 on the Ace and says 'three'. A, with a 2 and a 5 in his hand, now plays the 2 and says 'five'. B retaliates by playing the 4, saying 'nine'. Unless A has a 9, with which he can take all four cards, they will fall to B next time. Or, if A's remaining cards are an Ace and a 10, he can play the Ace, saying 'ten', and with his 10 will collect all five—A, 2, 2, 4 and A.

A player who has made a 'build' is obliged to win it, when next it is his turn, unless he wins something else or makes another 'build'.

4. A player can 'call' one (or more) combinations; that is, he earmarks cards for subsequent capture, unless anticipated by his adversary. Thus, if there are 4 and 5 on the table, he can play a 9 to the table, saying 'nines'; then, with a subsequent 9, can take them both. But if his opponent also has a 9, he will collect the earmarked cards first, so that calling is a dangerous game unless one is sure of success.

5. If none of these plays is possible, a player must just play one of his cards to the table.

When the four cards first dealt to each player are exhausted, four more are dealt as described; and the game goes on until all cards have been played. Any cards left on the table at the finish are taken by the winner of the last trick. This, however, does not count as a 'sweep'.

FIVE HUNDRED

At FIRST blush, this game may seem complicated, but with a little practise one can soon familiarize oneself with its rules.

Five Hundred is played with a Piquet pack of thirty-two cards, *ie* an ordinary pack from which the 2's, 3's, 4's, 5's and 6's have been removed. To these thirty-two cards is added a Joker, making thirty-three cards in all. If you have no Joker in your pack, the ♣ 2 will do.

The ranking order of the cards is peculiar to this game. First, ranking highest, comes the Joker. Then, if there is a trump suit, the Knave of trumps. This card (borrowing a term from Euchre) is known as the Right Bower.

Next, after the Right Bower, ranks the Left Bower, which is the Knave of the other suit of the same colour as the trump suit. Thus, if Hearts are trumps, the highest trump is the Joker, the next highest is the Knave of Hearts, the next highest is the Knave of Diamonds, which acquires temporary status as a Heart.

The remaining cards of the trump suit follow in their normal order, *ie* A K Q 10 9 8 7. Hence, if trumps have been declared, there are *ten* cards in the trump suit (the eight cards included in it initially plus the Joker and the Left Bower).

There are seven cards only in the second suit of that colour, the Left Bower having temporarily become a trump, and there are eight cards in each of the other two suits. In these two suits, the Knaves take their ordinary rank, *ie* next after the Queen.

If there are no trumps, these elaborations do not apply. The Joker is still top dog, but belongs to no specified suit. The player leading it can nominate the suit which it purports to represent, saying, for example: 'This is a Diamond,' when opponents who have Diamonds must follow suit. Alternatively, if it is played to a trick led by someone else, it takes the trick. There are, however, special rules applying to the use of the Joker in no trumps which I will explain in due course.

The three players begin by cutting for deal. The deal falls to whoever secures the lowest card. For this purpose the Joker ranks as lowest, then come the Aces, then the 7's, 8's, and so on, upwards to the Kings. If two players cut cards of the same denomination, Spades rank as lowest, then, in ascending order, come Clubs, Diamonds and Hearts.

The deal having been determined, the dealer deals three cards to each player, beginning with 'eldest hand', on his left. Then come two more rounds of three cards each followed by a single card to each player. Each has now ten cards. The remaining three cards are placed on the table face upwards; these three cards are known as the 'Widow'.

Bidding to secure the contract now begins. Eldest Hand, *ie* the player to the dealer's left, bids first. A contract is a contract to make so many out of the maximum of ten tricks, and the lowest bid that can be made is a bid of six. The suits rank, in ascending order: Spades, Clubs, Diamonds, Hearts, No Trumps. This, Bridge players will note, is the order in which they ranked at Bridge when that game was first introduced. Thus, the lowest possible bid is Six Spades—a contract to secure six tricks with Spades as trumps. Then come, in ascending order: Six Clubs, Six Diamonds, Six Hearts, Six No Trump; then Seven Spades, and so on up to Seven No Trump; then Eight Spades, etc, the highest possible bid being Ten No Trump.

The reason why it is possible for competitive bidding to be carried so far, *eg* Ten No Trump being bid over Ten of a suit, etc, is that the player who secures the final declaration will have the privilege of exchanging three cards from his hand for the three cards exposed in the Widow. Hence, if the Widow includes the Joker, and perhaps an Ace or so, whoever makes final declaration may find himself in a commanding position.

No player is bound to bid. Thus, the Eldest Hand, if he does not think he can take six tricks, even with the assistance of the Widow, will just pass. The chance of making the opening bid falls now to the next player, and, if he, in his turn, passes, the dealer may bid.

The bidding is competitive. A player who has made a bid may, if he is overcalled, bid again, but once he has passed, his right to continue to bid ceases. If no player makes a bid—which, of course, is quite a likely contingency—the deal is played out at No Trump. No one takes the Widow, and the Eldest Hand leads to the first trick. In this case, scoring is on a very modest basis, each player taking ten points for each trick that he wins.

When there *has* been bidding, whoever makes the highest bid becomes declarer and it will be he who has the lead to the first trick. Before doing so, he takes the three Widow cards into his hand, and then, discarding three cards, places these face downwards on the table. The other players are not entitled to look at his discard. He may, of course, return to the table one or more of the Widow cards, so that, until he plays them, it is a matter of conjecture whether or no he has them in his hand.

Now the other two players are, in a sense, combining against the declarer, since their first objective is to prevent him making his contract. Each of his adversaries, however, is also playing for his own hand, since he scores ten points for each trick that he takes. This consideration, specially towards the end of a game, can produce some very pretty tactics.

If the declarer makes his contract (or any greater number of tricks), he scores points according to the following schedule:

Bids	6 Tricks	7 Tricks	8 Tricks	9 Tricks	10 Tricks
In Spades	40	140	240	340	440
In Clubs	60	160	260	360	460
In Diamonds ..	80	180	280	380	480
In Hearts	100	200	300	400	500
In No Trump ..	120	220	320	420	520

If declarer fails to make his contract, he loses points to the same value. Thus, a player whose contract is, say, Eight Clubs, scores 260 if he takes eight or more of the ten tricks, while he loses 260 if he secures fewer than eight tricks.

A player whose contract is less than Eight Clubs gets extra points if he secures all ten tricks, for, in this case, whatever his contract, ten tricks give him 250 points. This 'bonus' rule, however, does not apply to contracts of Eight Clubs or over, which in any event carry a higher score.

Nothing is scored for making more tricks than one has declared, except in the above case.

The game is 500 up and may be attained in a very few deals (a player bidding Ten Hearts or Ten No Trump can win the game out of hand at the first deal), but is more likely to take quite a number of deals.

If, in the same deal, two players attain 500, the declarer wins the game if he is one of them. If, however, they are both opponents of the declarer, the winner is the player who first passes the five hundred mark.

For scoring purposes, each player should keep a plus and minus account. Thus, suppose one begins by bidding Seven Clubs and failing to make the contract, one puts down minus 160. Now suppose one plays against the declarer and takes four tricks, one scores plus 40, and one's net score is minus 120. And so on until the objective of plus 500 is attained.

Where a deal is played at No Trump, whoever has the Joker must be careful what he does with it. He cannot nominate it as belonging to a suit which he has already renounced in play. Thus, having said that he has no Spades, he can only make his Joker a member of one of the other suits.

It will be inferred from this that the rule in play is the same as in all games of the Whist family. That is to say, every player must follow suit if he can, and, should he revoke, is liable to penalties.

KNAVES: A Good Game for Three

'KNAVES,' like most good card games, admirably combines the elements of skill and chance.

Players cut for deal, the dealer giving seventeen cards to each player. The remaining card is turned face upwards on the table; the suit of this card is the trump suit.

The object of the game is to take as many tricks as possible (players following suit if they can do so, but otherwise discarding or trumping as they like), but penalties are incurred if any trick taken includes a Knave.

Thus the game is not (as is the case with Black Maria) purely a matter of 'avoidances', but, with each trick played (until the last Knave has appeared), a nice balance is struck between the incentive to take a trick and the fear of a disagreeable surprise.

The game is 20 points up. Each trick counts one point, while points for collecting Knaves are deducted as follows:

For taking the Knave of Hearts	4 points
" " " " " Diamonds	3 "
" " " " " Clubs	2 "
" " " " " Spades	1 "

Thus, if a player makes six tricks which include the Knaves of Hearts and Spades, his net score for the deal is one point.

A trick with the Knave of Spades only in it cancels itself out.
A trick may, of course, include two or even three Knaves.

The aggregate score for the deal (unless the card indicating
the trump suit happens to be a Knave) is 17 points for tricks,
minus 10 for the Knaves, or 7 points in all. A very lucky player
could go game in two deals, but, normally speaking, five or
six deals are required.

Obviously an important element in play is getting rid of high
cards, if there is a danger of their taking outstanding Knaves.
And yet, if one gets rid of them too precipitately, one loses one's
chance of the all-important trick points.

Below is set out a hand from play which illustrates the tactical
aspects of this game. Not least of its fascinations is that of
manœuvring to prevent the leading player from getting too far
ahead.

For example, if one player has scored 15 points, a second
one 8 points, and the third 7 points, these two—if they are
sensible—will endeavour to play into one another's hands rather
than concede more points to the leader.

Again, if two players are running neck-and-neck, while the
third is a good way behind them, the last-named will find himself
—for the time being—the object of a good deal of sympathetic
attention. Each of the leaders will endeavour to secure that
such points as he cannot win for himself are the perquisite of
the under-dog!

An Illustrative Deal

The players are Amy, Brenda and Charles. The last-named
deals the cards as under:

To Amy: ♠ K Q 10 6 5 2 ♡ Q 9 5 2 ◇ 9 6 5 ♣ Q J 4 2.
To Brenda: ♠ 8 4 3 ♡ A K 8 ◇ A K Q 10 7 4 3 ♣ 10 9 8 5.
To Charles: ♠ A J 9 7 ♡ J 10 7 6 4 3 ◇ J 8 ♣ A K 7 6 3.

The ◇ 2 is turned up to indicate the trump suit.

The Play

(The card underlined takes the trick. Remember that each
player scores one point for each trick taken, less:

      4 points if he takes the ♡ J
      3   ,,   ,,   ,,   ,,   ,, ◇ J
      2   ,,   ,,   ,,   ,,   ,, ♣ J
      1   ,,   ,,   ,,   ,,   ,, ♠ J)

Trick	Amy	Brenda	Charles
1	♠ 10	♠ 8	♠ A
2	♡ 5	♡ A	♡ 10
3	♣ Q	♣ 9	♣ 7
4	♠ 6	♠ 3	♠ 7
5	♡ 9	♡ K	♡ 6
6	♣ 4	♣ 8	♣ 6
7	♣ 2	♣ 10	♣ 3
8	♣ J	♣ 5	♣ A
9	♡ 2	♡ 8	♡ 7
10	◇ 5	◇ 10	◇ 8
11	◇ 6	◇ 3	◇ J
12	♡ Q	◇ 4	♡ 3
13	◇ 9	◇ 7	♡ J
14	♠ 5	♠ 4	♠ 9
15	♠ 2	◇ Q	♡ 4
16	♠ Q	◇ K	♣ K
17	♠ K	◇ A	♠ J

This deal will show, I trust, that there is room for some very pretty manœuvring. Brenda's plethora of trumps gives her a big pull, so far as the collection of tricks is concerned, but this is counterbalanced by the danger that she may be compelled to take Knaves.

The score on the deal is:

Amy: 2 tricks, less 4 for the ♡ J—minus 2 points.
Brenda: 10 tricks, less 1 for the ♠ J—9 points.
Charles: 5 tricks, less 3 for the ◇ J and 2 for the ♣ J—0 points.
(The total is always 7, unless a Knave is turned up as the trump card.)

Amy played badly—not throwing her ◇ 9 at trick 11. This cost her 4 points, and gave 4 to Brenda.

GAMES FOR FOUR PLAYERS

HASENPFEFFER

HASENPFEFFER IS a little-known, but quite good, game for four players. It will appeal to those who find Bridge or Whist too serious, and yet there is quite an element of skill in it.

A modest pack of twenty-five cards is required: Ace down to the 9 of each suit with a Joker added. If your pack has no Joker, the ♣ 2 or any rejected card will do.

Players begin by cutting for partners, the two cutting the highest cards playing against the two who cut the lowest. The player cutting the highest card then deals three cards at a time to each player, with the last card placed face downwards on the table. This card must not be exposed until a deal has been completed. There may thus be throughout the play an element of doubt as to whether a vital card is in the game or not.

When the deal is completed, calling begins. The player to the dealer's left calls first. He can call any number of tricks from one upwards, this being the number of tricks he hopes (with his partner's assistance) to make.

The next player can overcall him with a greater number of tricks, and similarly with the third and fourth players. The last player to call names one of the suits as trumps and leads to the first trick.

Players must follow suit, failing which they can either trump or discard, and the Joker counts as the highest trump. Next comes the Knave of trumps, followed by the A, K, Q, 10, 9 in sequence. In the three non-trump suits the Knave has its ordinary ranking.

If the declaring side makes its contract they score one point for each trick taken. If they fail, they lose one point in respect of each trick below the number named. Competition to secure a call is thus very keen, since one stands to gain more than one stands to lose, but for that very reason the bidding is frequently pushed beyond the level of safety.

Ten points, unless otherwise agreed, constitute a game.

GREEK HEARTS

BLACK MARIA, already fully described, is a development of the old game of Hearts. Here is another variant.

This game, 'Greek Hearts', is played by four people, though it can be played by five, the dealer in his turn sitting out, as in Solo Whist when five persons play.

The general principle of the game is the same as 'Hearts', namely, that any person taking a trick with a Heart or the Queen of Spades in it is debited with the pip value of the Hearts, all court cards counting 10, the Ace 15 and the Queen of Spades 50. If, however, a player takes all the Hearts and the Queen of Spades, he scores 450—*ie* is paid 150 points by each of the other three players.

At the beginning of the game the stake is agreed upon (sixpence a hundred will be found quite enough by all except hardy gamblers), the cards are dealt and each player passes on three cards to the player on his right. Whereas in 'Slippery Anne' it is advisable to get rid of your high cards, in 'Greek Hearts' you must be very careful. If you pass, let us say, the Ace of Hearts and the Ace, King of Diamonds, you may enable the player to whom you are passing the cards to take all the Hearts in which case you are heavily penalized. Again, you must consider the possibility that you yourself may do the same thing by keeping a long suit.

After the first few tricks it is usually possible to see which, if any, of the players is trying to make a corner in Hearts. Then the object of the rest of the players is to prevent this happening, though this may entail some sacrifice. For example, if a player leads out the Ace of Hearts and then the King of Hearts and you have three Hearts to the Queen, you must not discard the Queen on the Ace, but must keep it and *take* a trick with it. You will lose, perhaps, 20 or 30 points, but you will save over a hundred.

There is another variation of the game played in which each player pays into the pool a forfeit according to the pip value of the Hearts he has taken, and a player who has taken no trick with a Heart in it takes the pool. If there are two players who have taken no Hearts they divide the pool. If a player makes a

corner in Hearts, each other player forfeits 150 points. When
each of the four players has to pay a forfeit the pool is not taken,
but is added to the pool of the next hand, the first winner taking
the lot.

SLOBBERHANNES

THIS is a game that belongs to the same school as 'Black Maria'
and 'Hearts'. I have been trying to find out the origin of its
extraordinary name, but so far without success; probably it is a
corruption from Dutch or German.

Slobberhannes is a game for four, and, though not a partnership game, it could, of course, be adapted for partnership
purposes. Each player plays against the others and a Piquet
pack of thirty-two cards is used, *ie* an ordinary pack from which
the 2's, 3's, 4's, 5's and 6's have been removed. The cards rank as
at Whist (from the Ace downwards) and there is no trump suit.

The players cut, not for deal, but for the privilege of leading
to the first trick. The right to lead goes to the player who cuts
the highest card (Ace is high). The cards are then shuffled and
cut, and are dealt by the player to the right of whoever has
the lead.

The winner of each trick is the player playing the highest
card of the suit led, and he leads to the next one. Players must
follow suit if they can. If they cannot follow to the suit led,
they may discard from any other.

The object of the game is threefold:

1. To avoid taking the first trick.
2. To avoid taking the last trick.
3. To avoid taking a trick containing the Queen of Clubs.

Whoever does any of these three things is penalized one point.
One point is also scored against any player in respect of a revoke.

The most dangerous cards one can hold—apart from the
Queen of Clubs—are the Ace and King of that suit. These one
will normally seek to get rid of at the earliest opportunity.

Possession of the Queen of Clubs is, of course, not always
dangerous. If it is well 'guarded' one can rely on it not being
forced out by the Club leads of other players, and one will,
sooner or later, be able to discard it. As in Black Maria and
in those Misère hands which lend so much interest to Solo, one
wants to conserve as long as possible the low cards which control

the suit. The two illustrative hands which follow demonstrate the game's tactical principles.

ILLUSTRATIVE DEAL I

The players cut for lead. A wins. D (the player on A's right) now deals the cards as under:

```
                    B
              A           C
                    D
```

A: ♠ K   ♡ A 9 7   ◇ 10   ♣ A Q 8
B: ♠ A K 7   ♡ 10   ◇ Q 8   ♣ K 9
C: ♠ 9   ♡ K Q 8   ◇ J 9   ♣ 10 7
D: ♠ Q 10 8   ♡ J   ◇ A K 7   ♣ J

THE PLAY (the card underlined takes the trick)

Trick	A	B	C	D
1	♣ 8	♣ 9	♣ 7	<u>♣ J</u>
2	♠ K	<u>♠ A</u>	♠ 9	♠ 10
3	<u>♡ A</u>	♡ 10	♡ Q	♡ J
4	◇ 10	◇ Q	◇ J	<u>◇ K</u>
5	♣ Q	◇ 8	◇ 9	<u>◇ 7</u>
6	<u>♣ A</u>	♣ K	♣ 10	◇ A
7	♡ 9	♠ J	<u>♡ K</u>	♠ Q
8	♡ 7	♠ 7	<u>♡ 8</u>	♠ 8

PENALTY POINTS

1 against D (first trick).

2 against C (last trick), and trick 5, which contains the ♣ Q.

NOTES

1. A has an easy hand to play. His ♣ 8 is a perfectly safe lead, and conserves his best card, the ♡ 7. Keeping this card enables him to escape the last trick.

2. At trick 5, D has an awkward choice of lead between ◇ 7 and ♠ 8. As the cards lie, the latter lead would have proved fatal, as both the outstanding Spades are in one hand.

ILLUSTRATIVE DEAL II

The players cut for lead as before. B wins, and A deals the cards as under:

B: ♠ 9 ♡ K J 9 ◇ Q J 8 7 ♣ None
C: ♠ K Q 10 8 ♡ None ◇ K 10 ♣ A 10
D: ♠ None ♡ A Q 8 7 ◇ 9 ♣ J 9 8
A: ♠ A J 7 ♡ 10 ◇ A ♣ K Q 7

This deal illustrates a less 'balanced' distribution of the cards.

THE PLAY (the card underlined takes the trick)

Trick	B	C	D	A
1	♠ 9	♠ 8	♡ Q	♠ 7
2	◇ 8	◇ K	◇ 9	◇ A
3	♡ 9	♣ A	♡ A	♡ 10
4	♡ K	♣ 10	♣ 9	♣ K
5	♡ J	♠ 10	♣ J	♠ J
6	◇ Q	◇ 10	♣ 8	♣ 7
7	◇ J	♠ K	♡ 8	♠ A
8	◇ 7	♠ Q	♡ 7	♣ Q

PENALTY POINTS

1 against B (first trick).
2 against D (last trick), which includes the ♣ Q.

An amusing deal, which illustrates both good and bad play.
B's choice of the ♠ 9, as his opening lead, is unfortunate.
D makes a fatal mistake in discarding the ♡ Q instead of a
Club. Result, at trick 6 A puts him in with the ♣ 8, and his
carefully preserved low Hearts are useless.

GAMES FOR FROM THREE TO SEVEN PLAYERS

BRAG

Brag is a card game which is interesting for two reasons: in the first place it is very old; and in the second place, it is the ancestor of one of the greatest of card games—Poker.

Its essential principles are the same as those of Poker. For instance: 1. The best hand (as determined by certain arbitrary rules) wins; 2. Players can bet on the respective merits of their hands; and 3. If the player making the best bet is not 'seen' the hands are not exposed. Thus there can be, as in Poker, an element of bluff. Nevertheless, it is a far cry from Brag to Poker, as I shall explain.

Brag has various forms. The ordinary game is a three-card game played with a full pack. Three cards are known as 'braggers', *ie* they are, in effect, Jokers. These are the Ace of Diamonds, the Knave of Clubs and the Nine of Diamonds. Each of these can represent any other card.

To begin the game the dealer puts up any stake to the agreed limit. (This, incidentally, is one of those games which, unless played for stakes, are pointless.) Now three cards are dealt to each player, and each in turn must put up at least as much as the dealer's stake or else (as in Poker) retire. Successive players may raise the stake in accordance with whatever scheme has been agreed, and any player betting an amount which no one else is prepared to meet takes the pool without exposing his cards. Any player, however, who is 'called' or 'seen' by another must show his hand, and the best hand takes the pool.

The following is the order of value of the hands:

1. Three natural Aces (in a three-Ace hand, of course, the Ace of Diamonds ranks as a natural Ace).

2. Three Aces including one or more 'braggers', *eg* the Knave of Clubs and 9 of Diamonds, with any one Ace.

3. Three natural Kings.

4. Three Kings, including one or more 'braggers', and so on, down to three 2's.

After 3's come Pairs from Aces downwards, a natural pair taking precedence over a pair made with the aid of a 'bragger'.

If two players have similar pairs, the player with the higher third card wins. Lastly, if no player has a pair, the best single card.

If two players have absolutely equal cards, preference goes to the elder hand, *ie* to the player who is the first of these two to stake.

In the second form of the game, called Three Stake Brag, three separate and individual stakes are made in respect of each deal. In this variety of Brag, the third card is turned face upwards and the first stake goes—a matter of pure chance—to the holder of the best card. The second stake goes to the holder of the best hand, this being determined as above; this second stake is liable to increase in just the same manner as in single stake Brag.

The third stake goes to the player whose cards most nearly total 31; Aces count as 11 and each court card counts 10. Thus, one Ace and two court cards would be exactly 31 and would either take or divide the third stake. A player with less than 31 may, if he wishes, draw another card, as in Vingt-et-Un. If, however, after drawing this card, his total exceeds 31, his hand is dead.

Before any extra cards are drawn, all hands are exposed so that each player knows what he is up against.

THE FOUR KNAVES

ANY number from four to seven can play. If, however, there are seven players, the dealer deals cards to the other six but misses his own turn.

'The Four Knaves' is played with a Piquet pack—*ie* a pack of thirty-two cards, the 2's, 3's, 4's, 5's and 6's having been removed.

The cards are dealt singly, beginning with the player on the dealer's left. Thus, if there are four players, each will have eight cards; if there are five, two players will have seven each and the other three six each; if there are six players, two will have six each and the other four, five each. This discrepancy does not matter; in fact, it makes the game rather amusing.

When the cards have been dealt (face downwards) the players take up their hands, and whoever is on the dealer's left leads to the first trick. There are no trumps and everyone must follow suit if he can. The trick is won by whoever plays the highest card of the suit led, and the winner of it leads to the next trick.

The object of the game is to avoid taking a trick with a Knave in it. A player who 'wins' a Knave must place it face upwards on the table in front of him.

The Knaves of Hearts, Diamonds and Clubs each count one point against the player who 'wins' them, while the Knave of Spades counts two points against him.

One player keeps the score, and as soon as anyone has lost ten points he is out of the game; thus, if the number of players were seven, to begin with, it is now reduced to six. This goes on until there is only one player left who has not an adverse score of ten. He is the final winner, and if stakes are being played for he collects the pool.

Skill is required (a) in discarding intelligently when one is unable to follow suit; (b) in deciding whether or not to take a trick if one has the option; and (c) having taken a trick, in making the right lead to the next one.

Beginners will always throw their Knaves at the first opportunity, but very often it is much more important to get rid of high cards which may subsequently take tricks than to get rid of Knaves immediately.

HITTING THE MOON

THE following excellent game is a variety of 'Hearts', which will particularly interest those who play 'Black Maria'.

The objects are as usual:

(a) To take no Hearts in tricks (—one point each).

(b) To avoid the ♠ Q (—13 points);

(c) To take *all* Hearts and the ♠ Q, in which case all players *bar the one concerned* score —26.

One has therefore the Misère element and the take-all game going on at the same time, and the passing becomes very involved through the necessity of a safety element. Thus one seldom passes high Hearts, and the usual precaution is for everyone to pass a medium Heart to stop one's neighbour trying to 'hit the moon'.

The passing involves three cards, and takes place to left and right alternately.

Regarding odd cards after the deal (for, say, three or five players) these form a pool added to the first trick, and thus anyone trying to 'hit the moon' should make sure of taking the dummy, as it may contain a penalty card.

When it is suspected that someone is trying for the 'moon' (usually in every third deal or so), each one's object is to 'plant' a heart with two people so as to avoid it, and it usually only becomes evident halfway through that one person is trying for all penalty cards.

There is thus an amusing element of mystery in the deal. Nobody knows what anybody else is 'up to' until an informative trick lays bare the secret, usually too late.

The necessary qualifications for 'hitting the moon' are:

(a) A good hand improved by passing low and receiving high;

(b) Preferably high Hearts to draw all the outstanding Hearts, but in many cases the lead of a singleton $\heartsuit$ 10 (say) will be left alone with a smile, as an attempt at bluff to avoid -4 points or so, as a penalty for a normal Heart trick.

(c) Better players, of course, readily take the trick so as to make sure, but it involves a calculation of whether -5 paid to four or five or more people—(see scoring)—compensates well for a possible -26 paid to one only.

(d) Obviously, one can 'hit the moon' also with no Hearts, provided one can win every trick with Hearts in it at the start, and after a certain point lead out established winners right to the last trick.

This establishment of winners is easier than would appear. A suit such as $\clubsuit$ A J 9 3 may lose but one trick, eg lead 3 and K Q 10 may fall, as the holders are only too glad to be rid of them early in the deal, before they know what it is all about.

But, of course, if the receiver of the 'Moon-man's' three cards (at the start) holds the guarded $\clubsuit$ Q, he will not throw it light-heartedly away on the first trick, as he knows what is going on. The absence of the $\clubsuit$ Q early in the play may then cause others to suspect and to trace the culprit.

Finally, regarding scoring, take the following table:

A	B	C	D	E
0	-26	-26	-26	-26

(A 'hits the moon'.)

-25	-27	-26	-26	-26

(B stops A 'hitting the moon', by taking one Heart. A's high cards make his case hopeless after this and he gets stung for -25.)

-38	-35	-31	-26	-26

(A takes the Queen, B takes eight Heart cards, and C five ditto) and so on.

Now at the end, say, 200 up, the scores stand:

A	B	C	D	E
−140	−224	−97	−185	−108

B pays D the difference.

   ,, ,, A ,,   ,,

   ,, ,, E ,,   ,,

   ,, ,, C ,,   ,,

(D pays all those lower than himself, A ditto, and so on down to the player E, who receives three payments, and pays but one.)

NAPOLEON (or 'NAP')

THIS ever-popular game might be described as a poor relation of the Whist family. Nevertheless, it is not to be despised. There is quite enough play in it to keep the intelligence alert.

Nap is played with a full pack of fifty-two cards and any number from two to seven, or even eight, can take part. With these large numbers, however, the game becomes somewhat dull, as too high a proportion of the hands will be thrown in. I suggest, therefore, that six is the maximum number of players for a reasonably interesting game, and that the ideal numbers are four or five.

The game is simplicity itself. Before each deal, the pack is shuffled and cut and the dealer (each player dealing in turn) deals out five cards, face downwards, one at a time to each player. The players then look at their hands and each in turn (beginning with the Eldest Hand or player on the dealer's left) has the opportunity of making a call.

The calls are, in ascending order: Two, Three, Misère, Four, Nap, and (where Nap has been called) Wellington.

The call of Two is, in effect, an undertaking to take two of the five tricks; Three, which overcalls Two, is an undertaking to take three tricks; Four is an undertaking to take four tricks, and Nap is an undertaking to take all the tricks.

Wellington is equally an undertaking to take all the tricks and, as stated, can only be offered where there is already one five-trick candidate in the field.

Over Wellington there is no further call; should there be

three players, each of whom thinks he can take all the tricks, the third one must suffer in silence.

Misère is, as in Solo, an undertaking to take no tricks.

The player who makes the highest call leads to the first trick as soon as the other players have passed. The suit of the card which he first leads is the trump suit and the rules of play are the rules which obtain at Whist, *ie:*

1. The trick is taken by the highest card of the suit led, the Ace for this purpose ranking high.

2. The players must follow suit if they can; if they cannot follow suit they may either discard or trump.

3. The winner of a trick leads to the next one.

At Misère there is no trump suit, but otherwise the rules of play are the same.

Here is a specimen deal. Suppose there are five players and East has dealt the cards as follows:

A: ♥ J 6 4 ♦ A ♣ 3.
B: ♦ K J 10 9 ♣ A.
C: ♠ 5 ♥ 10 7 3 2.
D: ♠ A K Q 9 4.
E: ♥ A K Q 9 8.

The calling might well be:

A: (Eldest Hand): Pass.
B: Three.
C: Misère.
D: Nap.
E: Wellington.

These are all reasonable calls, having regard to the probable distribution of the other cards of each suit.

Nap is usually played for stakes, the caller paying or receiving from each of the other players. Thus, suppose the game is 'Penny Nap', a player calling three receives 3p from each player if he makes three (or more) tricks, and pays 3p to each player if he fails. If the call is Two, he pays or receives 2p; if Misère, 3p; or Four, 4p.

If, however, the call is Nap, the usual arrangement is that he pays 6p to each player if he fails but receives 10p from each if he succeeds.

The Wellington stakes, as patriotism demands, are double the stakes at Napoleon.

CHASE THE ACE

'CHASE THE ACE' is a simple little game, requiring no skill. Any number of players can participate.

Each player is given three counters, representing that number of lives. When he has lost his three counters he is out. The winner of the game is, of course, the last survivor.

The dealer deals one card to each player. The object of the game is to avoid being the holder of the lowest card, Ace counting lowest. If two players, at the finish, hold cards of the same denomination, *eg* if two players each hold a 2, Clubs rank lower than Diamonds, Diamonds than Hearts, and Hearts than Spades. Thus the King of Spades is the highest card and the Ace of Clubs is the lowest.

The player on the left of the dealer first looks at his card. If it is a King, he places it face upwards on the table, otherwise he either says 'stand' or exchanges the card with the player to his left. Other players, in turn, now do the same thing, so that a low card is passed round the table until it reaches some player who has given one even lower in exchange. (He will, naturally, say 'stand'.)

Finally, it comes to the dealer's turn. The dealer exposes his card, and has the option either of 'standing' or of cutting a card from the pack in front of him.

Now all the cards are shown, and whoever has the lowest hands in a counter. The deal then passes to the player on the original dealer's left.

VINGT-ET-UN (PONTOON)

THIS is quite an amusing round game and one which anyone can learn in a few minutes.

One pack of cards is required and any reasonable number can play. If, however, more than seven are in the game, I recommend two packs of cards shuffled together.

To begin with, one player is chosen as Banker. Each player should draw a card and whoever draws the highest takes the Bank.

Vingt-et-Un is played for stakes—not necessarily, of course, for money—and therefore each player should be provided with counters. If counters are not available, matches will do just as well. The cards having been duly shuffled and cut, the Banker deals one, face downwards, to each player, himself included. The players now look at their cards and each stakes one or more counters up to the permissible limit on the card which he has been dealt.

Now the object of the game is to secure a combination of two or more cards totalling 21, the Ace for this purpose counting as either 1 or 11, and each Court card as 10. Other cards carry their pip value. Hence the stake originally laid on one's card will depend upon one's chances of making 21, or of getting nearer to 21 than the Banker.

If the card is an Ace, one will stake the maximum, since any Court card or 10 will give one the best possible combination; if the card is a Court card or 10, one should stake, not the maximum, but something better than the minimum; 2's or 3's, for reasons which will appear in a moment, are also worth a better than minimum stake. On other cards, place the minimum.

The players having staked, the Dealer looks at his card, and, if he likes, can double the stakes laid. He will invariably do this if he has an Ace and, on balance, it will pay him to do it if he holds a Court card or a 2. The other players, in staking, will bear in mind the possibility of their being doubled by the Dealer.

Now the Dealer deals a second card, face downwards, to each player and to himself. If this second card gives any player a 'Natural' (*ie* an Ace and a Court card or a 10), the player at once exposes his cards and is entitled to be paid by the Dealer three times the amount of his stake, unless the Dealer also has a 'Natural'. A player who has a 'Natural', in addition to receiving three times his stake, takes the Bank for the next deal. If more players than one have 'Naturals', the Bank is taken by the one nearest to the Dealer's left.

Any 'Natural' or 'Naturals' having been turned up, the Dealer asks each player in turn, beginning with the player on his left, whether he wants any more cards. The player can either buy cards or can have them 'twisted'. A card which he buys (giving as many counters as he likes for it up to his original stake) is dealt face downwards and is only seen by the recipient; a card twisted is turned face upwards. As soon as a player reaches 21, or as soon as the total of his cards is so near to 21 that he does not like risking taking another one, he says 'stand'. If a card dealt him makes his total over 21, he exposes his hand and automatically forfeits his stake.

SOME ILLUSTRATIVE DEALS

A has been dealt a 9 and an 8; without exposing his cards, he says 'stand'.

B has a 9 and a 5; he says 'twist me one'. His score of 14 is unlikely to win and there are seven chances to six that one more card will still leave him in the game. The Dealer turns up a card for him; it is a 9, and he is out.

C has an Ace and a 3. He has originally staked two counters and he now says 'buy one for two'. This is another Ace, and C, who has prospects of getting five cards which total less than 21 (this is a very good combination to have), at once puts up two more counters for another card. Now he gets a 9, making his total 14 for the four cards, and he says 'twist me one'. He receives a 6 and has five cards totalling 20, which entitles him to receive double the total amount he has staked.

\ Note that a player who has bought one or more cards can have one or more cards twisted, but a player who has had a card twisted, cannot, after that, buy cards.

When each of the players has had the cards he wants (those who are 'busted' having disclosed the fact), the Dealer turns up his two cards. He can now deal himself as many more cards as he likes. His procedure will depend, in part, on what there is out against him. Thus, the Dealer, if he suspects that there are several good scores against him, must go all out to obtain 20 or 21; otherwise he will be content to stand at 17 or 18.

Settlement is now made along the following lines:

1. Players who have gone 'bust', *ie* exceeded 21, will have forfeited their stakes automatically.

2. If the Dealer has a 'Natural' he receives (a) single stake from any player who has a 'Natural'; (b) double stakes from any player who has 21 or 'five and under'; (c) three times their stake from each of the other players.

3. If the Dealer has 21 or 'five and under', he receives a single stake from any player similarly placed, and double stakes from each of the others.

4. Otherwise, the Dealer pays double stakes to any player having 21 or 'five and under' and single stakes to any player whose total is better than his own. Thus, if his total is 18, he says, in standing on this, 'pay 19'. He receives single stakes from

players whose total is inferior to his own. A player who has the same score as the Dealer also has to pay, thus the Bank holds a considerable advantage.

The following variant, that of 'splitting' cards, is optional. Beginners may find it complicated, but I think it adds to the interest of the game.

If the two cards first dealt to a player are the same, *ie* two Aces, two 7's, etc, he can say 'split', staking the same amount on each card. A second card is then dealt, face downwards, in respect of each. The player is now the owner of two independent hands, each of which is separately dealt with on the lines set out above.

The original Banker holds the Bank until someone else produces a 'Natural'. Then, unless the Banker also has a 'Natural', the Bank passes. A player who does not wish to take the Bank may put it up for auction, but unless one is very short of counters, the Bank should not be rejected. The odds are heavily in favour of the Banker.

The Bank does not pass on a 'split' natural.

Two Deals from Actual Play

1. There were seven players, A being the Banker. The maximum stake on any one card was three chips. The cards having been duly shuffled and cut, A dealt one card to each player as follows:

B	C	D	E	F	G
7	4	6	6	2	A
(1)	(1)	(1)	(1)	(2)	(3)

(In brackets is shown the number of chips staked by each player.)

A then dealt a 2 to himself and announced that the stakes were doubled. He now deals a second card to each player as follows:

B	C	D	E	F	G
4	2	4	8	Q	7

A dealt a Knave to himself and then asked each of the players what further cards were required.

B bought one for two chips and received a 3; he now said 'twist one', received another 3 and said 'stand'. B's total was 17 with four chips staked.

C bought a third card for two chips, receiving a 3, and a fourth card for two chips, receiving a 10. He stood at 19 with six chips staked.

D bought a third card for two chips, receiving a King. He stood at 20 with four chips staked.

E (his two cards totalling 14) said 'twist one'; he received a 4 and stood at 18 with a stake of two chips.

F (his two cards totalling 12) said 'twist one'; he received a 10 and forfeited his four chips, being over 21.

G (holding a 7 and an Ace and with six chips already staked) said 'twist one'; he received a 9 and stood at 17.

The Dealer, of course, was not aware what the totals of B, C, D, E and G were.

The Dealer now exposed his own hand—a 2 and a Knave. He dealt himself another card, a King, and thus had to pay a single stake to everyone except F. On balance, therefore, the deal cost him 18 chips.

2. This time A dealt the following cards (the staked chips being shown in brackets as before):

B	C	D	E	F	G
A	4	2	3	10	6
(3)	(1)	(2)	(2)	(2)	(1)

A dealt himself a Queen and doubled the stakes.

A second card was now dealt to each player, as under:

B	C	D	E	F	G
5	Q	8	4	2	5

To himself the Dealer dealt a 9.

Cards were taken as follows:

B bought one for two and received a Knave and said 'stand'.

C said 'twist one', received a Knave, and forfeited his stake.

D bought one for two, received an Ace and said 'stand'. D, with 2, 8 and Ace, had made 21.

E bought one for two, received a Queen and said 'stand'.

F said 'twist one', and received a 3; he then said 'twist another', and received an 8 and had to forfeit his stake.

G (holding 11) bought one for two, received a 7 and said 'stand'.

A now exposed his hand (Q 9) and said 'pay 20'.

In addition to the two chips he had received from C, and the four chips from F, he collected eight chips from B, six chips from E and four chips from G. He thus received twenty-four chips, less twelve paid out to D who, having scored 21, was entitled to double his stake. Thus A gained twelve chips on the deal.

CATCH-THE-TEN

A good round game is 'Catch-the-Ten', or Scotch Whist.

Any number from two to eight can play. Normally the pack used is a shortened pack of thirty-six cards, the 2's, 3's, 4's and 5's being removed.

If there are eight players, all four 6's are also removed (reducing the pack to one of thirty-two cards), and if there are five or seven players the 6 of Spades is removed, thus producing a thirty-five card pack.

Normally each player plays against each, but partnerships are permissible; thus, where six are playing, there may be either two partnerships of three (seated alternately) or three partnerships of two; and similarly, where eight are playing, there may be four competing pairs, or two 'sides' of four each.

The cards are dealt in a somewhat peculiar way. Where there are two players, each will have eighteen cards, and the dealer, dealing one card only at a time, deals three packets of six cards each to each player. Each of these packets of six is a separate hand, and they are played out independently; a player does not look at his second and third hands until the first has been played out. Where there are three players there are similarly two separate hands of six cards dealt to each. With more than three players, there is only one hand consisting of nine, seven, six, five or four cards, according to the number played.

The last card is turned up, as at Whist, to represent the trump suit.

The order in which the cards rank is also as in Whist (*ie* the Ace is the highest card), except that, in the trump suit, the Knave is the highest card.

The object of the game is to take as many tricks as possible, but particularly to take tricks which contain certain *scoring cards*. The *scoring cards* are the honour cards of the trump suit. The Knave of trumps scores 11 points (which must go, of course, to the player to whom this card is originally dealt), the 10 of trumps scores 10 points (but the 10 can be captured by the Knave, Ace, King or Queen), and the Ace, King, Queen of trumps score respectively 4, 3 and 2 points.

Thus there are always 30 points to be distributed in respect of these five cards. In addition, the number of tricks taken by each player (or side) is counted at the end of a hand and each player (or side) scores one point for every card taken in excess of those originally dealt. Thus if, in a two-handed game, a player at the end of the first hand has taken four tricks, he has two cards in excess of the six with which he started and his score for cards is two points. Or, if there are seven players and one of them collects three tricks, he has twenty-one cards where he only started with five, and his score for cards is sixteen.

It will be seen that this game, while it has the merit of simplicity, involves a large element of luck. On the other hand, there is a good deal of interest in the play of the trump cards, particularly in manœuvring to 'catch the Ten', and there is also scope for considerable skill—particularly in the partnership game—in playing for tricks when the scoring cards are exhausted. Players must, of course, follow suit as at Whist.

The score should be checked at the end of every hand and recorded on a 'plus and minus' basis.

NEWMARKET

THIS is one of the easier round games, yet it has a definite skill element; players who have concentration and card sense will always show up well at it. An example deal will be easier to follow than any amount of explanation.

Let us suppose there are five players: Alice (dealer), Basil, Claire, David and Ernest. Before the game begins an agreed number of counters (say, 50) are given to each player.

Four 'luxury' cards from a different pack are set out on the table before the cards are dealt. The luxuries consist of one Ace, one King, one Queen and one Knave, each from a different suit. (It does not matter which card is taken from which suit.)

On these cards each player stakes, say, six counters. Players can stake as they wish and this part of the game is, of course, a pure gamble. Thus, Alice may put all six counters on the ♠ A; Basil may put two each on the ♡ K, ♣ Q and ◇ J, and so on. There is no possible means of telling what will prove the most profitable investment.

When all have staked, Alice deals the cards, beginning with the player to her left. She deals one card (face downwards) to each player in rotation, and one to a dummy hand. Cards left over (four in this case) are given to the dummy.

Now the players look at their cards and the play of the hand begins. We will suppose the cards dealt are:

To Basil: ♠ 3   ♡ 9 6 3   ◇ 9 8   ♣ 10 3.
To Claire: ♠ Q J 7   ♡ 10   ◇ None   ♣ Q J 7 5.
To David: ♠ K 6   ♡ 5   ◇ A K J   ♣ K 4.
To Ernest: ♠ 8 2   ♡ A 4   ◇ 10 5 2   ♣ 2.
To Alice: ♠ A 9 5   ♡ Q J   ◇ 6 3   ♣ 9.
To Dummy: ♠ 10 4   ♡ K 8 7 2   ◇ Q 7 4   ♣ A 8 6.

Dummy's hand remains face downwards.

The object of the game, which each player will have in mind, is to exhaust his cards as quickly as possible. As soon as a player is 'out', the deal is over. But each player also aims at playing any luxury-card in his hand (*eg* Alice's first objective will be to play the ♠ A) because if she can do so she takes the counters that have been staked on it. Thus each player has also a third objective: to get out, or to help some other player out, before a well-backed luxury-card can be played.

The rule of play is simple. The player to the dealer's left leads off. He may select any suit, but must lead the *lowest* card of it. Naturally, if he has a luxury-card, that is the suit he will select; if not, he uses his judgment.

As soon as a card is played, the next card above it must be played by whoever holds it. If, however, a card is in the dummy hand, the last-played card is a 'stop'. After a 'stop', a player plays again, and may, if he wishes, change the suit. Clearly, to be successful, a player must hold 'stop' cards.

Now let us see how all this works out:

Basil leads off with ♡ 3.

Ernest plays ♡ 4; David ♡ 5; Basil ♡ 6 (stop).

Basil now plays ♣ 3; David ♣ 4; Claire ♣ 5 (stop).

Claire (holding ♣ Q) now plays ♣ 7 (stop). Claire now plays ♣ J, ♣ Q, and collects the stakes on the ♣ Q. David plays ♣ K (stop).

David plays ◇ J (a luxury) and collects the stakes on this card. The ◇ J is a stop. Now David plays ◇ K, ◇ A.

Next, David plays ♠ 6; Clair ♠ 7; Ernest ♠ 8; Alice ♠ 9 (stop). Alice plays ♠ 5 (stop), followed by ♠ A (a luxury), on which she collects the stakes.

Now Alice plays ♡ J ♡ Q (stop). Next, ♣ 9; Basil plays ♣ 10 (stop). Basil plays ♡ 9 and Clair ♡ 10 (stop). Claire now plays ♠ J ♠ Q, and is out.

The other players now pay one counter to Claire in respect of each card left in their hands. Thus:

    Basil pays 3 counters.
    David pays 1 counter.
    Ernest pays 6 counters.
    Alice pays 2 counters.

So Claire collects 12 counters in all.

Now the deal passes to Basil, and each player stakes as above.

Note that stakes on the ♡ K (held by dummy) are unclaimed. These stakes remain. Often a 'luxury' is not played for several deals in succession, and quite a large stake accumulates. It is this that makes Newmarket a very exciting game.

AN ILLUSTRATIVE DEAL

The players are seven—Arthur, Betty, Clare, Donald, Enid, Frank and George.

George (dealer) takes an Ace, a King, a Queen and a Knave from another pack, and lays them face upwards in the centre of the table, as shown in the diagram.

(Any Ace, King, Queen, Knave will do, but each should be of a different suit.)

Each player proceeds to stake an agreed number of chips—say, 10. Chips are staked as under:

	♠ A	♡ K	◇ Q	♣ J	Total
Arthur	—	10	—	—	10
Betty	5	—	5	—	10
Clare	4	3	—	3	10
Donald	—	—	10	—	10
Enid	5	2	2	1	10
Frank	—	10	—	—	10
George	—	5	2	3	10
Total	14	30	19	7	70

As the above table shows, a player can either 'plump' for one card, or can distribute his favours among one or more of them.

George now deals the cards as under:

Arthur: ♠ 5 3 ♡ A 4 ◇ 8 ♣ J 9.
Betty: ♠ A 4 ♡ 7 ◇ A ♣ 10 3 2.
Clare: ♠ Q J ♡ 5 ◇ K ♣ 8 5 4.
Donald: ♠ K ♡ 6 ◇ 10 9 7 ♣ K 7.
Enid: ♠ 10 2 ♡ K 8 3 ◇ 3 ♣ None.
Frank: ♠ 6 ♡ None ◇ 6 4 2 ♣ A Q.
George: ♠ 8 ♡ J 9 2 ◇ J 5 ♣ None.
One dummy hand: ♠ 9 7 ♡ Q 10 ◇ Q ♣ 6.

NOTE.—1. The pack is dealt out, and four players get extra cards. This is not unfair, as the deal passes each time.

2. The cards are dealt face downwards; when all are dealt, each player picks up his hand.

3. The dummy hand is not exposed.

THE PLAY

Arthur leads ♣ 9.

Betty plays ♣ 10.

Arthur plays ♣ J and secures the 7 chips staked on it.

Frank plays ♣ Q, Donald ♣ K, Frank ♣ A.

Frank now leads ◇ 2.

The Diamonds are now played, by those holding them, as far as the ◇ J, which is a 'stop', as the ◇ Q is in the dummy hand.

George, who played the ◇ J, leads next the ♡ 2.

The Hearts are now played as far as the ♡ 9, which is a 'stop'. George next plays the ♠ 8—another 'stop'. And now George plays the ♡ J, and is out.

Players with cards remaining in their hand now give George one chip in respect of each card remaining. Thus he gets:

            3 chips from Arthur
            6   „   „   Betty
            6   „   „   Clare
            2   „   „   Donald
            3   „   „   Enid
            1   „   „   Frank
            —
            21 chips in all.

The chips staked on the ♠ A and ♡ K remain there, as do the chips on dummy hand's ◇ Q. The deal passes to Arthur, and each player stakes ten chips more.

HOGGENHEIMER

FOR a carefree after-dinner game requiring very little skill and hardly any knowledge of cards, there is nothing better than Hoggenheimer. It is, of course, a pure gamble, but it can be played for any stakes from nuts or counters upwards.

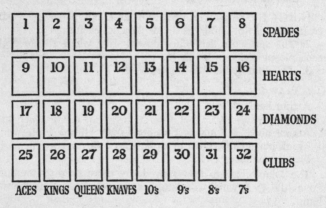

The game is played with a Piquet pack (the thirty-two cards from Ace to 7 inclusive) and one other card—say, the 2 of Clubs —in addition. Each player in turn acts as banker.

To begin with, the cards are thoroughly shuffled and are then cut by the player on the banker's left. He now deals out thirty-two cards, face downwards, in four rows of eight.

The thirty-third card is placed face downwards on the table.

The banker now explains his dispositions to any who have not played Hoggenheimer before. The game consists in turning up cards successively, each card, as it is turned up, occupying its appropriate space.

Where card No 1 is will go the Ace of Spades; where 2, the King of Spades; and so on down to the 7. The Ace of Hearts is at 9, directly under the Ace of Spades.

What players can do is to back single cards, groups of two

or four cards, complete columns, or complete rows, to turn up.
Thus a player can back the Knave of Diamonds (No 20), and,
if it turns up, will receive what he has staked. Or he can back,
say, the Knave and 10 of Diamonds (receiving, if successful,
twice his stake); or the Knave, 10 of Diamonds and Knave, 10
of Clubs (receiving four times his stake); or all the Knaves
(receiving four times his stake), or all the Diamonds (receiving
eight times his stake). The banker sets a limit to the amount
that each player can stake.

When all have staked—different coloured counters are
useful—the excitement begins. The banker turns up his thirty-
third card. If it is the ♣ 2 he takes all the stakes (amid groans
of disappointment) and the bank passes to the next player.
But this will not happen often.

Suppose, then, that he turns up the ♡ 8. He places this
card in its appropriate place (No 15) and turns up the card
occupying that position. Suppose that is the ♣ J. It is duly
placed face upwards at 28, and *that* card is turned up. And so it
goes on until the ♣ 2 is reached, when the deal automatically
terminates.

The Banker now collects the stakes from cards which have
not turned up; also stakes placed on rows, columns, etc, which
have not materialized *in toto*. He pays out, according to the
scale set out above, to those who have been successful.

Sometimes the ♣ 2 is the very last card to show up, and then
the banker will pay everybody. The excitement of those who
have backed columns or rows, and who see their favourites
gradually coming home—only, perhaps, to be thwarted at the
eleventh hour—is one of the most amusing features of the game.

PARTY GAMES

CHEAT

CHEAT IS one of the most lighthearted of card games and provides grand entertainment for children of all ages.

It should be played with two packs well shuffled together (or three packs if there are more than eight at the table). Any number of people can take part.

The cards having been dealt out as far as they will go, the game begins.

The player to the dealer's left leads off. He takes any card he likes from his hand and places it face downwards on the table, at the same time naming its denomination. Thus, if his card is a 5, he says 'Five'. He does not, however, show it. The next player must now play a 6 on top of the 5, again face downwards; if he has no 6 (as, of course, may well be the case), he must still play a card, at the same time saying 'Six', and must do his best to look as if there is nothing wrong.

So the play goes on. Seven follows 6, 8 follows 7, and so on. When a King is reached, the next card declared is 'Ace'. Thus, the pile of cards in the centre of the table goes on continuously accruing.

Where, then, does the fun come in? In this way. Any player having played his card may be challenged by anyone else at the table. The challenge takes the form of a shout of 'Cheat', and quite likely more than one player will challenge, especially towards the end of the game, so it is advisable to appoint someone as umpire. Naturally, if the game is a family affair, Father will act in this capacity, and perhaps will play as well. But, normally, it is best to let each player, in turn, stand out for one round so that all his energies can be devoted to umpiring.

As soon as 'Cheat' is called, the card last played must be turned up. If the challenge is successful (*ie* if the player actually has cheated) he has to take into his hand all the cards on the table. If, however, the challenge is unsuccessful, the player who has first called 'Cheat' is awarded the stock of cards. And it is from this point of view that an umpire's services are required.

After a challenge, the player next to the one challenged plays a card to the table. He can play any card he likes.

It is legitimate to cheat not only by playing a card not of the denomination named, but also by playing two cards at once if one can get away with it. But here, again, of course, one is liable to be challenged.

The game is full of interesting possibilities. It is quite an art looking innocent when, in fact, one is guilty, and, equally, looking guilty, when, in fact, one is innocent. Expert players, moreover, will calculate what cards will be required from them next time round and will take care to conserve these, cheating for preference in the earlier stages of the game when they are less likely to be challenged.

The player who first gets rid of all his cards is the winner; but as it is normally difficult to do this without cheating, a deal may go on for quite a long time.

ROCKAWAY

ROCKAWAY is an excellent party game; it belongs to the same school as Rummy, but is even simpler. It can be learnt in five minutes and is thus eminently suitable for those who are unfamiliar with cards, while there is just enough play in it to give some scope to those who take their card games seriously.

Any number can play. Take two packs of cards and shuffle them well together. Now the dealer deals seven cards (face downwards) to each player and one card (face upwards) to the centre of the table. This is known as the 'kitty' card. As each player discards, he places his discard, face upwards, on to the 'kitty' card, and the card so played becomes the 'kitty' in its turn.

The object of the game is to get rid of all one's cards as quickly as possible. To this end, each player may discard either: (1) a card of the same denomination as the 'kitty' card; (2) a card of the same suit; or (3) any Ace, all Aces being Jokers. Thus, if the 'kitty' card is the ♣ 10, a player can discard: (1) any 10; (2) any Club; or (3) any Ace. If the 'kitty' card is the ◇ Ace, the only cards that can be discarded are Aces or Diamonds.

Where the element of skill comes in is in watching the denominations and suits of cards discarded and keeping those which are more likely to be useful in subsequent rounds. For example, one would never discard an Ace if some other choice is available, nor should one normally choose a suit discard in preference to that of a denomination.

Cards not dealt to players originally are placed, face downwards, in the centre of the table and form the stock. A player who cannot discard when his turn comes to him must draw a card from the stock and must continue to draw cards until he can discard.

When the stock is exhausted the drawing of cards ceases and the players play out their hands, merely missing their turn if they have no discard to make.

As soon as one player has played all his cards, the others put their hands down, face upwards, and the pip values of the cards that remain are totalled. These are scored against the various players as in Rummy. An Ace counts 15 against a player, Court cards 10, and each other card its pip value. A game should consist of an agreed number of deals.

Here is an illustrative deal at Rockaway which should make the game quite clear. The seven players are: Aline, Bob, Clara, Dick, Eva, Fred and Gracie. Cards are dealt as under:

Aline: ♠ A J ♡ K 5 2 ◇ 3 ♣ A.
Bob: ♠ Q 10 5 ♡ 7 ◇ 7 6 4 ♣ None.
Clara: ♠ 6 ♡ Q 4 ◇ A 10 ♣ 10 4.
Dick: ♠ K 7 ♡ None ◇ 2 ♣ Q 5 4 2.
Eva: ♠ 4 2 ♡ Q 10 ◇ None ♣ 9 3 2.
Fred: ♠ A 8 ♡ A 4 3 ◇ 4 ♣ J.
Gracie: ♠ None ♡ 10 8 ◇ 9 ♣ A 8 7 6.

The 'kitty' card is the ◇ 6; it is Aline's initial lead.

The play went:

Aline	Bob	Clara	Dick	Eva	Fred	Gracie
◇ 3	◇ 7	◇ 10	◇ 2	♣ 2	♣ J	♣ 8
♠ A	♠ Q	♡ Q	♣ Q	♡ Q	♡ 4	♡ 10
♡ K	♡ 7	♡ 4	♣ 4	♣ 9	♡ A	♡ 8
♡ 5	♠ 5	♠ 6	♠ K	♠ 4	♠ 8	♣ A
♣ A	Cannot go.	♣ 10	♣ 5	♣ 3	♠ A	Cannot go.
	Draws and plays ♣ 8					Draws, in succession, ♡ 6, ◇ K, ♡ J, ◇ 8, ◇ 5, ♡ 9. Draws and plays ♠ 3.

♠ J   ♠ 10   ◇ A Cannot go. ♡ 10   ♡ 3   ♡ J
                   Draws and
                   plays ◇ 10
♡ 2
Out

Pip values of remaining cards are now added up and scored against the various players:

Aline	Bob	Clara	Dick	Eva	Fred	Gracie
—	◇ 6 4	♣ 4	♠ 7 ♣ 2	♠ 2	◇ 4	◇ K 9 8 5
						♡ 9 6
						♣ 7 6
0	10	4	9	2	4	60

Gracie's bad luck is the cause of much amusement. Gracie doesn't mind; it will be someone else's turn next time!

MINORU

THE game Minoru was produced soon after King Edward the Seventh won the Derby with a horse of that name. That game required a special cloth with a number of lead horses. Here is the same game, but played with just an ordinary pack of cards, a piece of brown paper, and a piece of chalk.

First of all, mark your sheet of paper with the chalk as follows:

	Black			Red		
2—1	5—1		2—1	7—1	10—1
___	___		___	___	___
___	___		___	___	___
___	___		___	___	___
				___	___
					___
□	□		□	□	□

Allow enough space above each of the columns and on the 'Black' and 'Red' to permit of the stakes being placed. The Banker is chosen either by cutting for the lowest card or by choice. Each player should hold the Bank for six deals.

When the Banker has been chosen, each player (any number can play) puts his stake on the horse he fancies, and the race is then run as follows:

Five cards—the horses—are dealt, face downwards, on each

of the bottom squares. The Banker then deals out five cards, one at a time, from left to right, immediately beneath the horses, but face upwards.

The horse immediately above the highest card of the five (Ace high) is moved up so that the top of the card touches the first line of the column. Then five more cards are dealt out, and again the horse in front of the highest card moves up one space. The horse that touches the top line first wins, and the Banker pays out the odds as shown.

It is obvious that the two columns with only two lines, where a horse has only to move twice to win, are much more likely to prove the winning paths than the 7—1 or 10—1 columns, where the horses have to move four and six times respectively.

Instead of backing a horse, or additionally, players can back Black or Red. In this case the Banker pays even money, and if the winning horse is on the left of the dividing line, he pays on Black, and on the right Red. The Banker takes all stakes laid on losing horses or losing colours.

It is simple to employ counters, and, if possible, counters of two or three different colours, each colour representing a different coin. The odds are almost correct mathematically but with a very slight advantage to the Banker.

Before beginning, a limit should be agreed upon.

RACING DEMON

A GOOD family card game is the old favourite, Racing Demon. This is a game which appeals particularly to young people, who, being naturally quick (once they have got the hang of the game), are almost invariably successful against the older generation. For the essence of this game is speed.

It should be played with the oldest packs of cards available, since any pack is apt to get damaged in the course of play. Any number can play and one pack is required for each player. Each pack, moreover, should be distinctive, for reasons which will appear in a moment.

At the outset, each player has his own pack of cards, conscientiously shuffled, in front of him. When the players are ready, each deals a stack of thirteen cards and turns this over so that the cards lie in front of him, face upwards, with only the top one visible. Then he lays out four other cards, face upwards, side by side in a row.

The players should be sitting round a large table with their cards arranged in front of them and there should be plenty of room in the middle of the table.

At the word 'Go' (one of the players should act as starter) each player plays into the middle any of the Aces exposed in front of him, *ie* any of the four cards in his row or the top card of his stack. Now any 2's that are exposed are played on to the appropriate Aces; 3's are played on to 2's, and so on.

In playing these cards into the middle, the packs from which the cards that are played are taken is a matter of indifference; thus, if your left-hand neighbour puts the Ace of Hearts into the middle, you can at once play your 2 of Hearts upon it. And this is where speed is so important. There may be only one Ace of Hearts available and two or more 2's of Hearts waiting to be played. The one that gets there first wins.

As soon as a player has played one of the four cards from his row, he plays into it the top card from his stack of thirteen; the stack of thirty-five cards he holds in his hand. Also, as soon as he has no card in front of him which he can play, he starts turning over the cards in his hand, three at a time, playing out, as he comes to them, any Aces or other appropriate cards, and at the same time filling in any gaps in his row of four cards from the top of his stack of thirteen.

In addition to doing all this, each player may get rid of the cards in his original stack of thirteen by building on the cards in the row in front of him. This he does in the manner familiar to Patience players, by building in descending sequence with cards alternating in colour, *ie* a red Queen can be played on a Black King, a black 9 on a red 10, and so on.

Where this building is taking place, only the last played card of each sequence can be played from the row on to the growing piles in the middle of the table.

All this sounds extremely complicated, but with a little practice it becomes quite easy and even the youngest members of the family will soon learn to play with astonishing celerity.

The object of the game is twofold: to get rid of all the cards in the stack of thirteen (either by playing them into the middle of the table or by playing them on to cards in the row of four), *and* to play as many cards as possible into the middle of the table. This twofold object finds expression in the scoring rules, which are as follows:

When a player has got rid of all the thirteen cards in his stack, he calls 'Out'. Play immediately stops. The cards in the centre of the table are taken up and sorted (that is why each player must have his own distinctive pack) and are returned to their owners. Then, each player's score is the number of cards which he has played into the middle *less* the number of cards which he has left in his stack of thirteen.

Thus, suppose the player on one's left has been the first to call 'Out'. Suppose it is found when the cards are sorted that he has played eighteen cards into the middle of the table. His score is 18.

Suppose, on the other hand, that one has played twenty-three cards into the middle of the table but six of one's stack of thirteen are still left; one's score is 23 minus 6, or 17, and the player who went out first has won by one pip.

It is desirable, by the way—especially if young people are playing—that there should be a referee. And if there is a large number of players I recommend that the referee should not himself participate. He will have quite enough to do without engaging in the *fracas* himself.

AUTHORS

'AUTHORS' is quite an easy card game. Why it should be called 'Authors' I have never been able to discover, but the name does not take away from the attractions of the game.

Little knowledge of cards is required—merely an ability to recognize the different suits and the various card-denominations. It may thus serve (like 'Old Maid' or 'Beggar-my-Neighbour') as an introduction to cards for the very young.

Any number up to eight or nine can play. The cards are dealt to each player one at a time, as far as they will go. It does not matter if some players have more cards than others, so the whole pack can be dealt out.

The object of the game is to collect sets of four cards of the same denomination, *eg* four Queens or four 5's. (The game is thus, in essentials, not unlike 'Happy Families.')

The player to the left of the dealer begins. He may ask any other player for any particular card; he must, however, hold in his own hand a card of the same denomination. Thus, suppose one is first to speak in this game and one's original hand is: ♠ A 9 ♡ K 9 5 ◇ Q ♣ 9, one notes with satisfaction that one has three 9's, and begins by asking any other player (chosen at random) if he or she has the ◇ 9.

If the player asked has the card asked for, it must be handed over; the successful player has another turn. If his shot misses the target, the player asked may ask for a card in his turn, and so the game goes on until each of the thirteen 'sets' has been collected.

As soon as a player has secured a set he lays it, face downwards, on the table in front of him. Each set counts one point. At the end of the game (an agreed number of deals), the player with most points has won.

If a player, on completing a set, has no more cards in his hand, he has finished so far as that deal is concerned. The right to ask for a card now passes to the player from whom his last card was obtained.

There is obviously scope in 'Authors' for the exercise of the deductive faculties. Suppose one holds ♡ Q and ♣ Q, and another player, A, asks B for the ♠ Q and gets it. When it comes to one's turn, one can confidently demand from A the ♠ Q and also the ◇ Q. In the long run the player who observes most, and turns his knowledge to best advantage, will win.

GREAT EXPECTATIONS

'GREAT EXPECTATIONS' is an excellent game for parties. It is very amusing, and, at the same time, is one of the simplest of games to play, as there is no element of skill in it.

Each player is given so many counters. Then the pack is dealt out as far as it will go. Thus:

If there are five players, each receives ten cards and there are two over.

If there are six players, each receives eight cards and there are four over.

If there are seven players, each receives seven cards and there are three over,

and so on. The odd cards are successively auctioned to the players by the dealer; the buyer of each card is the player who offers the most chips for it.

Now the dealer takes a second pack. This is well shuffled and the top five cards from it are then placed in front of the dealer, face downwards. Now each player pays his stake to the dealer as follows:

> Where there are three players, each pays eight counters.
> Where there are four players, each pays six counters.
> Where there are five players, each pays five counters.
> Where there are six or seven players, each pays four counters.
> Where there are eight, nine or ten players, each pays three counters.

These counters are placed on the backs of the five cards in front of the dealer. If there are three, four, six or eight players (*ie* 24 counters in all), 1 is placed on the first card, 2 on the second, 4 on the third, 7 on the fourth, and 10 on the fifth. If there are five players (*ie* 25 counters in all), the distribution is 1, 2, 4, 8, 10. If there are seven players (*ie* 28 counters in all) it is 1, 3, 5, 8, 11. If there are nine players (*ie* 27 counters in all), it is 1, 3, 4, 8, 11. If there are ten players (*ie* 30 counters in all), it is 1, 3, 5, 9, 12. To these counters are added, at the dealer's discretion, the proceeds of the auction.

And now the fun begins. The dealer takes the remainder of the second pack and deals out each card in turn, at the same time calling out what it is. The player holding the corresponding card, puts it down in front of him. Gradually this stock of forty-seven useless cards diminishes and each player's hope of holding one of the lucky five cards correspondingly increases.

When the forty-seven useless cards have been dealt, the first of the five hidden cards is turned up. The player holding that card claims the stake, and, similarly with the other four.

The game, obviously, can be played for money or otherwise— just as those participating may desire.

In its essentials, 'Great Expectations' bears a close resemblance to the well-known game of 'Keno'.

PARLIAMENT

'PARLIAMENT' is another good game for an evening party—a game in which from three to eight players can take part. It is also known as 'Card Dominoes' and 'Sevens'.

A single pack of cards is used and is dealt out one card at a time. (It does not matter if some players have more cards than others.)

The cards are dealt face downwards; the players then take them up, look at their hands and sort their suits.

The object of the game is to get rid of your cards as quickly as possible and the player who is out first either wins outright or scores some agreed number of points.

When all are ready, the dealer asks: 'Who has the 7 of Diamonds?' This is the key card. Whoever has this 7 places it face upwards in the centre of the table. The player to his left may now play either (1) the 6 or 8 of Diamonds, or (2) any other 7.

If he plays the 6 or 8 of Diamonds, he lays it down, endways on to the 7 on the table. If he plays another 7, he lays it alongside the 7 of Diamonds. Thus the cards are laid out in an ordered pattern, radiating outwards from the 7 of Diamonds, and the other 7's which have been placed in line with it.

If the second player has none of the five cards which will enable him to put one down he says 'Go', and the player to his left steps into the breach.

Suppose the latter player plays the 7 of Clubs, the next player now has more options: he can put down not only one of the remaining 7's or the 6 or 8 of Diamonds, but also the 6 or 8 of Clubs. When the 6 of Clubs is played, the 5 of Clubs becomes an eligible card, and so on.

The principle of the game, it will be seen, is simplicity itself. Nevertheless, there is scope for concentration and skill. You should look at the cards in your hand, and, if able to play more than one of them, should consider carefully which of them gives one a better opportunity for being able to play next round; and also which of them gives the other players the least chance of getting rid of their own cards.

Thus, suppose you hold—as cards which you are eligible to play—the 6 of Diamonds and the 9 of Clubs, and suppose you also have the 10 of Clubs in your hand, the 9 of Clubs is obviously the card to put down first. For, next time, you can follow it up with the 10, still retaining the 6 of Diamonds to the annoyance of your adversaries.

If you have a large party—say, from eight to a dozen players—you can play 'Parliament' with two packs of cards shuffled together.

COMMIT

THE name of this old family game was originally Comet, but, like many card terms, it became corrupted by usage.

The connection with a comet is obvious: the cards, as they are played, spread themselves across the table rather in the manner of a comet's tail.

Commit is played with one pack of cards, from which the ◇ 8 has been removed, and any number of players from two to eight can participate.

The cards are dealt, face downwards, so far as they will go. (The fact that some players may have more cards than others does not matter, as the deal passes after each hand has been played out.)

The player to the left of the dealer plays any card he likes from his hand, placing it, face upwards, on the table. For example, he might begin with the ♡ 5, laying this card on the table, and, at the same time, calling out its name.

The object of the game is to get rid of the cards in one's hand as quickly as possible.

As soon as the ♡ 5 (say) is played, the player holding the 6 calls out 'Six of Hearts' and plays it. This goes on until the King of Hearts has been played; that is a 'stop' card, and whoever has played it can next play any card he chooses.

It will be noticed that the game bears some resemblance to Newmarket, but you do not have, as in Newmarket, to remember which cards are 'stops', because all the cards played are spread out on the table in front of you.

Note that, in the Diamond suit, the ◇ 7 is a 'stop' as well as the ◇ K.

The ◇ 9 plays a special part in the game. Whoever holds this card can play it at any time he likes, at the same time calling out 'Commit'. This enables the holder of the ◇ 9 to stop the current sequences and next to play any card he chooses.

Where a suit has been opened with a card higher than the Ace, the card immediately below it is obviously a 'stop' card. For example, if the first card played is the ♡ 5, the suit is played out up to the King. Now the holder of the ♡ K may have the ♡ 4 2 in his hand; he plays the ♡ 2, then, in his turn, the ♡ 4, and can now embark on some other suit. Whoever has the ♡ A will play it later if he is able to get the lead.

As soon as a player has got rid of all his cards he calls 'Out', and receives one counter from each of the others in respect of every card not yet played, and two counters in respect of the ◇ 9 if the holder of that card has failed to play it.

Commit is a simple game, but it has a sufficient skill factor to be called interesting.

OH! WELL

'OH! WELL' is one of the best round games. It will appeal both to expert players who, playing against one another, will find plenty of opportunities for the development of an interesting technique, and it will also appeal to beginners and to the young, who will appreciate the simplicity of its rules.

The game is played by three, four, five, six or seven players. When three are playing, the bottom card of the pack is discarded but not exposed. When four are playing, the whole pack is used. If five, six, or seven people are playing, then two, four and three cards respectively are discarded from the bottom of the pack. The remaining cards are dealt out, the dealer's last card being exposed, and the suit of that card is declared trumps.

The player on the left of the dealer then states how many tricks he can make out of his own hand. If he thinks he can make none, he declares 'None'. The second player then calls, and so on, in turn, until each player has stated how many tricks he undertakes to make. The calls are thus written down on the score-sheet by the dealer, or whoever is nominated scorer.

The player on the left of the dealer leads, and the game is played in exactly the same manner as Solo Whist or Nap; that is to say, each player must follow the suit led, or, having none of that suit, he may either play a trump or discard a card of another suit.

The winner of the trick leads the next card, and each, in turn, starting always on the left of the dealer, plays until the hand is completed. The tricks of each player are then counted, and any player who makes the exact number of tricks he nominated at the beginning receives a bonus of ten points in addition to one point for each trick made.

If a player makes either more or less than the tricks he bid, then he only scores one for each trick made by him. The first player to score 100 wins the game. If the game is being played for money, either the players pay the differences at so much a point, or, better still, each player pays a given sum at the beginning into a pool, all of which is taken by the eventual winner.

When the game is played by a number other than four, it is essential that at the end of each hand the discarded cards shall be returned to the pack, and the bottom card, or cards, again discarded on the fresh deal after reshuffling. If this is not done the discards are known and some interest is lost.

This round game, played without partners, will be found interesting and amusing, and one which needs a certain amount of ingenuity. At first blush it may be thought wise tactics to declare 'None' as frequently as possible in order to win the bonus by avoiding the taking of tricks. In practice it will be found none too easy to do this, unless there are at least six persons playing, because the remaining players will combine to force you to take a trick if possible.

Again, if you have called 'Two' and have already made that number of tricks, your opponents will do their best to see to it that you score one more and so rob you of your bonus.

PIP-PIP!

'PIP-PIP' is one of the liveliest (and noisiest) of party games.

Two packs shuffled together are required, and any reasonable number can play. A trump suit is first selected by cutting the pack, after which seven cards are dealt to each player.

The object of the game is to win tricks containing any of the following cards: 2's, Aces, Kings, Queens and Knaves. I mention them in this order because, in taking tricks, 2's rank before Aces; that is to say, the Ace of a suit can be captured by the 2. When it comes to scoring at the end of the game, 2's count more than Aces, scoring being as follows:

For each 2	..	..	..	11 points
„ „ Ace	..	..	..	10 „
„ „ King	..	..	..	5 „
„ „ Queen	..	..	..	4 „
„ „ Knave	..	..	..	3 „

Thus, a player who, at the end of the game, has won tricks which contain one 2, two Aces, one Queen and one Knave, scores 11 + 20 + 4 + 3 or 38 points in all.

The player on the left of the dealer leads to the first trick and everyone must follow suit. A player who cannot follow

suit may trump or discard, as he pleases. The winner of a trick
leads to the next one. If two identical cards (*eg* two Kings of
Hearts) are played to the same trick, the player of the second
one is assumed to have played the higher card. It is thus important
to note carefully what winning cards are out.

Now for the feature which gives the game its name and its
distinctive character. After playing to a trick, each player draws
a card from the top of the pack, the pack after the deal being
placed in the centre of the table. If, after the draw, he finds he
has in his hand a King and Queen of the same suit, he calls
'Pip-Pip', laying his King and Queen face upwards on the
table. Trumps now change (as from the end of the current trick)
to the suit in which a player has 'Pip-Pipped', and he scores 50
points for effecting the change.

Various points of controversy are apt to arise in this game:

1. If, at the beginning of a game, a player has a King and
Queen of a suit (other than the trump suit) in his hand, he can
'Pip-Pip' at once and trumps change before the first trick has
been played.

2. If two players both find they have the King and Queen
of a suit (other than the trump suit) both score 50 points, but
the trump suit is changed to that of whoever calls 'Pip-Pip'
last.

3. There is nothing to prevent a player from 'Pip-Pipping'
twice in the same suit, but, to do so, he must have both Kings
and both Queens. He cannot pair his King with each of the
two Queens in turn.

4. There is no obligation on a player to 'Pip-Pip' the moment
he finds himself with the King and Queen of a suit. He can hold
them up if he thinks it is tactically advantageous to do so. But,
of course, by so doing, he runs a risk of losing a 50-point bonus.

5. Drawing cards ceases when the number of cards left in the
pack is less than the number of players taking part. The residue
of cards is turned face upwards and these do not count to anybody; the tricks in hand are then played out.

AN ILLUSTRATIVE DEAL

Let us suppose there are nine players. The cards are dealt as under:

Anne	Betty	Carol
♠ J 9 7	♠ None	♠ 10 8 5 5
♡ 2 Q	♡ K J 9	♡ A Q
◇ 10	◇ A J	◇ None
♣ 4	♣ 2 Q	♣ K

David	Enid	Frank
♠ 2 A J	♠ 4 3	♠ 2 K 10
♡ 10	♡ J 8 7	♡ 10 7
◇ 9 6 4	◇ 5	◇ None
♣ None	♣ 3	♣ 2 10

Gerald	Hilda	John
♠ Q 7	♠ None	♠ Q 6
♡ 9	♡ 2 6 5	♡ 5
◇ 2 10 6	◇ 3	◇ K J 8 7
♣ 5	♣ A J 10	♣ None

Don't forget that the 2 is the best card of a suit. Hence it is shown here *before* the Ace.

Points are gained for taking tricks containing: 2's (11 each), Aces (10 each), Kings (5 each), Queens (4 each), Knaves (3 each).

To follow this deal, cancel, with a pencil, each card as it is played. It is then easy to see what cards remain in each player's hand.

Spades are made trumps (by cutting).

Round 1. Anne leads:

♣ 4   ♣ 2   ♣ K   ♠ J   ♣ 3   ♣ 10   ♣ 5   ♣ 10   <u>♠ Q</u>

John takes the trick, scoring 23 points. Cards drawn:

♣ 7   ♣ 9   ♡ K   ♡ 4   ♣ Q   ♣ 3   ♠ K   ♡ A   ♡ 8

Carol and Gerald simultaneously shout 'Pip-Pip!' each having now the King and Queen of a suit. Carol's call takes precedence, as she is the first to play. Both score 50 points and Hearts become trumps.

Round 2. John leads:

♠ 7   ♡ 9   ♠ 5   ♠ A   ♠ 3   ♠ 10   ♠ 7   <u>♡ 2</u>   ♠ 6

Hilda takes the trick, scoring 21 points. Cards drawn:

♣J ♣9 ♡3 ◇Q ♣K ◇A ◇K ♠9 ♡4
A   B   C   D   E   F   G   H   J

Enid, having the luck in two successive draws to collect the ♣ K Q, now shouts 'Pip-Pip!' Clubs are made trumps (and, as it happens, remain trumps for the rest of the game). Enid scores 50 points.

Round 3. Hilda leads:

◇ 10 ◇ J ♡ 3 ◇ 4 ◇ 5 ◇ A ◇ 2 ◇ 3 ◇ 7

Gerald takes the trick, scoring 24 points. Cards drawn:

♣A ◇Q ♠A ♠6 ♠4 ◇3 ◇4 ♣8 ♣8

Round 4. Gerald leads:

♡ 2 ♡ J ♡ Q ♡ 4 ♡ 7 ♡ 7 ♡ 9 ♡ 5 ♡ 5

Anne takes the trick, scoring 18 points. Last round of cards is now drawn:

♠ 8 ♣ 6 ♣ 5 ♣ 4 ◇ 2 ♣ 6 ♣ 7 ♡ 3 ♡ 6

The remaining cards are exposed face upwards, as there are not enough to go round again. They are ♠ 3 ◇ 9 8 7 5.

Round 5. Anne leads:

♠ 8 ♠ 9 ♠ 5 ♠ 6 ♠ 4 ♠ K ♠ Q ♠ 9 ♡ 4

Betty takes the trick (9 points) and leads (Round 6):

♠ 9 ◇ Q ♣ 5 ◇ 6 ◇ 2 ◇ 3 ◇ 4 ♣ 8 ◇ 8

Hilda takes the trick (15 points) and leads (Round 7):

♡ Q ♡ K ♡ K ♡ 10 ♡ 8 ♡ 10 ♣ 7 ♡ 3 ♡ 6

Gerald takes the trick (14 points) and leads (Round 8).

♣ A ◇ A ♠ 8 ◇ 9 ♠ 4 ♣ 2 ◇ 6 ♣ J ◇ J

Frank takes the trick (37 points). High-scoring cards which have been unsuccessfully held up to now begin to be gathered in. Frank leads (Round 9):

♣ 7 ♣ 6 ♠ 10 ♣ 4 ♣ Q ♣ 3 ◇ 10 ♣ A ♣ 8
A   B   C   D   E   F   G   H   J

Hilda takes the trick (14 points) and leads (Round 10):

♠ J ♣ 9 ♡ A ◇ Q ♡ J ♣ 6 ◇ K ♡ 6 ♡ 8

Betty takes the trick (25 points) and leads for the eleventh and last Round:

♣ J ♣ Q ♠ A ♠ 2 ♣ K ♠ 2 ♠ K ♡ A ◇ K

Enid collects this valuable trick, every card in which scores—a total of 64 points.

Points for the deal are now totalled. They are:

A	B	C	D	E	F	G	H	J
18	34	—	—	64	37	38	50	23
	and for 'Pip-Pip!'							
—	—	50	—	50	—	50	—	—
18	34	50	0	114	37	88	50	23

The above deal will show, I hope, to what extent luck and skill, respectively, enter into the game. It will also serve to emphasize how important it is that, if young people are playing, there should be a suitable 'manager' and scorer!

TWO PUZZLING CARD TRICKS

(1) Naming Two Cards

HERE is a simple little card trick which will amuse—and puzzle—non-mathematicians.

The explanation is quite obvious—when you know it—but if you have not the mathematical sort of brain you may be baffled for quite a long while before you find out how it is done.

Get a pack of cards and ask one of your audience to deal out twenty, face downwards.

Then ask someone else to take these twenty cards and arrange them in ten pairs (still keeping them face downwards). By a pair of cards I merely mean two cards placed one on top of another. They do not need to be of the same suit or the same denomination; indeed, the person arranging them does not look at the faces of the cards. Now get someone to look at the faces of the cards (which should not be shown to you) and to make a mental note of the cards which constitute any particular pair.

Next, you collect all twenty cards, taking them up haphazard, but taking care not to separate the cards of any pair, and deal them out, face upwards, according to some such scheme as the following:

Here 1—1 represents the first pair of cards, 2—2 the second pair, and so on.

All you have to do now is to ask whoever looked at one of the pairs to tell you in which row or rows his cards are to be found. You then pick them out; for inspection of the plan set out will show that each of the ten pairs is differently located.

1	1	2	3	4
2	5	5	6	7
3	6	8	8	9
4	7	9	10	10

Thus the two cards of Pair No 1 are both in the top row; hence, if your friend says, 'Both in the first row', you select the cards 1, 1. If he says, 'Third and fourth rows', you select 9, 9; and so on. *The secret of success with this trick is to think up new ways of arranging your twenty cards.*

Thus, a second time you might start at the bottom left-hand corner; next, operate in terms of files instead of rows, and so forth. A little experiment will suggest all manner of amusing variations.

1	1	2	3	4	5	6
2	7	7	8	9	10	11
3	8	12	12	13	14	15
4	9	13	16	16	17	18
5	10	14	17	19	19	20
6	11	15	18	20	21	21

Similar tricks can be performed with other numbers of cards. For example, with 21 pairs:

Here, again, the arrangement can be varied in a number of fairly obvious ways.

The trick can also be performed, both with pairs and trios, by means of 'magic sentences'.

(2) Naming a Selected Card

HERE is a trick (requiring no sleight of hand) which will mystify quite a number of people. Try it at the card table next time you are waiting for a fourth.

Take up some number of cards which is a multiple of three—say, 27. You should not, by the way, mention that you have chosen this number. Then announce that you will name any card selected by a member of your audience. Ask him or her to choose a card, as you turn over your pack (face upwards), and to write down what it is, but to give no inkling to you of the card chosen.

Now turn over the pack and deal the cards quickly into three heaps, placing one card in each heap in rotation. To make the trick more mystifying, *do not yourself look at their faces.* Then ask your 'client', having selected his card, to tell you which of the three heaps it is in.

Now comes the crucial part of the performance. Pick up the three heaps and place them face downwards again. You should pick them up with every appearance of casualness (if possible, cover your actions with a little 'patter') *but make sure, in fact, that the named pack is in the middle.*

Repeat the process a second time, a third, and a fourth. At the end of the fourth performance, you will know which the selected card is. *It is the middle card of the middle pack.*

Do not, however, blurt out this fact, but approach the identity of the card obliquely, for example, having noted the card, shuffle the pack, get someone to cut it, deal out the cards and inspect them with an air of profound cogitation before you finally select your 'client's' card.

THE EXPLANATION

The trick is simplicity itself—once you know how it is done! Let the cards—in the order in which they are dealt—be 1, 2, 3, etc. Suppose your 'client' chooses the ♣ 2, which is the 25th card dealt. Then you deal them in three heaps as follows:

1st heap:	1	4	7	10	13	16	19	22	25
2nd heap:	2	5	8	11	14	17	20	23	26
3rd heap:	3	6	9	12	15	18	21	24	27

Now the 1st heap is named as being the one which contains

your card. You put it in the middle (*it does not matter which of the others you deal first*) and you get:

1st heap: 2   11   20   1   10   19   3   12   21
2nd heap: 5   14   23   4   13   22   6   15   24
3rd heap: 8   17   26   7   16   25   9   18   27

This time the 3rd heap goes to the middle:

1st heap: 5   4   6   8   7   9   2   1   3
2nd heap: 14   13   15   17   16   18   11   10   12
3rd heap: 23   22   24   26   25   27   20   19   21

And now for the final rearrangement, with the 3rd heap again in the middle:

1st heap: 5   8   2   23   26   20   14   17   11
2nd heap: 4   7   1   22   25   19   13   16   10
3rd heap: 6   9   3   24   27   21   15   18   12

These diagrams should make clear how, by a process of selective promotion, the chosen card reaches the middle.

PATIENCE GAMES

ALTERNATIONS

'ALTERNATIONS' IS a two-pack Patience which combines two well-known themes.

First, shuffle the packs together, cut, and deal, from left to right, a row of seven cards, face upwards; then a second row, face downwards, overlapping the first row; and then, similarly, five more rows, making seven in all. The first, third, fifth and seventh rows will then be face upwards, and the second, fourth and sixth face downwards. The cards thus dealt form seven vertical 'depots'.

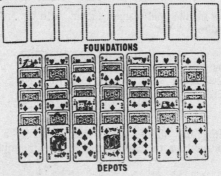

FOUNDATIONS

DEPOTS

The object of the Patience is to build in ascending sequence of suit on foundations. 'Exposed' Aces, and Aces exposed in play, are placed to form foundations. Exposed cards are the cards of depots not overlapped by another card, and the top card, for the time being, of the 'rubbish heap'.

Exposed cards may be played in ascending sequence of suit on foundations, or in descending sequence, *irrespective* of suit, on depots.

A sequence of cards, or any portion of a sequence, may be played bodily from one depot to another, provided the highest card of the sequence is in descending sequence (irrespective of suit) with the card upon which it is played. Deal, playing available cards to foundations and depots, and unplayable cards to a rubbish heap.

A 'space' occurs when all the cards of a vertical depot have been played. A space may, but need not necessarily, be filled with an exposed card or sequence of cards.

One deal only is allowed. If the Patience goes through, all cards will be built in sequence of suit on foundations.

AS YOU LIKE IT

HERE is a somewhat 'different' two-pack Patience which embodies two unusual features. Patience addicts who do not know it will, I think, derive pleasure from it.

Shuffle the packs together, and cut. Deal eight 'depots' of thirteen cards each, face downwards; then turn the top cards of the depots face upwards, and place them, as 'index cards', immediately above the depots from which they came, thus forming a row of eight index cards; then turn all the depots face upwards.

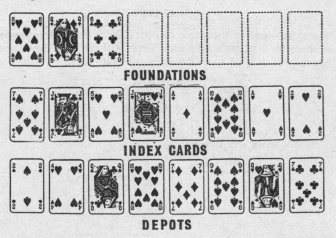

FOUNDATIONS

INDEX CARDS

DEPOTS

The object of the Patience is to build in ascending sequence, *irrespective of suit*, on 'foundations', which are placed in a row immediately above the index cards. Each foundation follows in sequence, irrespective of suit, the index card immediately below it.

'Exposed' cards are the top cards, for the time being, of the eight depots. Exposed cards can be played, *irrespective of suit*, to foundations.

In building up on foundations, when the King is reached, the ascending sequence is continued by the Ace. Each foundation is completed when a card, one lower in value than its index card, is reached. Thus, if the index card is 10, the foundation is completed with 9.

When all available cards have been played, the left-hand depot is taken up, turned face downwards, and re-dealt from left to right, face upwards, on the eight depots, starting with the original left-hand depot, and dealing to any 'spaces' that may have occurred by playing.

When *all* the cards of the first depot have been dealt, play available cards; then take up the cards of the second depot, deal, starting at the left-hand depot, and play in a similar manner, until all the depots have been dealt once each.

If the Patience goes through, all cards, except the index cards, will be built in sequence, irrespective of suit, on the foundations.

CARLTON

'CARLTON'—one of the staple two-pack Patiences—offers plenty of scope for a player's ingenuity. There will often be alternative 'moves' which need to be carefully thought out.

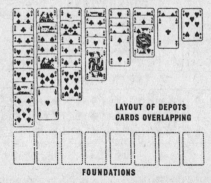

LAYOUT OF DEPOTS
CARDS OVERLAPPING

FOUNDATIONS

First, shuffle the pack and cut. Deal, from left to right, a row of eight cards, face upwards; then deal a row of seven cards, face upwards, overlapping the top row. Continue similarly dealing the cards in rows, diminishing by one the cards dealt in each row, until the layout is completed by dealing one card face upwards on the first column, as shown in the diagram. The first vertical column will then consist of eight cards.

The cards thus dealt form eight vertical 'depots'. The depot cards must all be dealt before play is commenced.

The object of the Patience is to build up in ascending sequence of suit on 'foundations'. 'Exposed' cards are cards of depots not overlapped by other cards. Exposed Aces, and Aces subsequently exposed in play or dealing, are taken and placed to form foundations.

Exposed cards may, if available, be played in ascending sequence of suit on foundations, or in descending sequence of alternating colour on other depots. A sequence of cards, or any portion of a sequence, may be played bodily, at any time, from one depot to another, provided the proper sequence and alternation of colour are preserved, or to a 'space', if one exists.

A space occurs when all the cards of a depot have been played and it must be filled with the exposed card or sequence of cards from a depot.

When all available cards have been played, deal, from left to right, a *complete* row of cards, face upwards, on the depots, overlapping the other cards. Continue to play available exposed cards and, when blocked, deal another complete row, face upwards; and so on, until all the cards have been dealt.

One deal only is allowed; if the Patience goes through, all cards will be built in ascending sequence of suit on foundations.

CASTLES IN SPAIN

ONLY one pack of cards is required.

Shuffle the pack, and cut. Deal from left to right, a row of five cards, face downwards; then, above it, a row of four cards; then a row of three cards above the second row; and finally, one card above the third row. All cards should be face downwards. Next, deal on the top of the cards already dealt, two more complete sets of cards, face downwards; and finally, a complete set, face upwards, as shown in the diagram.

The cards thus dealt form thirteen 'depots'. 'Exposed' Aces, and Aces subsequently exposed in play, are taken and placed to form 'foundations'.

The object of the Patience is to build in ascending sequence of suit on foundations. Exposed cards are cards of depots not covered by other cards.

When the exposed card of a depot is played, the card under it is turned face upwards, and becomes exposed.

Exposed cards may, if available, be played in ascending sequence of suit on foundations, or in descending sequence of alternating colour on other depots. A sequence of cards, or any

DEPOTS

portion of a sequence, may be played at any time from one depot to another, provided the proper sequence and alternation of colour are preserved; or to a 'space', if one exists.

A space occurs when all the cards of a depot have been played.

A space must be filled with the exposed card, or sequence of cards, from a depot.

One deal only is allowed. If the Patience goes through, all cards will be built in ascending sequence of suit on foundations.

DEAUVILLE

THIS is a two-pack Patience of which the technique is simple and easily remembered. There is, however, scope for a good deal of skill and judgment in play.

Shuffle the packs together and cut. Deal out, from left to right, face downwards, a row of ten 'depot' cards; then a second row of ten cards, overlapping the first row; then a third row, overlapping the second row—all face downwards; and, lastly, a fourth row of ten cards, face upwards, overlapping the third row, as shown in the diagram opposite.

The cards thus dealt form ten vertical depots. The card of a depot not overlapped by another card is 'exposed'.

Exposed Aces, and Aces as exposed in play, are moved into a row below the depots, as 'foundations'.

The object is to build in ascending sequence of suit on foundations. Exposed cards may be played in ascending sequence of suit to foundations, in descending sequence of alternating colour to depots, or to 'spaces'.

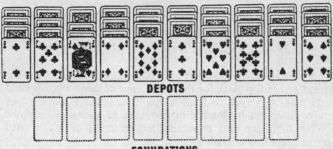

DEPOTS

FOUNDATIONS

Single cards only may be moved at a time from one depot to another, or to a space, and not sequences.

When the exposed card of a depot has been played, the card immediately below it must be turned face upwards, and so becomes exposed and available for play.

The cards in hand are turned up one at a time and only one deal is allowed.

DEMON

DEMON is a popular Patience game, and is the basis of the round game, 'Racing Demon', though it differs from the latter in some respects. It is sure to become a favourite with those who have not tried it, as there is considerable scope for skill.

Shuffle two packs together, cut, and deal forty cards, face upwards, to a 'stock'; then deal eight cards, face upwards, to a 'depot' row; after which, deal one card, face upwards, as a 'foundation' card, to a row above the depots.

Any 'exposed' card, or any card exposed in play, of the same value as the foundation card, is put into the foundation row.

The object of the Patience is to build in ascending sequence of suit on foundations.

When the foundation is other than Ace, and, in building up, King is reached, the sequence is continued by playing Ace. If the foundation card is 10, the building up is completed with 9.

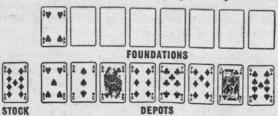

FOUNDATIONS

STOCK   DEPOTS

Exposed cards are the cards of depots not overlapped by other cards, and the top card, for the time being of the stock. Exposed cards may be played to foundations in ascending sequence of suit, or to depots in descending sequence of alternating colour.

When there are only two cards left in the stock, either card may be played, if available.

A sequence of cards, or portion of a sequence, may be played bodily at any time from one depot to another, provided the proper sequence and alternation of colour are preserved.

A 'space' occurs when all the cards in a depot have been played. A space must be filled by the top card of the stock, until the stock is exhausted; after which it may, but need not necessarily, be filled with any exposed card.

The cards remaining in hand are dealt in batches of three, face upwards, to a 'rubbish heap', and every third card (*ie* the top card of each batch) becomes an exposed card, and can be played on foundations or depots; if it is played, the card immediately below it becomes exposed and playable, and so on with each top card in turn.

When only two cards of the pack are left in hand, they are dealt separately, and either or both may be played, if available.

Pick up the rubbish heap, turn it face downwards, re-deal, and play in the manner described above, and so on, until such time as no more cards can be played, in which case the order of the cards would not be altered in a re-deal, and therefore the Patience is blocked.

If the Patience goes through, the cards will all be built up in sequence on the foundations.

FORTY-NINE

'FORTY-NINE' is played with two full packs of cards.

Shuffle the packs together and cut. Deal face upwards from left to right a row of seven cards; then a second row of seven cards, overlapping the row above it; and then, similarly, five more rows, making in all seven rows of seven cards each, which must be completely dealt before commencing play. (See diagram.) The cards thus dealt form seven vertical 'depots'.

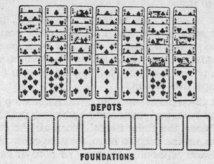

DEPOTS

FOUNDATIONS

'Exposed' cards are the card of a depot not overlapped by another card, and the top card for the time being, of the 'rubbish heap'. Exposed Aces, and Aces as exposed in play, must be taken and placed to form 'foundations'.

The object of the Patience is to build in ascending sequence of suit on foundations.

Exposed cards must be played in ascending sequence of suit on foundations, or in descending sequence, *irrespective of suit*, on depots.

When all available cards from those originally dealt have been played, deal the cards remaining in hand, playing available cards, when desired, to foundations or depots; and unplayable cards, and such cards as the dealer does not desire to play to foundations or depots, to a rubbish heap.

A 'space' occurs when all the cards of a vertical depot have been played. A space may, but need not necessarily, be filled with any exposed card.

It is desirable not to fill a space unless absolutely necessary; for, to carry the Patience through, spaces are usually required to enable the cards to be shifted about. Single cards only may be movèd, and not sequences or portions of sequences.

A 'merci' consists in borrowing a whole foundation pack and placing it diagonally on the exposed card of any depot with which the top card of the foundation is in descending sequence, *irrespective of suit*. Any card of lower value, irrespective of suit, may be played on the exposed card of the borrowed foundation. Thus, assuming 9 to be the exposed card of the borrowed foundation, an 8, or a 7, or indeed any card down to a 2, could be played on to it.

Any number of mercis can be taken, at any time, and played on any or the same depot, and this, of course, opens up the game immensely. When once a card has been played on a borrowed foundation, such card becomes an ordinary exposed card and can only have another card played on it in descending sequence, irrespective of suit.

When all the cards played on a borrowed foundation have been disposed of, the borrowed foundation becomes exposed, and can be replaced among the foundations. When all the cards have been dealt, pick up the rubbish heap, turn the cards face downwards, and re-deal without shuffling. The bottom card of the rubbish heap may be looked at before turning the cards, in order to see if it is desirable to play the exposed card of the rubbish heap before turning.

In the second deal no rubbish heap is allowed and all cards, as dealt, must be played to foundations, depots or spaces; failing which, the Patience is blocked.

If the Patience goes through, all cards will be built in sequence of suit on the eight Aces.

KINGS

'KINGS' is a somewhat tricky two-pack Patience. The instructions should be carefully followed.

Take the eight Aces and place them to form 'foundations' as shown in the diagram.

Shuffle the remaining cards together, cut, and deal four horizontal rows of two cards each to the left of the 'foundations', to form 'left depots', and four similar rows to the right of the foundations to form 'right depots'.

The object of the Patience is to build in ascending sequence, irrespective of suit, on foundations.

'Exposed' cards are the outside cards, for the time being, of each horizontal row of left depots, and the outside cards, for the time being, of each horizontal row of right depots.

| **LEFT DEPOTS** | **FOUNDATIONS** | **RIGHT DEPOTS** |

An exposed card, *during dealing*, can only be played to a foundation if it is on a depot absolutely alongside the foundation. Thus, an exposed card from a left depot can only be played to a left-hand column foundation in the same horizontal row as itself; and similarly, an exposed card from a right depot can only be played to a right-hand column foundation in the same horizontal row as itself.

Deal single cards, overlapping the eight depot cards, commencing at the top left depot, going down the left depots and up the right depots. Play any available card during dealing, and replace it with the next card dealt.

Continue dealing and playing in a similar manner until all the cards are exhausted.

When *all the cards have been dealt*, exposed cards may be played to *any* foundation, in ascending sequence, irrespective of suit; to any other depot, in either ascending or descending sequence, irrespective of suit; or to a space. Cards may only be moved singly, and not in sequences.

A space occurs when all the cards in a horizontal row of either left depots or right depots have been played. A space may, but need not necessarily, be filled with any exposed card.

One deal only is allowed. If the Patience goes through, all cards will be built in sequence, irrespective of suit, on foundations.

LABYRINTH

THOUGH 'Labyrinth', the name of this one-pack Patience, may be suggestive of complications, the game is, in fact, a fairly simple affair. On the other hand, a good many attempts at it are likely before one gets it out.

First, take the four Aces from the pack and place them to form 'foundations'. Now shuffle and cut the remaining cards and deal, face upwards, from left to right, a row of eight cards.

The object of the Patience is to build in ascending sequence of suit on foundations. Any available cards in the first row dealt are played to foundations, after which any 'spaces' in the row are filled by dealing cards, from left to right, into them.

When all available cards have been played and spaces filled in, deal another row of eight cards immediately below the first row, and play as before; then continue dealing and playing in a similar manner, until all the cards are exhausted.

Spaces caused by playing cards from any rows, except the first row dealt, are not filled in; thus, in play, there may be many gaps in the rows, giving the layout of rows the appearance of a 'labyrinth'. Each row must be completely dealt before playing.

'Exposed' cards are the cards in the top and bottom rows. If a card is played from the top row, it exposes the card immediately below it, and so on; in a similar manner, if a card is played from the bottom row, it exposes the card immediately above it, and so on. Exposed cards, if available, are played to foundations.

If the Patience becomes blocked, any *one* card may be taken from any row for play to a foundation.

One deal only is allowed. If the Patience goes through, all cards will be built in sequence of suit on foundations.

LADY PALK

WHO Lady Palk was is one of the mysteries of the card world which I have not been able to solve. But she has given her name to an interesting two-pack Patience.

First, shuffle the packs together and cut. Deal, face upwards, four horizontal rows of four cards each to 'left depots'; then

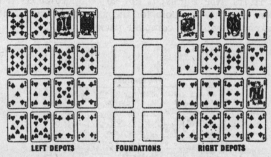

LEFT DEPOTS FOUNDATIONS RIGHT DEPOTS

deal four horizontal rows of four cards each to 'right depots', leaving a good space between the left and right depots for the 'foundations'.

The left-hand outside card, for the time being, of each horizontal row of left depots, and the right-hand outside card, for the time being, of each horizontal row of right depots, are 'exposed'.

Exposed Aces, and Aces subsequently exposed in play, are placed, face upwards, to form foundations.

The object of the Patience is to build in ascending sequence of suit on the Ace foundations.

'Spaces' occur when all the cards have been played from a

horizontal row of either left depots or right depots. A space must be filled by playing a King into it; and if a King is not available, it is left until a King becomes exposed.

Exposed cards can be played in ascending sequence of suit on foundations, or in descending sequence, irrespective of suit, on the exposed cards of depots.

Deal, playing available cards to foundations and depots, and unplayable cards, face upwards, to a 'rubbish heap'. The top card, for the time being, of the rubbish heap is exposed.

A card, or cards, may, at any time, be played back from foundations to depots, provided the cards played back are in sequence, irrespective of suit.

One deal only is allowed; and if the Patience goes through all cards will be built in sequence of suit on the foundations.

LES HUITS

'LES HUITS' (the Eights) is not so complicated as it looks, but there is plenty of room for the exercise of judgment. The game is played with two complete packs of cards.

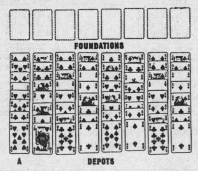

First, shuffle the packs together, cut and deal, from left to right, eight rows of eight cards each, face upwards, and overlapping. These eight rows must be completely dealt before commencing play. The cards thus dealt form eight vertical 'depots'. The card of a depot not overlapped by another card is 'exposed'.

Exposed Aces, and Aces exposed in play, are placed to form 'foundations'.

The object of the Patience is to build in ascending sequence of suit on foundations.

Exposed cards, if available, may be played to foundations in ascending sequence of suit, or to depots (including depot A) in descending sequence, irrespective of suit.

A sequence in suit, or a portion of such sequence, can at any time be played from one depot to another, provided the highest card of the sequence so used is in descending sequence, irrespective of suit, with the card upon which it is played. Sequences *not in suit* must not be played.

A 'space' occurs when all the cards of a vertical depot have been played. A space may, but need not necessarily, be filled with an exposed card, or sequence of cards, *in suit*.

Deal, playing available cards to foundations or depots, and all unplayable cards to the left-hand depot A.

It is important to arrange cards, as far as possible, in sequence of suits on depots, otherwise the Patience is liable to become blocked.

One deal only is allowed; and if the Patience goes through, all cards will be built in sequence of suit on foundations.

MILLIGAN HARP

'MILLIGAN HARP', a two-pack Patience, is, as its name suggests, a derivative of the popular 'Miss Milligan'.

First, shuffle the packs together and cut. Deal, from left to right, a row of eight cards, the first face upwards, and the remaining seven face downwards; then deal a row of seven cards, the first face upwards, on the second card of the first row, and the remaining six cards face downwards. Continue similarly dealing the cards in rows, diminishing by one the cards dealt in each row, until the Harp is completed by dealing one card face upwards on the last column, as shown in the diagram. The last vertical column will then consist of eight cards.

The cards thus dealt form eight vertical 'depots'. The depot cards must all be dealt before play is commenced.

'Exposed' Aces, and Aces subsequently exposed in play or dealing, are taken and placed to form foundations.

The object of the Patience is to build up in ascending sequence of suit on foundations.

Exposed cards are cards of depots not overlapped by other

cards. When the exposed card of a depot is played, the card immediately under it is turned face upwards and becomes exposed. Exposed cards may, if available, be played in ascending sequence of suit on foundations, or in descending sequence of alternating colour on other depots.

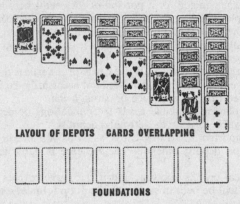

LAYOUT OF DEPOTS   CARDS OVERLAPPING

FOUNDATIONS

A sequence of cards, or any portion of a sequence, may be played bodily, at any time, from one depot to another, provided the proper sequence and alternation of colour are preserved, or to a space if one exists.

A 'space' occurs when all the cards of a depot have been played. A space must be filled with the exposed card or sequence of cards from a depot.

When all available cards have been played, deal, from left to right, a *complete* row of cards, face upwards, on the depots, overlapping the other cards. Continue to play available exposed cards, and, when blocked, deal another complete row, face upwards, and so on, until all the cards have been dealt.

One deal only is allowed; if the Patience goes through, all the cards will be built in ascending sequence of suit on foundations.

MONTE CARLO

MONTE CARLO is a one-pack Patience of a different type from most of those I have shown. Its object is not to build up sequences of cards, but to eliminate cards altogether.

First, shuffle the pack thoroughly, and cut. Deal, face upwards,

as many rows of five cards each as the operations described
below require; but the rows must never exceed four in all.

Any cards, during dealing to the 'lay-out', which pair are
taken and cast aside, provided they are next each other in any
direction—viz, alongside, above, below, or in the same diagonal.
For example, card E in diagram may be paired with a card in
position A, B, C, D, F, G, H, or I, if both of them are of the
same denomination.

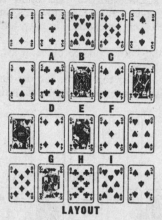

LAYOUT

When two cards have been paired and cast aside, their places
must be filled by closing up the row or rows; after closing up,
left-hand cards from the lower row must be moved (in the order
as dealt) to fill the row above; after which, the lower row is
again closed up. The rows are closed up by moving cards to the
left.

Only one pair (even if two are available) must be played
before closing up the layout.

Continue dealing and playing, as described above. If all four
rows of five cards each have been dealt, without any pairing
being possible, the Patience is blocked. If the Patience goes
through, no cards will be left in the rows, as they will all have
been paired and cast aside.

MYSTERY

HERE is a simple and very amusing one-pack Patience. Uncertainty as to what the 'blind' card is lends an element of surprise which will be appreciated.

Shuffle the pack, cut, and deal one 'blind' card, face downwards; then deal seven cards, face upwards, in a row to form 'depots'. Aces are taken, as exposed in play, and placed to form 'foundations'.

The object of the Patience is to build in ascending sequence of suit on foundations.

Exposed cards are the top cards, for the time being, of the depots. Exposed cards are, if available, played to foundations.

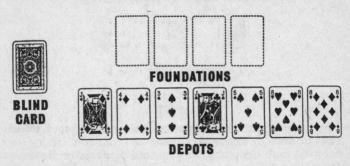

FOUNDATIONS

BLIND CARD

DEPOTS

Deal the cards in hand, playing available cards to foundations, and other cards to any of the seven depots.

Judgment is necessary in deciding to which depot to play the card, for it is undesirable to play a higher card of a suit on a lower one of the same suit.

A player may look through the depots before deciding where to play a card.

A space occurs when all the cards of a depot have been played. A space must be filled by an exposed card, or the next card dealt.

If the Patience becomes blocked, the 'blind' card is turned face upwards, and is playable.

One deal only is allowed. If the Patience goes through, the cards will all be built in sequence of suit on the foundations.

ONE FOUNDATION

ONE FOUNDATION is a comparatively simple one-pack Patience. It is different in principle from the majority, and is, I find, very little known.

First, shuffle the pack, cut and deal, face upwards, from right to left, a row of seven cards; then a second row, face upwards, from left to right, overlapping the first seven cards dealt; and so on, until five rows have been dealt. Thus, the first, third, and fifth rows are dealt from right to left and the second and fourth rows from left to right.

The cards thus dealt form seven vertical 'depots'.

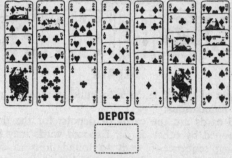

DEPOTS

FOUNDATION

Now deal a card lengthwise, face upwards, to form a 'foundation'. Only one foundation is allowed.

The object of the Patience is to build cards on the foundation.

The card of a depot not overlapped by another card is 'exposed'. Exposed cards may be built in either ascending or descending sequence, irrespective of suit, on the foundation. In building on the foundation, an ascending sequence may, at any time, be changed into a descending sequence, and vice versa, with the exception that an Ace cannot be played on a King, nor a King on an Ace. Exposed cards can only be played to the foundation.

When all available cards have been played from the depots to the foundation, deal another card, face upwards, on the foundation and play available exposed cards, as before, on to this new foundation card; continue to play in the same manner until all the cards are dealt.

If the Patience goes through, the cards will all be built on the foundation.

PAS SEUL

THIS is a Patience played with one complete pack of cards:

Shuffle the pack, cut and deal, from left to right, six cards in a horizontal row to form 'depots'.

'Exposed' Aces, and Aces subsequently exposed in play, are placed to form 'foundations'.

FOUNDATIONS

DEPOTS

The object of the Patience is to build in ascending sequence of suit on foundations.

Exposed cards are the cards of depots, for the time being, not overlapped by other cards. Exposed cards may be played in ascending sequence of suit to foundations in descending sequence of alternating colour to depots or to spaces.

A sequence, or portion of sequence, of cards may be played from one depot to another, provided the proper sequence and alternation of colour are maintained; or to a space.

A space occurs when all the cards of a depot have been played. A space may, but need not necessarily, be filled with any exposed card or sequence of cards; but if not so filled, it must be filled in dealing.

RAGLAN

RAGLAN is an interesting and unusual one-pack Patience in that the whole of the pack is dealt out at the beginning of play.

First, take the four Aces and place them to form 'foundations'; then shuffle and cut the pack. Now deal six 'stock' cards lengthways, and place them in any convenient position, face upwards, on the table.

Next deal, face upwards, a horizontal row of nine cards, followed by rows of eight, seven, six, five, four, and, lastly,

three cards, as shown in the diagram. The cards thus dealt form
nine vertical 'depots'.

The bottom card, for the time being, of each vertical depot
is 'exposed'.

The object of the Patience is to build in ascending sequence
of suit on foundations.

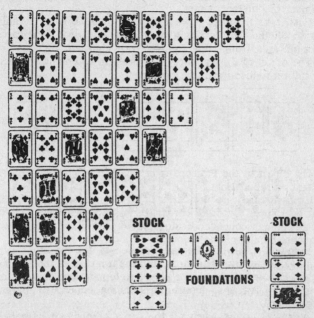

The six stock cards are exposed, and playable, when available,
to foundations or depots. Cards must not be played to stock,
which consequently disappears when the cards originally dealt
to it have been played.

Exposed cards may, if available, be played singly (but not in
sequences) to foundations in ascending sequences of suit, or to
depots in descending sequence of alternating colour.

A 'space' occurs when all the cards of a vertical depot have
been played. A space may, but need not necessarily, be filled
with any exposed card.

If the Patience goes through, all cards will be built in sequence
of suit on the foundations.

RED AND BLACK

OF the two-pack Patiences, Red and Black is probably one of the simplest and best known. I have seen it played under a number of different names.

First, take the eight Aces and place them to form 'foundations'. Shuffle the remaining cards, cut, and deal eight cards, face upwards, from left to right, to form eight 'depots'.

The object of the Patience is to build in ascending sequence of suit on foundations.

FOUNDATIONS

DEPOTS

'Exposed' cards are the cards of depots, for the time being, not overlapped by other cards, and the top card of the 'rubbish heap'. Exposed cards may be played to foundations in ascending sequence of suit, or to depots in descending sequence of alternating colour.

A 'space' occurs when all the cards of a depot have been played. Cards may only be moved singly, and not in sequences.

A space must immediately be filled by dealing a card into it; but when all the cards have been dealt, it must be filled with the top card of the rubbish heap; when the rubbish heap is also exhausted, a space must be left, as it must not be filled with a card from another depot.

Deal, playing available cards to foundations or to depots and unplayable cards, face upwards, to a rubbish heap. When all available cards have been played, pick up the rubbish heap, turn it face downwards, re-deal, and play as before.

One re-deal only is allowed. If the Patience goes through, all cards will be built in sequence on the foundations.

REFORM

'REFORM' is an ingenious and elaborate Patience played with
two full packs. The instructions which follow need to be carefully read and memorized. There is ample scope for skill.

Shuffle the packs together and cut. Deal, from left to right,
a row of eleven cards, face upwards.

The object of the Patience is to build in ascending sequence
of suit on 'Ace foundations', and in descending sequence of
suit on 'King foundations'.

FIRST TWO DEPOTS

ACE FOUNDATIONS   **KING FOUNDATIONS**

One Ace of each suit and one King of each suit are taken, as
dealt, to form 'foundations'. Any cards in the first row playable
on foundations may be played before dealing the second row.
The 'spaces' so caused must be filled by dealing from left to
right, and the cards so dealt may, if available, be played, when
the spaces must again be filled before continuing the deal.

Deal, face upwards, a second row of eleven cards, overlapping
the first row, and so on. During the deal play is only allowed
after each row is completely dealt, but (excepting Aces and
Kings required for foundations, which may be taken) only
the end left-hand card and the last two right-hand cards of the
row are 'exposed' and playable.

Spaces caused by taking Aces and Kings, and by playing
exposed cards from the end depots as described, must at once
be filled by playing from left to right. Cards dealt into spaces
in the left-hand depot, or the last two right-hand depots, may
be played, if available, in which case the spaces must again be
filled before continuing the deal.

If a card in the row last dealt is played, it exposes the card previously overlapped by it, and so on.

When *all* the cards have been dealt, they form eleven vertical depots, and any card not overlapped by another card is exposed and playable.

Exposed cards can be played to foundations as described, to depots in *either* ascending *or* descending sequence of suit (an ascending sequence may, at any time, be changed into a descending sequence of suit, and vice versa—an Ace being played on a King, or a King on an Ace), or to spaces.

Cards may only be moved singly, and not in sequences.

A space occurs when all the cards of a vertical depot have been played. A space may, but need not necessarily, be filled.

When all available cards have been played, pick up the vertical depots from left to right, so that the left-hand depot is at the top and the right-hand depot at the bottom of the pack when turned face downwards.

Deal and play exactly as in the first deal.

If the Patience goes through, all cards will be built in sequence of suit on foundations.

Merci —One 'merci' is allowed in each deal in each suit. If a ♠ 7 were on one foundation, and a ♠ 8 on the other, the 8 might be moved on the seven in ascending sequence, or the 7 on the 8 in descending sequence. This moving across of a card from one foundation to another constitutes a 'merci'.

REGIMENT

'REGIMENT' is a two-pack Patience in which Aces and Kings, as foundations, are in friendly competition.

First, shuffle the packs together, cut and deal, face upwards, two depot rows of eight cards each, leaving room between them for a third row; then deal between them, face upwards, eight stock packets of eleven cards each.

One Ace and one King of each suit are taken, as exposed in play, and placed to form foundations.

The object of the Patience is to build in ascending sequence of suit on 'Ace foundations', and in descending sequence of suit on 'King foundations'.

Exposed cards are the cards of depots not overlapped by other cards. Exposed cards may be played, if available, to foundations or in ascending or descending sequence of suit on the exposed

cards of other depots. An ascending sequence may at any time
be changed into a descending sequence of suit, or vice versa.

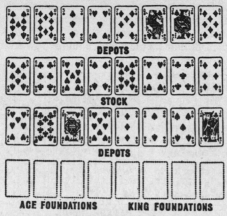

DEPOTS

STOCK

DEPOTS

ACE FOUNDATIONS   KING FOUNDATIONS

Cards may only be moved singly, and not in sequences.

A space occurs when the card, or cards, have been played
from a depot. A space must be filled with the top cards from
the stock packet nearest to it. If a stock packet becomes exhausted
the space must be filled with the top card taken from a stock
packet next to it, either on the right or left-hand side.

One deal only is allowed. If the Patience goes through, all
cards will be built on foundations.

ROYAL PARADE

ROYAL PARADE is a novel two-pack Patience in that the eight
Aces are removed. The object is to produce, at the finish, the
'Grand Parade' of twenty-four Court cards.

First, remove the eight Aces, and then shuffle the packs
together and cut. Now deal, face upwards, three rows of eight
cards each, as 'Parade Cards'.

The object of the Patience is to build up as follows:

On 2 put 5, then 8, and finally Knave of a suit.
On 3 put 6, then 9, and finally Queen of a suit.
On 4 put 7, then 10, and finally King of a suit.

Thus, in building up, a card three higher in value must always
be played.

In play, the 3's must always be in the centre row before

commencing the building up; the 2's and 4's may be either in the top or bottom row, but they may not be mixed in a row.

The building-up proceeds as far as possible with the twenty-four cards dealt out; thus, if a ◇ 2 occurs in the top row, and a ◇ 5 in any of the three rows, the 5 would be taken and put upon the 2, and thus create a 'space' in the row from which it is taken.

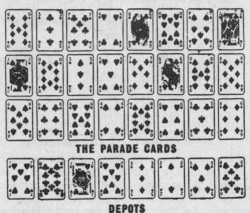

THE PARADE CARDS

DEPOTS

If the space occurs in the top row, any 'exposed' 2 can be moved into it; if the space occurs in the centre row, any exposed 3 could be moved into it. And if the space occurs in the bottom row, any exposed 4 could be moved into it.

Spaces may only be filled by moving the cards 2, 3 or 4 into them, the object being to get the 3's in the centre row, the 2's and the 4's in the top or bottom rows, as explained above.

When all moves with the twenty-four cards originally dealt out are completed, eight cards are dealt out in a row, from left to right, face upwards, to create eight 'depots'.

Any 2, 3 or 4, being the top card of a depot, can be put to a space in its proper 'Parade' row, and any exposed card (*ie* the top card of any depot) or any available Parade card, can be used in building up on the 2's, 3's and 4's as described above.

When all available cards have been played, deal another row of eight cards on the top of the depots and proceed in the same manner. Only the twenty-four cards originally dealt out, and the exposed (*ie* top) cards of the depots, can be played.

If the Patience goes through, no cards will be left in the depots and the top row will be all Knaves or Kings, the centre row all Queens, and the bottom row all Kings or Knaves. If, when commencing play, the 4's are played in the top row, and 2's in the bottom row, then the top row would come out all Kings and the bottom row all Knaves.

SIX BY SIX

'SIX BY SIX' is quite a fascinating one-pack Patience, which will, I expect, be new to most of my readers.

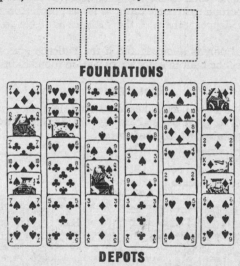

FOUNDATIONS

DEPOTS

First, shuffle the pack, cut, and deal from left to right six rows of six cards each, face upwards and overlapping. These six rows must be completely dealt before commencing play.

The cards thus dealt form six vertical 'depots', and the card of a depot not overlapped by another card is 'Exposed'.

Exposed Aces, and Aces exposed in play, are placed to form 'foundations'.

The object of the Patience is to build in ascending sequence of suit on foundations.

Exposed cards, if available, may be played to foundations in ascending sequence of suit, or to depots (including the first depot) in descending sequence, irrespective of suit.

A sequence in suit, or a portion of such a sequence, can at any time be played from one depot to another, provided the highest card of the sequence so used is in descending sequence, irrespective of suit, to the card upon which it is played. Sequences not in suit must not be played.

A 'space' occurs when all the cards of a vertical depot have been played. A space may, but need not necessarily, be filled by an exposed card, or sequence of cards, in suit.

Deal, playing available cards to foundations or depots, and all unplayable cards to the left-hand depot.

It is important to arrange cards, as far as possible, in sequence of suit on depots, otherwise the Patience is liable to become blocked.

One deal only is allowed; and if the Patience goes through, all cards will be built in sequence of suit on foundations.

SQUADRON

SQUADRON is a two-pack Patience with the eight Aces as foundation cards. To get it out successfully will, I think, prove a real trial of ingenuity and 'staying power'.

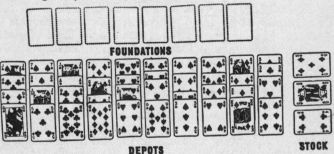

FOUNDATIONS

DEPOTS   **STOCK**

Shuffle the packs together, cut, and deal, face upwards, from left to right, a row of ten 'depot' cards; then a second row of ten cards overlapping the row above it; and then, similarly, two more rows, making four rows in all. The cards thus dealt form ten vertical depots.

Now deal three cards, face upwards, to a 'stock'.

'Exposed' cards are the card of a depot not overlapped by another card, the three stock cards, and the top card, for the time being, of the 'rubbish heap'.

Exposed Aces, and Aces as exposed in play, must be taken and placed to form 'foundations'.

The object of the game is to build in ascending sequence of suit on foundations.

Exposed cards may be played in ascending sequence of suit on foundations, or in descending sequence of suit on depots.

Cards may only be moved singly, and not in sequences or portions of sequences.

When all available cards have been played from the four rows, deal the cards remaining in hand, playing available cards to foundations or depots and unplayable cards to a rubbish heap.

A 'space' occurs when all the cards of a vertical depot have been played, or when a stock card has been played. A space may be filled with any exposed card; but the stock must never exceed three cards.

Only one deal is allowed. If the Patience goes through, the cards will all be built in sequence on the foundations.

STREETS

'STREETS' is a little-known and rather difficult Patience. It is tactically interesting and is played with two full packs of cards.

First, shuffle the packs together and cut. Deal, face upwards, from left to right, a row of ten 'depot' cards; then a second row of ten cards overlapping the row above it; and then, similarly, two more rows, making four rows in all. The cards thus dealt form ten vertical depots.

'Exposed' cards are the card of a depot not overlapped by another card, and the top card, for the time being, of the 'rubbish heap'. Exposed Aces, and Aces as exposed in play, must be taken and placed to form 'foundations'.

The object of the game is to build in ascending sequence of suit on foundations.

Exposed cards may be played in ascending sequence of suit on foundations, or in descending sequence of alternating colour on depots.

When all available cards have been played from the four rows, deal the cards remaining in hand, playing available cards to foundations or depots, and unplayable cards to a rubbish heap. A 'space' occurs when all the cards of a vertical depot have been played. A space may, but need not necessarily, be filled with any exposed card.

It is desirable not to fill a space unless absolutely necessary, for to carry through the Patience spaces are usually required

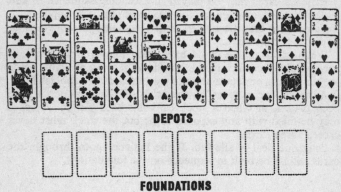

DEPOTS

FOUNDATIONS

in order to enable the cards to be shifted about. Single cards only may be moved, and not sequences or portions of sequences.

Only one deal is allowed. If the Patience goes through, the cards will all be built in sequence of suit on the foundations.

SULTAN

SULTAN is a somewhat fanciful two-pack Patience, the object of which is to produce, pictorially, a representation of a harem.

First, take all the Kings and one Ace of Hearts and place them to 'foundations', as shown in the diagram; then shuffle the packs together, and cut.

The object of the Patience is to build in ascending sequence of suit on all foundations, except on the central King of Hearts, called the 'Sultan', upon which no cards must be played.

The ascending sequences on the 'King foundations' are commenced by playing Aces on to them.

Deal eight cards to eight 'depots', as shown in the diagram. Any available cards of the depots must be played to foundations.

A 'space' occurs when a card is played from a depot; it may, but need not necessarily, be filled with an 'exposed' card.

Deal the cards remaining in hand, playing available cards to foundations or spaces and unplayable cards, face upwards, to a 'rubbish heap'. The top card, for the time being, of the rubbish heap is exposed and playable. Cards must not be played on to depot cards.

When all the cards have been dealt, shuffle the rubbish heap, cut, and re-deal. Three deals in all are allowed.

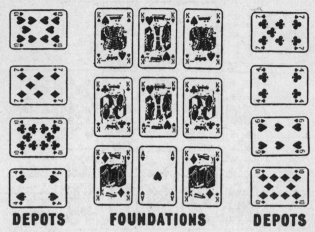

DEPOTS   FOUNDATIONS   DEPOTS

If the Patience goes through, the cards will be built in sequences of suits to the Queen on all the foundations, except the 'Sultan', who will then be surrounded by his eight wives.

THIRTY

THIRTY is a Patience which differs from any so far presented in that it is played with a short (Bezique) pack, viz, 2's to 6's inclusive, omitted.

First, shuffle the pack, cut and deal, face upwards, from left to right, six columns each of five cards, overlapping. Place the two cards left over, face upwards, to a 'stock'. The cards thus dealt form six vertical 'depots'.

The object of the Patience is to build in ascending sequence of suit on 'Ace foundations', commencing the sequence by playing a 7 on an Ace.

'Exposed' cards are the cards of depots not overlapped by

other cards, and the two stock cards. The stock disappears when
the two cards have been played.

Exposed Aces, and Aces exposed in play, are placed to form
foundations. Exposed cards can be played to foundations in
ascending sequence of suit, or to depots in descending sequence,
irrespective of suit.

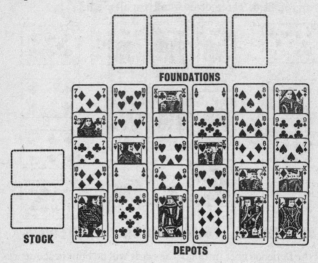

A sequence, or any portion of a sequence, can be played from
one depot to another, provided the proper sequence is maintained.

A 'space' occurs when all the cards of a vertical depot have
been played. A space may, but need not necessarily, be filled
with an exposed card or sequence of cards.

If the Patience goes through, all cards will be built in sequence
of suit on foundations.

TRIANGLE

TRIANGLE is another of the more picturesque Patiences, for which
two full packs are required.

First, shuffle the packs together, and cut. Deal (removing
Aces during dealing, and placing them to 'foundations') from
left to right, a row of eight cards, face upwards; then rows of
seven, six, five, four, three, and two cards respectively: lastly,

a single card at the bottom of the first vertical column, as shown
in the diagram.

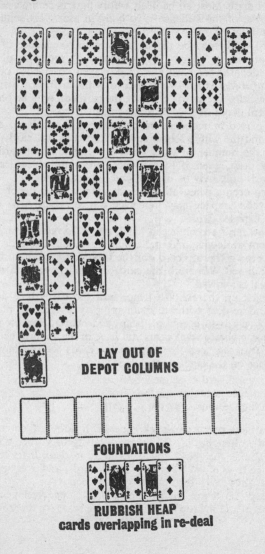

**LAY OUT OF
DEPOT COLUMNS**

FOUNDATIONS

**RUBBISH HEAP
cards overlapping in re-deal**

The cards thus dealt form eight vertical 'depots' and the bottom card, for the time being, of each depot is 'exposed'. The depot cards must all be dealt before play is commenced.

The object of the Patience is to build in ascending sequence of suit on foundations.

Exposed cards may be played in ascending sequence of suit to foundations, to 'spaces', or in descending sequence of suit to other depots, provided they are played to depots of *the same or of a higher row—ie* if a card is taken from a vertical depot consisting of, say, four cards, the card can only be played to a vertical depot of four or fewer cards.

Cards played in sequence on depots should be placed overlapping, and the whole sequence is reckoned as one card when counting the number of cards in a depot; but depot cards as originally dealt, even if in sequence, are counted separately. Single cards only may be moved, and not sequences.

A space occurs when all the cards of a vertical depot have been played. A space may, but need not necessarily, be filled with any exposed card.

Deal the cards remaining in hand, playing available cards to foundations or depots, and unplayable cards, face upwards, to a 'rubbish heap'. The top card, for the time being, of the rubbish heap is exposed. When all the cards in hand have been dealt, one re-deal is allowed.

Now pick up the rubbish heap, turn the cards face downwards, and re-deal without shuffling; play as before, placing unplayable cards to a rubbish heap, and overlapping them, so as to see at a glance what cards you have in the rubbish heap.

If the Patience goes through, all the cards will be built up in sequence on the eight Aces.

TRIPLE LINE

This is rather a pretty two-pack Patience. It does not 'come out' particularly often, but it is all the more satisfactory when it does.

First, shuffle the packs together, cut, and deal, from left to right, three rows of twelve cards, face upwards, and overlapping. The cards thus dealt form twelve vertical 'depots'.

'Exposed' cards are the card of a depot not overlapped by another card and the top card, for the time being, of the 'rubbish heap'.

Exposed Aces, and Aces as exposed in play, must be taken and placed to form 'foundations'.

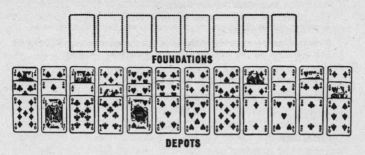

FOUNDATIONS

DEPOTS

The object of the Patience is to build in ascending sequence of suit on foundations. Packing on the board is restricted, *ie* any exposed (bottom row) card may have one of lower consecutive exposed cards placed upon it, taken either from other exposed cards on the board or from the waste-heap, but *only* one; and the couple thus made may not be moved till taking their place on their proper Ace-packet. Single available cards as turned up from stock can build on their foundation Ace-packets at once.

When stock is finished you are allowed a restricted second turn, being granted four 'grace' cards. These are set out in a line, and if you can place any of them in a column, or a vacancy, or on an Ace-packet, you do so; once more fill up the 'grace' row to four and so proceed till none of the 'graces' will fit.

As a final respite, you may look at the fifth card; but if that fails you, all is over. A vacancy made in the top row can be filled by any single exposed card, but need not be filled at once.

All Pan books are available at your local bookshop or newsagent, or can be ordered direct from the publisher. Indicate the number of copies required and fill in the form below.

Send to: Pan C. S. Dept
            Macmillan Distribution Ltd
            Houndmills Basingstoke RG21 2XS
or phone: 0256 29242, quoting title, author and Credit Card number.

Please enclose a remittance* to the value of the cover price plus: £1.00 for the first book plus 50p per copy for each additional book ordered.

*Payment may be made in sterling by UK personal cheque, postal order, sterling draft or international money order, made payable to Pan Books Ltd.

Alternatively by Barclaycard/Access/Amex/Diners

Card No.

Expiry Date

Signature:

Applicable only in the UK and BFPO addresses

While every effort is made to keep prices low, it is sometimes necessary to increase prices at short notice. Pan Books reserve the right to show on covers and charge new retail prices which may differ from those advertised in the text or elsewhere.

NAME AND ADDRESS IN BLOCK LETTERS PLEASE:

....

Name _____

Address _____

_____

_____

_____

6/92